THEORIZING MOTHERHOOD AND EMERGING ADULTHOOD

REPRESENTATIONS, EXPLORATIONS, AND CONTENTIONS

EDITED BY MAYA E. BHAVE, TALIA ESNARD, AND KAE SOLOMON

DEMETER

Theorizing Motherhood and Emerging Adulthood
Representations, Explorations, and Contentions
Edited by Maya E. Bhave, Talia Esnard, and Kae Solomon

Copyright © 2025 Demeter Press

Individual copyright to their work is retained by the authors. All rights reserved. No part of this book may be reproduced or transmitted in any form by any means without permission in writing from the publisher.

Demeter Press
PO Box 197
Coe Hill, Ontario
Canada
K0L 1P0
Tel: 289-383-0134
Email: info@demeterpress.org
Website: www.demeterpress.org

Demeter Press logo based on the sculpture "Demeter" by Maria-Luise Bodirsky www.keramik-atelier.bodirsky.de

Printed and Bound in Canada

Cover image: *Parent Connection* by Andrew Ostrovsky (agsandrew)
Cover design and typesetting: Michelle Pirovich
Proof reading: Jena Woodhouse

Library and Archives Canada Cataloguing in Publication
Title: Theorizing motherhood and emerging adulthood: representations, explorations, and contentions / edited by Maya E. Bhave, Talia Esnard, and Kae Solomon.
Names: Bhave, Maya Elizabeth, editor | Esnard, Talia, editor | Solomon, Kae, editor.
Description: Includes bibliographical references.
Identifiers: Canadiana 20250184869 | ISBN 9781772585407 (softcover)
Subjects: LCSH: Motherhood. | LCSH: Adulthood.
Classification: LCC HQ759.T47 2025 | DDC 306.874/3—dc23

 The publisher gratefully acknowledges the support of the Government of Canada

We dedicate this volume to all the mothers around the globe who are deeply loving and resilient through the fluctuations and changes across the entire mothering arc.

Contents

Prologue
Maya E. Bhave, Talia Esnard, and Kae Solomon
9

Introduction
Situating Motherhood and Emerging Adulthood
Maya E. Bhave, Talia Esnard, and Kae Solomon
21

1.
AITA: Navigating between Chinese and American Dating
Belief Systems across Two Generations and Two Cultures
Catherine Ma
41

2.
Enduring Love:
Maternal Experiences of Child-to-Mother Abuse
Laura Rite
57

3.
In Her Reflection: The Effect of Daughters' Educational Pursuits
and Career Exploration on Maternal Career Aspirations and Roles
*Lisa H. Rosen, Linda J. Rubin, Isabella Iven, Maritza Marquez,
Savannah Dali, and Dante Jackson*
75

4.
Ellipsis: Making Sense of Non-proximate Mothering
Maya E. Bhave
95

5.
Challenges of Being a Mother to Adolescents in Brazil:
A Review of the Indexed Literature
Irene Rocha Kalil and Martha Silvia Martinez-Silveira
101

6.
Working through Adolescence and Motherhood:
A Sociopoetic and Evocative Caribbean-Centered Reflection
Talia Esnard and Faith Flavius
127

7.
Motherhood Transitions:
Menopause, Teenagers, Gender Identity, and Disability
Carmen G. Farrell
149

8.
Outsmarting Giants
Teresa Cavanaugh Donkin
163

9.
Poems
Victoria Bailey
175

10.
On Tiger Mothering
Wendy M. Thompson
181

11.
Mothering: The Voices in My Head
Kae Solomon
195

12.
Spiderlings and Butterfly Wings: A Métis Maternal Response
to Teenage Nature Disconnection and Ecoapathy
Josée Bergeron
209

13.
Healing the Blame and Shame in Motherhood:
Tokens of Resistance
Vanessa Marr
219

Epilogue
Maya E. Bhave, Talia Esnard, and Kae Solomon
235

Notes on Contributors
243

Prologue

Maya E. Bhave, Talia Esnard, and Kae Solomon

Andrea O'Reilly, who coined the term "matricentric feminism"—that is, a mother-centered feminism—argues that since the publication of Adrienne Rich's formative and groundbreaking classic, *Of Woman Born: Motherhood as Experience and Institution* (1986), motherhood and maternal studies have become a burgeoning, scholarly field. She documents, in her pivotal book *Matricentric Feminism,* how over the last several decades the broad expanse of maternal research has grown to include research on:

- analysis of the mother-daughter connection (Rich; Collins);
- the concept of "intensive mothering" in which mothers are central caregivers devoting copious amounts of energy, time, and personal resources to their children (Hays 8–9);
- the theoretical framework of maternal thinking in which motherhood is framed as an experience (as opposed to an institution); maternal thinking focusses on the preservation, nurturance, and training of children, and the maternal values, attitudes, and beliefs arising from such maternal practices (Ruddick);
- the post-second-wave shift affecting gender assumptions and family configurations (O'Brien-Hallstein and O'Reilly);
- and racial standpoints on mothering (Collins; hooks);
- However, this edited volume looks at a much more specific period within the mothering arc: mothering teens and young adults. This research area lacks theorization, with needed interrogation across diverse contexts.

As coeditors, we each came to this volume with our divergent professional backgrounds, skills, expertise, and experiences. We were pulled together through a common interest and concern for the lack of scholarship on mothering teens and young adults and the need to make visible the silenced and constructed narratives of mothering. As we began this collaborative journey, it became evident that our mothering stories grounded and unsettled us. The complexity and histories in our stories gave us much to connect on and work through together. Although it was no surprise that we found ourselves quickly and animatedly sharing stories about our respective children, their ups and downs and our responses, we became intrigued by the diverse but unspoken realities, defying how we encountered and worked through motherhood. We knew then the importance of speaking through and sharing these stories. We see sharing our stories as mothers of teens or young adults as an important aspect of building on the scholarship and advancing understanding of this issue. We first share our stories and the major themes unfolding across our experiences.

Kae

I always wanted to be a mother, specifically a mother to a daughter. I imagined the closeness, the wonderful mother-daughter bonding, and the extraordinary love I would feel for this little creature created from my body. The biology of the craving was almost my undoing; many times, I physically desired to be pregnant. The maternal feeling extended to my hips, which felt empty and aching without the soft yet solid body of a young child to cleave to them. In the past generations, I likely would have had a large family confined by societal expectations. Would I have been worn out from toil and worry, cared for in my old age by their many-faceted branches that my love and care had made possible? Or would I have succumbed to the "nerves," as it was called then, that ran rampant in my maternal family?

Growing up in the shadows of mental illness, my perspective on families and mothering was a bit skewed. Most women performed traditional roles during my childhood in the late 1960s and 70s in small Canadian cities. Not in our family, however. When my mother discovered feminism, she used it for her purposes. Other mothers made meals, but not mine. Other moms got up in the mornings. My mom stayed up all night, surfacing late afternoon and already behind schedule for her piano students. She did not drive, rarely left the house, and had few responsibilities. Everything was on her terms. She controlled the household by how she lived; the rest of us were often afterthoughts. Somewhere my dad lost the fight. Depression took him under for a long time. Shock treatments and medication brought him back, but he rarely spoke and rarely showed emotion. It became easier to enable her dysfunctions. My brother and I learned to live without a stable foundation. I hid and dismissed my problems, as there were already too many around me.

As this history of mental illness was rarely acknowledged, I subsumed my problems until that became the norm. I was determined to do it differently and escape that history. It was not going to happen to me. It was only upon writing my memoirs that I realized that I, too, have been living with mental health issues most of my life. There was also the feeling of wanting to do it better because of what I lacked in my relationship with my mother. But life circumstances forced me to wait longer than I wanted to. Had I known the extent of mental illness in our family, would I still have chosen to have offspring? Mental health problems are in my partner's family, too. We aimed for one perfect child and succeeded in so many ways, but genetics won despite our best intentions. My poor girl has struggled at times with depression and anxiety and was recently diagnosed with attention deficit hyperactivity disorder. I feel guilt, helplessness, and anger watching another generation suffer. But yes, I would have still chosen to have her. We have tackled each challenge as they have come, not always nobly but with strength enough.

Thankfully, late motherhood has had the benefits of experience and wisdom, unlike my young mother, who failed to understand her illness and trusted whatever drugs were thrown at her. We have been fortunate to have access to excellent mental health practitioners and other health supports. I am so grateful to be able to give my daughter a better measure of what I grew up with.

So determined was I not to be my mother that my dreams took me far and away—beyond her judgements, hostilities, jealousies, and control. She wanted my dreams to be much smaller, and I could not bear those limitations. Despite her insisting on my continuing musical education, my choice of a musical career shocked and horrified her. She made no bones about not approving of my free-spirited lifestyle.

I want my daughter to dream big but cannot help but worry that she is reaching too far, just as I did. Teens are as vulnerable as toddlers but in different ways, as we cannot hover and must let them make their own painful mistakes. How do I save her from the fall? How many safety nets should I provide? The childproofing devices are long gone from our cupboards and sharp edges around the furniture, but the painful contusions are now internal. When I bend down to kiss her newly washed head goodnight, as she still sleeps in her small childhood bed, she smells like gum, and strawberry conditioner and hormones. Now a teenager, she is lovely and blooming at seventeen. If she gets into her choice of university this fall, we will have an empty nest much sooner than expected. We have had a few practice runs this past year, as she has taken a few trips while her dad and I get used to having more space around us. In occasional moments, I long for space, as inevitable but normal clashes and frustrations leave me weary, questioning my abilities as a good mother and role model. Over and over, I have told her that I do not want her to make the kind of mistakes I did. If I had to suffer to learn all this wisdom, then the least I could do is pass it down and give her the benefits of my experiences. Sometimes, it seems she may even be listening.

Talia

It was the year 2003. I was a young, recently married, and excited young girl ready to start a new project and journey: the start of my doctoral journey in a neighbouring Caribbean country. After two months, I struggled to find a rhythm and mental clarity to focus, and my journey took a completely different turn.

I still remember the events of the day. I sat on the fourth floor of the library reading a book on research methods. As I tried to read through the material on case studies, I experienced a sudden feeling of lightheadedness, which struck me as odd. I waited for a few minutes and thought the feeling would go away, but the feeling persisted, pushing me to pack up my belongings and walk towards the university health care center. The elevator felt different, as did the walk. I barely made it to the centre.

Waiting at the centre only encouraged wild speculation and fear. I had no idea of their source. I would soon discover that although there are many potential causes of lightheadedness, my symptoms were caused by early pregnancy. "Congratulations," the doctor said, "You are pregnant." She then asked whether I had planned or expected this. No, was my response. I was stunned and worried. She spent some time counselling me on the ways to prepare for pregnancy, but I could not move past the shock. Questions and uncertainty all rushed in. How would I continue my doctoral journey? Should I forget it? Should I pause it and return later? The questions were just too confusing and scary. I felt lost, disappointed, and torn between the pathways I wanted to create and the one where I had planted a seed but with no readiness to water.

I must admit that a little bit of excitement crept in slowly. I had to decide. I chose to enjoy the moment. I chose to return to my homeland and to my then-husband and family to share this experience and excitement. During the following months, that initial fear turned into pure delight. The many milestones and learning more about this unborn child created a bond which only strengthened as time progressed. The bond strengthened after birth, as my daughter grew from a baby to a toddler and then a teenager. My role over time was to show love and care as she blossomed into this life. I enjoyed that. The many years that followed allowed for this kind of peace and love.

As she turned sixteen, however, I noted the change in how we interacted, how often she reached out, and how she began to present herself, not so much to me but to others who grew in importance to her. Over time, the teenage years introduced more changes with visible implications for the mother-child relationship. The changes surprised me, or perhaps I should say I had not prepared myself for these transitory years. There were so many questions, concerns, and moments of relearning. For some reason, this period of adjusting to being a mom relieved me. I was learning to understand the changes unfolding before me and how to support and grow. I often thought of the changing butterfly and experiencing the metamorphosis that results in great, beautiful changes. I saw my daughter, the butterfly, change right before me into a beautiful person.

She recently turned twenty-one, so the years of adolescence have now closed. But there are still many questions and silences that remain. What does it mean to raise teenage daughters into adulthood? What changes occur, and what are the challenges for them? What connections do they form? And what about mothers and their experiences? Why is there so much silence around this period? These stories are still untold. The mask is still worn. I am still learning.

Maya

Before becoming a mother, I thought about motherhood as a social role that I could and wanted to do; it was one I fully believed would bring me joy, fullness, and happiness. Motherhood certainly did give me those things, but looking back, I realize I had a naïve, idealized version of normative motherhood in my head. I thought about what motherhood would add or bring to my life and what I could give to my kids in terms of physical, emotional, and social support. My vision was about social nurturing, connections, and bonds and incorporated little of anything negative. I imagined there would be difficult periods as my children grew and matured, but in my mental ruminations, I never fully understood motherhood could also be punctuated by deep, multi-layered levels of maternal loss.

When my first child, a son, named Andrew, was stillborn at term, my beliefs about motherhood came crashing down around me; my preset mothering beliefs shattered into pieces like sharp-edged ornaments from a toppled, December Christmas tree. Motherhood no longer felt bright, joyful, or pretty. Trauma, inequality, and medical gaslighting became glaringly evident and all too clear to me. Yet later when my second son, Kieran, and third son, Eric, were born, motherhood filled my life again with incredible joy, purpose, and definition. I loved watching the trajectory of their respective journeys, although I enjoyed it more when they were far beyond the toddler stage. I desperately wanted them to become teenagers—engaging, energetic, and interactive young adults. I had had enough of the messy Play-Doh afternoons, the strewn Cheerios all over the counter and floor, and the struggles to make sure we got in the toddler nap. I wanted young adults who could talk about politics, economics, and social life. I did eventually get that and more. Over the years, I have deeply relished their personal growth, academic successes, and thousands of hours of sporting events that dictated our weekly and monthly schedules.

So, it was a complete shock to my maternal self when my oldest headed off to college, and I suddenly felt like I had fallen off a cliff. His college was only a forty-eight-minute drive from our house, yet it felt like he was a thousand miles away. I felt upended, unsure of my role as a non-proximate mother, and uncertain about this new, modified social role. Once again, a fierce wave of maternal loss hit me in a way that I didn't see coming. I felt the same when my second son left. Not having both in the house felt disruptive and unsettling.

I spent hours questioning why I was so unsettled about this common American transition. I also wondered what other women thought about this period in their mothering arc. I fled to my local bookstore only to find hundreds of books on getting my kid into college, paying for it, and how to help them succeed once there, but there was nothing about my struggles in letting them go. I was dumbstruck. Why did it seem that mothering books focussed so much on the baby, toddler, and elementary school years? I wondered what the impact is of the teenager or college-aged child in the mothering arc, and why those long-standing tenets of normative motherhood focussed so much on the mothering of younger children. What happens when we mother older teens or young adults?

I returned home and threw my efforts into what I always do when I feel stymied: I studied it from a sociological point of view. I sought out mothers' voices across the country and constructed a broad qualitative research project to explore how our maternal thinking shifts or modulates when kids go to college. I began interviews in New England in January 2019 and continued on Zoom (due to COVID-19) through September 2022 to determine how women's maternal thinking changes or modulates when their kids leave home. I wanted to unearth the stories and experiences from this one slice in our motherhood arc—that seemingly had been studied very little. A few of the central ideas found in that research are included in this book in my creative essay titled "Ellipsis... Making Sense of Non-Proximate Mothering," which introduces my ideas on the intersection of non-proximate mothering, e-mothering, and our always-changing adult children.

Some Reflections

Although we share different histories, racial backgrounds, and personal lives, five themes connect our narratives: normative motherhood, struggle, silence, transitions, and maternal regret.

Normative Motherhood

Motherhood studies have long investigated mothers' relationships with their children in the family home. Normative motherhood, the dominant discourse in motherhood studies, posits that the relationship between mother and child is natural, necessary, and all-consuming. As such,

O'Reilly (2023) points out that normative motherhood is a social discourse "used to oppress and regulate mothers and their mothering" (*Normative Motherhood* 11). O'Reilly notes this mothering framework is built on ten tenets: essentialization, privatization, individualization, naturalization, normalization, idealization, biologicalization, expertization, intensification, and depoliticalization. These tenets combine to frame mothering as a process that women must do in the home. It assumes motherhood is nurturing and natural to all women and restricts this identity to the nuclear family. These tenets also create notions of intensive mothering, which is all-consuming and expert-driven, and has unattainable expectations.

Maternal Regret

Orna Donath's book *Regretting Motherhood* is the earliest scholarly book on maternal regret. Based upon interviews with Israeli women, Donath argues maternal regret is often studied within confines of the early part of our mothering arc, with little analysis of broader ways of envisioning maternal regret. O'Reilly in "*Maternal Regret: Resistances, Renunciations, and Reflections*" reflects on Donath's work which shows how "maternal regret…maternal remorse, resentment, dissatisfaction and disappointment—troubles the assumptions and mandates of normative motherhood" (9). O'Reilly uses Donath's work to investigate normative and oppressive motherhood scripts and asks what happens if motherhood does not look like normative motherhood. As such, she argues that Donath's work on maternal regret opens "the space for maternal erudition, enlightenment and evolution" (9).

Anne Kingston asks similar questions and examines how mothers challenge the taboo of regretting motherhood. She notes maternal regret has typically been "viewed as the purview of the childless," (2), yet there is a growing group of women who openly state they wish they did not have children. Kingston reflects on the work of Donath, O'Reilly, and others, arguing that the expectations placed upon women today are extensive, overarching, and unattainable. They demand mothers to be "the perfect Pinterest mom" (4). Kingston calls on us to reject the "idealized script" of motherhood (4) and understand maternal regret to include regretting having kids and the constraints and pressures surrounding motherhood.

Silences

Our narratives highlight the silences defining our experiences and perspectives on mothering teens. Although our frame of reference differs across the stories, they collectively speak to the contestations and confrontations that go unspoken but hold significant value in how mothers construct and locate their experiences. In all cases, our narratives point to the concept of "intensive mothering" (Hays), which dictates that mothering must be all-consuming. This experience of maternal loss is not isolated but represents a larger challenge around the (mis)treatment and silencing of birthing mothers by healthcare professionals, compromising possible health outcomes (Beck; Bohren et al.). Both the experiences of normative mothering and maternal loss still go untroubled.

Yet the inability to share the tensions around mothering speaks to discomfort and nondisclosure. The normative motherhood framework (O'Reilly, "Labour Signs") also does not correlate neatly with this later period of adolescence. This normative mothering experience captures the battle between the expectations to care and the nature of children. However, there is a lack of research on the challenges associated with maternal care and that of integrating or developing a career, which goes against normative ideologies (Hays; O'Brien-Hallstein). Although extensive literature exists on the restricted career outcomes following motherhood (e.g., Warren and Brewis), there is little storytelling about this process's struggles and sense-making aspect. This all reflects what Jane Waldfogel refers to as the penalty of motherhood, which structures and limits the experiences of mothers.

These narratives underscore the social norms or moral grammar around mothering (Morris et al.), the narratives or messages built within that discourse, the adverse childhood and family experiences going against these expectations, and the lack of pathways to speak through these experiences. These reflections suggest a need for greater examinations of the struggles mothers face as they engage with the institution and practice of mothering (Read et al.) and the level of ambivalence, confusion and emotional turmoil that unfolds as part of this process (Brookes et al.).

Struggles and Transitions

This sense of normative and intense mothering remains a point of contention for us all. The narratives speak to the significance of history and social status to mothering experiences (Hamilton). The need for alternative mothering strategies is also connected to that prior experience (Caitlyn Collins). Yet the stories also highlight the struggle of emerging from that history and working through the resources and the level of support at hand (Elliott et al.). The transition from free spirit, powerful in our embodied maternal selves, to all-consuming motherhood makes the journeys difficult for us all. We ask the questions therefore: (i) What is our role as mothers when kids are adults? How do we stay involved yet not overbearing? How do we continue to matter when our kids become emerging adults and need us less daily? The matricentric literature is sparse on this significant part of our latter mothering arc. This volume attempts to address this empirical gap.

Works Cited

Beck, Cheryl Tatano. "A Secondary Analysis of Mistreatment of Women During Childbirth in Health Care Facilities." *Journal of Obstetric Gynecologic Neonatal Nursing*, vol. 47, no. 1, 2018, pp. 94–104.

Bohren, Meghan, et al. "The Mistreatment of Women During Childbirth in Health Facilities Globally: A Mixed-methods Systematic Review." *PLoS Medicine*, vol. 12, no. 6, 2015, pp. 1–32.

Brookes, Gavin, et al. "'Off to the Best Start?' A Multimodal Critique of Breast and Formula Feeding Health Promotional Discourse." *Gender and Language*, vol. 10, no. 3, 2016, pp. 340–363.

Collins, Caitlyn. "Is Maternal Guilt a Cross-National Experience?" *Qualitative Sociology*, vol. 44, no. 1, 2021, pp. 1–29.

Collins, Patricia Hill. *Black Feminist Thought: Knowledge, Consciousness and the Politics of Empowerment*. Routledge, 1991.

Collins, Patricia Hill. "The Meaning of Motherhood in Black Culture and Black Mother-Daughter Relationships." *Double Stitch: Black Women Write About Mothers and Daughters*, Edited by Patricia Bell-Scott, et al. Harper Perennial, 1993, pp. 42–60.

Donath, Orna. *Regretting Motherhood: A Study.* North Atlantic Books, 2017.

Elliott, Sinikka, et al. "Being a Good Mom: Low-Income, Black Single Mothers Negotiate Intensive Mothering." *Journal of Family Issues*, vol. 36, no. 3, 2015, pp. 351–70.

Hamilton, Patricia. "The 'Good' Attached Mother: An Analysis of Post Maternal and Post Racial Thinking in Birth and Breastfeeding Policy in Neoliberal Britain." *Australian Feminist Studies*, vol. 31, no. 90, 2016, pp. 410–431.

Hays, Sharon. *The Cultural Contradictions of Motherhood.* Yale University Press, 1996.

hooks, bell. *Yearning: Race, Gender, and Cultural Politics.* South End Press, 1990.

Kingston, Anne. "'I Regret Having Children': Pushing the Boundaries of Accepted Maternal Response, Women Are Challenging an Explosive Taboo—And Reframing Motherhood in The Process." *CityNews Toronto.* 11 Jan. 2018, https://toronto.citynews.ca/2018/01/11/i-regret-having-children/. Accessed 10 Mar. 2025.

Morris, Michael, Ying-yi, Hong, Chi-Yue Chiu and Zhi Liu. "Normology: Integrating insights about social norms to understand cultural dynamics." *Organizational Behavior and Human Decision Processes*, 129, 2015, pp. 1–13, https://doi.org/10.1016/j.obhdp.2015.03.001.

O'Brien, Hallstein, D. Lynn, and Andrea O'Reilly, editors. *Academic Motherhood in a Post-Second Wave Context: Challenges, Strategies and Possibilities.* Demeter Press, 2012.

O'Reilly, Andrea. "Labour Signs: The Semiotics of Birthing." *Journal of the Motherhood Initiative for Research and Community Involvement*, vol. 3, no. 1, 2001, pp. 216–23.

O'Reilly, Andrea. *Matricentric Feminism: Theory, Activism, Practice.* Demeter Press, 2016.

O'Reilly, Andrea. *Maternal Regret: Resistances, Renunciations, and Reflections.* Demeter Press, 2022.

O'Reilly, Andrea. *Normative Motherhood: Regulations, Representations and Reclamations.* Demeter Press, 2023.

Read, Donna, et al. "'It Was a Horrible Shock': The Experience of Motherhood and Women's Family Size Preferences." *Women's Studies International Forum*, vol. 35, no. 1, 2012, pp. 12–21.

Rich, Adrienne. *Of Woman Born: Motherhood as Experience and Institution.* W. W. Norton and Company, 1976.

Ruddick, Sara. *Maternal Thinking: Toward a Politics of Peace.* Beacon Press, 1989.

Waldfogel, Jane. "Parental Work Arrangements and Child Development." *Canadian Public Policy*, vol. 33, no. 2, 2007, pp. 251–72.

Warren, Samantha, and Joanna Brewis. "Matter over Mind? Examining the Experience of Pregnancy." *Sociology*, vol. 38, no. 2, 2004, pp. 219–36.

Introduction

Situating Motherhood and Emerging Adulthood

Maya E. Bhave, Talia Esnard, and Kae Solomon

Introduction

Jeffrey Jensen Arnett coined the concept of "emerging adulthood" to refer to the child development period of the late teen years to the mid-twenties. Much sociological and psychological literature has explored emerging adulthood with attention to the often tumultuous and transitional years. Yet how mothering changes once children become young adults has unfortunately not been widely studied. Most mothering studies have focused on the transition to becoming a mother and the challenges of raising young children. There is also a dearth of literature on the "empty nest" phenomenon and the wider experiences and challenges related to mothering during periods of emerging adulthood. Those of us still living with older teens and adults in their twenties realize that our roles have changed. We are still very much parenting, only differently. Even as our children move away, we cannot walk away from our mothering roles, yet we continue to mother, though differently, from afar.

These discussions have centered around research on motherhood and emerging adults. Recent scholarly work has presented at times messy conversations about what constitutes mothering in this latter period of the mothering arc and how these experiences are understood. Elizabeth B. Francis-Connolly and Katherine Sytniak, for instance, interviewed fourteen white, middle-class, and mid-Western married mothers of emerging adults aged eighteen to twenty-nine to explore issues of mothering work, specifically the practices of providing emotional or financial support, the ongoing worrying that comes with mothering work, and the dynamics of mother-child relationships. The study considered the different stages of child and adolescent development, the types of support given, and how mothering practices change across this period. The authors call for more situated research that captures the cultural and historical aspects of mothering. This type of research calls for a focus on contextual representations that capture some of the key constructions and practices related to mothering across institutions, such as the family and the media. A call is also for explorations of motherhood for diverse peoples, and in particular for those within varied family structures and dynamics. or both. Such nuancing of mothering expectations are needed to center the different realities of motherhood, mothering and mother work.

Janet B. Hibbs and Anthony Rostain also look at the contested experiences of parenting and transition periods, noting that the time when kids move into emerging adulthood is confusing for kids and parents. They argue that as their kids are about to launch into adulthood "the roster of expert advice evaporates, leaving parents adrift" (3). They note that the age of eighteen, once seen as the beginning of adulthood, is an "outdated cultural storyline" and is when "paradoxically, the longest stage of parenting unfolds" (3–4). They argue that, historically, kids reached adulthood, got jobs, married, and were independent. However, they emphasize that today young adults face increasing levels of anxiety, depression (127), and economic uncertainty (120) and are often unsure of how to advance; thus, the period of adulthood is delayed. Their work, which resonates with the aforementioned study by Elizabeth Francis-Connelly and Katherine Sytniak, reveals the social reality that the "generational baton-pass into adulthood" is taking longer than it used to (Hibbs and Rostain 4). Both works examine the changing climates and patterns of engagement for children and adolescents and the need for a more nuanced understanding of how these landscapes and patterns of engagement for emerging adults have affected young adults and mothers.

This is a need for a deeper exploration of the complexities and contradictions within the thinking and practice of mothering emerging adults. These existing studies of mothering adolescents introduce many questions related to how motherhood is understood and practised. Additionally, these studies point to the need to situate the many discourses and institutions framing notions and practices of mothering and how these insights can be extended to advance the scholarship and activism within this field. We tackle these questions through this chapter and address some representations, concepts, and contentions related to maternal thinking, intensive, normative, feminist, and matricentric mothering. These questions are discussed to explore the breadth of the broader scholarship on mothering, specifically mothering teens and emerging adults. We explore these issues in the subsections of this chapter.

Motherhood Studies

Andrea O'Reilly, who coined the foundational terms "motherhood studies" in 2006 and "matricentric feminism" in 2016, points to Adrienne Rich's, *Of Woman Born: Motherhood as experience and Institution*, as a foundational underpinning for much of matricentric research. Through her work on motherhood as institution and experience, Rich differentiates "between two meanings of motherhood, one superimposed on the other: the *potential relationship* of any woman to her powers of reproduction and to children; and the *institution*, which aims at ensuring that that potential —and all women—shall remain under male control" (13). Rich stresses that "the patriarchal institution of motherhood is not the "human condition" any more than rape, prostitution and slavery are…. [and that] Motherhood…has a history, it has an ideology" (33). She elaborates that women's mothering is defined and controlled by the larger patriarchal society in which they live. Her work suggests that their identity, rules, and practices reinforce broader oppressive and patriarchal value systems built within cultural practices of mothering, which may also vary across contexts.

In her pivotal work, *Matricentric Feminism as Scholarship: Maternal Theory, Activism, Practice*, O'Reilly details the broad expanse of maternal theory, which includes issues of gender formation, expectations, practices, and social class variations of mothering. Within this expanse of theory, five concepts emerge as critical to motherhood studies: maternal thinking, intensive mothering, normative motherhood, matricentric feminism, and feminist mothering. We turn briefly to these framework conceptualizations to understand both the empirical and creative pieces within this current volume.

Maternal Thinking

A key concept within the motherhood literature is that of Sara Ruddick's notion of "maternal thinking" which is explored in her groundbreaking book of the same name. Her central argument is that maternal practice involves thinking, and that a discipline of thought emerges from this multilayered process (O'Reilly, "I Envision a Future" 296). Ruddick posits that early on in the motherhood journeys, "passions of maternity are so sudden, intense and confusing that women themselves remain ignorant of the perspective, the thought, that develops from mothering" (10). She notes mothers' lack of focus on maternal thinking derives from the fact that they believe maternal thinking is done by experts, not themselves, and that, additionally, mothers are powerless in society. Ruddick finds this ironic and troubling, since mothers have great input and control over their children's lives (35). Therefore, she urges mothers to tell and share their significant and diverse maternal stories (54).

Ruddick asserts that at the heart of this maternal practice are three demands: preservation, growth, and social acceptability, all of which are influenced culturally and contextually. Her work speaks to how a mother is expected to both preserve a child's life and nurture emotional and intellectual growth, processes Ruddick labels as "protection," "nurturance," and "training." She argues that the word "mother" moves from being a noun to a verb, what she calls an active, ongoing process of "becoming." It is in this "becoming" that women's full identities are revealed as they begin to "transform the thought they are beginning to articulate and the knowledge they are determined to share" (40). Ruddick notes, however, that not all moms engage in these practices in the same way, given their different social locations and contexts, and that the broad voices of mothers have been silenced, distorted, and ignored. Additionally, she notes how when mothers engage in maternal thinking, they often do so in isolation (101), and, at times, they fear the gaze of others, what she calls a type of "self-loss" (111). Coupled with this self-loss are the complexities and ambivalences involved in the practices of preservative love, types of control and protectiveness, as well as the uncertainty that comes with fostering growth in children, what she calls "growing away" (91). Such concepts are critical in our analysis of the transitional changes for mothers and their emerging adult children.

In the second part of her book, Ruddick looks at how maternal thinking is a natural resource for peace politics. She argues that there is a presiding and highly problematic myth in society of moms as peacemakers without power. She frames such dichotomous thinking as problematic, particularly given the fact that women and men have made war together (185) and that women are not innately peaceful (217). Although the possibility for violence exists within the relationships mothers and children share, Ruddick situates mothers as spectators of their children's nonviolent battles while acknowledging moments of anger, uncharitable thoughts, and impatience. Peacekeeping for moms, then, becomes the art of avoiding a battle (172-73), what she calls "conflict resolution through mutual concessions" (CRTMC) (178). Although she exposes how the peacemaker mother myth is intoxicating, she contends that the real promise of maternal peacefulness lies in "the work and love to which mothers are committed [to]" (221) and that a broader feminist consciousness and solidarity arises out of this maternal work.

Although some scholars, such as Ranjana Khanna, argue that the two halves of Ruddick's book do not connect tightly, recent academics have still found ways to apply maternal thinking to other social contexts, particularly global politics. Fiona Robinson, for example, looks at how maternal thinking can be applied to the construction of women and women's health in global health policy, whereas Catia Confortini and Abigail E. Ruane use Ruddick's work to examine restorative justice practices and the importance of contextuality (77) for women within a global context. Confortini and Ruane argue that understanding maternal thinking helps us see flexible ways of knowing and new understandings of the self and relationships with others.

Fiona Robinson also argues that maternal thinking can be read as feminist political theory, refuting the widespread critique that Ruddick valorizes women working in the home, thus, relegating them back to the private sphere without power, value, or significance. Robinson argues that the relationship between mothers and feminism is not antagonistic but "constitutive" (106), as mothers have unique power and leverage in society, thus framing new ways of understanding mothers' social roles and contentions. Sally J. Scholz agrees, arguing that the domestic sphere is a place of value and a site and arena of solidarity for women. Scholz posits what she calls a model of "integrative work or living work" (383), which transforms "what is and what ought to be meant by work" (384) by bringing the self into the home-work analysis.

Although Ruddick's work has inherent value and usefulness in application, some researchers, such as Alison Bailey, believe Ruddick falls short concerning racial diversity in her analysis of mothering. Bailey, using Patricia Hill Collins's concept of mother work, argues that Ruddick, though claiming to be a standpoint theorist, neglects to examine differences among mothers, which Bailey states "are equally as philosophically interesting and ought to be addressed more deeply" (188). Jean Keller, another of Ruddick's critics, argues that Ruddick's focus may be "child-centric, not mother-centric" (847). Such criticisms lend strength and validity to the need for this edited volume and the vital importance of hearing mothers' detailed stories and narratives.

Intensive Mothering

Another key concept within maternal scholarship is Sharon Hays's "intensive mothering," in which caregivers are conceptualized as only mothers who lavish "copious amounts of time, energy, and material resources on [their children]" (8). Hays argues that intensive mothering is the dominant ideology of socially appropriate childrearing presently in the United States. She suggests that parents using this parenting model are protective and child-focused, thus opposing the Western logic of homoeconomicus (10–11) in which individuals in Western societies are rational and self-interested. Within Hays's framework mothers develop an all-consuming, maternal intensity, not surprisingly reflected in the fact that the amount of time that working moms spend in "primary child care" with kids has nearly doubled since the 1970s (Milkie et al. 277).

Within intensive mothering, a cultural contradiction arises in which mothers attempt to live up to the constraints of *good* mothering of their "sacred children" within the opposing forces of a rationalized market economy (Hays 97). Hays's work also brings attention to the weight of motherhood on women, the responsibility they bear for their motherwork, and the ideological constructions of mothers as selfless caregivers. Through this representation, motherhood is positioned as more important than formal sources of employment and with expectations for visible attachment between mother and children. This ideology of intensive mothering also renders illegitimate other practices of mothering. Emily Jeremiah suggests therefore that the notion of "mothering as an ambivalent, even hostile, undertaking has been a significant focus of recent feminist thinking on maternity" (59), a reality which is certainly within

Rich's account of maternal hostility and violence. This point is similarly expressed by Rich who argues that this type of violence often leads to a manipulation of the mother-child relationship with representations of a harmonious order upheld within this relationship. Rich underscores that this occurs without choice and has the potential to affect the psyche and wellbeing of mothers.

Susan Douglas and Meredith W. Michaels expand upon Hays's work and argue that mothers are tired of the myth that motherhood is eternally fulfilling and rewarding. They call this myth "new momism," which is a "set of ideals, norms and practices, most frequently and powerfully represented in the media, that seem on the surface to celebrate motherhood, but which in reality promulgate standards of perfection that are beyond [our] reach" (4–5). Arguing that intensive mothering has only become more entrenched, invasive, and disturbing for mothers, Douglas and Michaels show that social media has been the driving force in perpetuating these ideals. New momism is the central ideology of post feminism, a concept acknowledging the progress women have made but arguing that women feel lonely and bitter because of it (24).

Linda Rose Ennis's edited volume and Miriam Liss and Holly H. Schiffrin's work on finding happiness, work, and family balance examine the continued prominence of intensive mothering in the twenty-first century. Liss and Schiffrin's broad, sweeping analysis of mothering, identity, and children found that college students with intensive, heavily involved mothers had "increased depressive symptoms and decreased satisfaction with life" (53). On the flip side, they found that women are intrinsically motivated but lose "autonomy when they become parents" (16). Subsequently, Liss and Schiffrin argue that mothers need to find happiness and meaning by intentional activity and self-care, and that these issues regarding inequality in motherhood need to be addressed not just by families but also by everyone in society (135). Their advice: Do what you love, carve out choices, do activities that show your competence, challenge yourself, and foster meaningful relationships with others. Such pleas are important for women, yet we ask in this current volume, how do mothers currently take care of themselves given their changing lives with emerging adult children coupled with societal and economic constraints—particularly rising levels of anxiety among youngsters—in today's global marketplace?

Ennis's volume addresses intensive mothering by examining motherhood and its relationship to the broader social and economic culture. Solveig Brown's chapter assesses the market economy in relation to intensive mothering, showing mothers feel they do not have enough "hours in the day to get everything done" (38). Thus, intensive mothering becomes a critical mothering action, as Brown notes it provides children with "two of our culture's scarcest [maternal] resources, time and attention" (38) and is an adaptive response to our cultural environment (39–40). Tatjana Takševa, in turn, looks at the choices mothers make within this market economy due to the increasing commercialization of motherhood (216–18). Kim Huisman and Elizabeth Joy examine microlevel constraints for mothers; they show that most mothers in their study had internalized the ideology of intensive mothering (97) and judged themselves, despite feeling that professional experts did not have all the answers.

Such analyses of culture, constraint, and contention emerge as critical aspects within the research. Patrice DiQuinzio recognizes, for instance, the significance of culture-and-context-bound constructions of motherhood, where issues of patriarchy determine such social organization of mothering and their positionality. In the *Myths of Motherhood*, Shari Thurer argues mothering can be seen as culturally derived and endemic of wider societal mythology replete with beliefs, expectations, and symbolic manifestations of how this is being defined and practised. For DiQuinzio, mothering in such a context emerges as a contentious issue and an oppressive experience.

Hays's work is pivotal to the conceptualization of intensive mothering, yet her research in 1996 focused on mothering children two to four years old. But what of mothers of emerging teens and young adults? Does intensive mothering exist during this part of the mothering arc? Several authors have examined intensive mothering, but they have largely used quantitative methodologies and statistical analyses of mothers and college-age children, showing a negative relationship between intensive parenting and child outcomes. Intensive parenting results in higher rates of medication use for anxiety and use of pain pills without a prescription (LeMoyne and Buchanan), problematic development for emerging adults (Padilla-Walker and Nelson), increased stress and poor coping skills (Segrin et al.), higher levels of depression, and less satisfaction with life (Schiffrin et al.).

Though valuable, these studies do not delve into some of the intricacies of motherhood, including those related to the experiences and practices representing the everyday lives of global mothers.

Feminist Mothering

Feminist mothering resists these normative notions of mothering. O'Reilly highlights the need to address how mothers are perceived when they deviate from normative constructions of motherhood and how their agency and positionality are influenced by these constructions within cultural contexts (*From Motherhood to Mothering*). She pushes for alternative framings of empowering mothering, including those that promote authentic, feminist, radical, or gynocentric mothering. She advocates for deconstructing and critiquing the cultural, social, and economic underpinnings of mothering. Through her work, O'Reilly argues for feminist mothering to facilitate "new progressive styles of mothering and generated maternal activism" that deviates from its concern with childrearing to focus instead on "the empowerment of mothers" (*Between the Baby and the Bathwater*, 324–25). This type of deviance seeks to affect change within the meaning and practice of mothering.

O'Reilly speaks therefore to the concept of feminist mothering as "any practice of mothering that seeks to challenge and change various aspects of patriarchal motherhood that cause mothering to be limited or oppressive to women" (*Feminist Mothering* 796). Here, feminist mothering consists of understanding that motherhood has a dual definition, which requires resisting the institutionalized and oppressive good mother ideal and redefining this space using counternarratives (O'Reilly, *From Motherhood to Mothering*). The notion of feminist mothering suggests that this institution is guided by Eurocentric norms, in which the so-called good mother is conceptualized as "white, heterosexual, able-bodied, married and in a nuclear family ... [and is] the primary caregiver of their children" (O'Reilly, *From Motherhood to Mothering* 4). Other scholars have similarly spoken of how this ideal perception of motherhood remains oblivious of mothers' desires, limitations, and contexts (Thurer), a reality leaving mothers feeling guilty when they cannot meet societal expectations (Ruddick). Without generalizing across contexts, Elizabeth Silva's *Good Enough Mothering* speaks to the rise of women's independence, the push for gender equality, increased participation of women within the labour force, the low status of mothers in the labour force, and the stigmatization of lone mothers. A central argument therefore is that "motherhood is an increasingly devalued activity within capitalism and patriarchy" (Silva 31) that is loosely defined around the high quality of care required for children, the increasing participation of women in waged labour, and the tendency for women to respond to struggle with notions of the embodied worker.

The scholarship on feminist mothering calls on researchers to acknowledge that "the institution affects mothers differently depending on their social location" (Green, "Feminist Mothering" 89) or their social status. Amy Middleton argues that feminist mothering theorists have ignored a population of marginalized and disadvantaged women including those from low socio-economic backgrounds, in abusive relationships or who suffer from mental illness. O'Reilly also argues that the literature on feminist mothering can be placed into two categories: antisexist childrearing and maternal activism. The former takes place at home, where feminist mothers permit "children to grow out-side and beyond the gender straight jackets of a patriarchal culture" (*Feminist Mothering* 811). This involves accounting for the ideas of difference and inclusivity to raise children "to be conscientious citizens for social justice" (Green, "Feminist Mothering" 83). This idea further challenges the Western notion of motherhood as a private act; feminist mothers attempt to redefine motherhood by using "their position as mothers to lobby for social and political change, usually for and on behalf of their children" (O'Reilly, *Between the Baby and the Bathwater* 326).

Other scholars have added to the conversation on feminist mothering. Fiona Green speaks of feminist mothering to underscore how women negotiate the tension between motherhood as an institution and experience ("Feminist Mothers"). She starts by acknowledging motherhood as a "complex site of women's oppression and a potential location for women's creativity and joy" ("Feminist Mothers" 125). Green illuminates how motherhood can empower women and be a site of political activism. These lenses represent an opportunity to move from the oppressive realms of mothering to more liberatory and engaging experiences. Green declares that feminist mothers understand they work within patriarchal societies, that they are idealized by certain standards that make them authentic, and that this ideology is adopted through how mothers are framed. However, she suggests that experiences of motherhood can be liberating as mothers exercise agency and resistance.

This emancipatory view of and vision for mothering unearths a feminist consciousness, a mixture of love for their children, consciousness of the parameters they are working within, and an understanding of the potential to choose to mother in ways challenging the status quo. Through such a consciousness, mothers resist the images and representations of themselves and use their positions as mothers in more subversive ways. The core aspect of feminist mothering is becoming conscious of their positionalities as mothers and the potential to resist or to change the parameters wherein they function and experience motherhood. The strategies within this choice remain diverse, such as choosing to be or not to become a mother, challenging patriarchal representations of mothering, creating alternative methods of mothering outside of patriarchal standards, and avoiding normative notions of mothering. The central goals here are devising emancipatory alternatives to patriarchal motherhood.

Normative Motherhood

In *Matricentric Feminism: Theory, Activism and Practice*, O'Reilly outlines the ten dictates of normative motherhood:

- Essentialization: Mothers have a female identity
- Privatization: Mothering is done in the home
- Individualization: Mothering is the work of one person, the female mother
- Naturalization: Maternity and mothering are natural
- Normalization: Mothers nurture both the husband and children
- Idealization: Mothering involves unrealistic expectations
- Biologicalization: Mothering is related to biological and blood ties
- Expertization: Mothering is an expert-driven process
- Intensification: Mothering is all-consuming and financially expensive
- Depoliticalization: Mothering is a private and nonpolitical undertaking

More recently, in *Normative Motherhood: Regulations, Representations and Reclamations*, O'Reilly argues that examining and theorizing normative mothering is the central aim of motherhood studies (8). She asks what the features are of this mothering framework, where it comes from, the impact of it on our individual mothering experiences, and how we possibly resist it. O'Reilly points out that Rich's term motherhood relates to a male-defined patriarchal institution, while "mothering" is a term that is more "empowering" to women (9). Normative motherhood in O'Reilly's opinion operates "as a regulatory institution, both discursively and materially" (10) and becomes seen as the "only legitimate discourse and practice of motherhood" (11). O'Reilly states that intensive motherhood is a contemporary enactment of normative mothering as professional women continue their busy lives by filling schedules and calendars around their children's lives. Intensive mothering then compensates for time away from our kids (*Normative Motherhood* 19). In addition, she notes that "demands made on mothers today are unparalleled in history" (*Normative Motherhood* 20). She notes that women strive to have a sense of accomplishment at work and home yet sometimes see themselves as failures.

For O'Reilly, understanding the framework of normative motherhood is critical to feminists, given that its tenets are the constraining and often invisible expectations that mothers face. Subsequently, she argues that we must look to a broader feminism, one she calls matricentric feminism, which is less confining, controlling, and thus more rewarding for mothers.

Matricentric Feminism

O'Reilly identifies matricentric feminism as the unfinished business of feminism. Matricentric feminism couples theoretical frameworks to inform a scholarship on motherhood focussed on microlevel narratives and experiences. In this work, she is "positioning mothers' needs and concerns as the starting point for a theory and politics on and for women's empowerment" (*Matricentric Feminism: A Feminism for Mothers* 14). This theory acknowledges the "social, economic, political, cultural, psychological" challenges that disempower mothers and emerge from their specific roles and identity. Through matricentric feminism, O'Reilly calls for the theorization of mothers and motherhood and the scrutiny of the idealization of normative motherhood (such as the notion that a woman's identity can be reduced to her reproductive capacity) and the presumption that motherhood is natural to women as opposed to being a learned skill.

Rejecting motherhood as natural within matricentric feminism is similar to Evelyn Glenn's argument: "By depicting motherhood as natural, a patriarchal ideology of mothering locks women into biological reproduction and denies them identities and selfhood outside mothering" (9). In many ways, this representation of mothers speaks to a dialectic struggle for an agency with the need for alternative expressions. O'Reilly suggests that feminist mothers should hold a perception of the self beyond that of a mother, acknowledging the importance of their intersecting identities. This feminist framing of mothers advocates for "a matrifocal narrative," which refers to narratives where "a mother plays a role of cultural and social significance and in which motherhood is thematically elaborated and valued" (*Matricentric Feminism* 17), Such discourse accounts for other sites of oppression which intersect with the identity of "mother women." This can create a "socially engaged enterprise and site of power" to further support the establishment of "maternal theory and motherhood studies" (*Matricentric Feminism* 18).

Collectively, O'Reilly outlines alternative ways in which women can carry out mothering in ways that "affords and affirms maternal agency, authority, autonomy and authenticity which confers and confirms power to and for mothers" (*From Motherhood to Mothering* 15). Middleton makes a similar argument, suggesting that agency and autonomy allow mothers to freely and confidently make independent choices about their practices while resisting scrutiny, stigmatization, and input from others in self-sustaining ways. While these conditions may seem ideal, Middleton calls for the authenticity in mothering practices to allow women opportunities to gain fulfillment outside of mothering or that of sacrificial notions of motherhood. She also advances notions of authority around motherhood to ensure that women can have the confidence that their "power and voice" as mother will be acknowledged in all settings. Alternatively, Green suggests that women can choose how they wish to engage or respond to the notion of the good mother and how they can work to empower themselves within that space.

Despite these hopes for theorizations of motherhood, DiQuinzio notes that the lack of consensus among maternal scholars on the meaning and significance of key concepts (such as embodiment, oppression, and freedom) and the lack of deliberations about motherhood within broader feminist scholarship remain major obstacles to advancing this field. This impossibility of motherhood therefore becomes a reflection of the difficulty within the debates and connections made between notions of individualism, gender neutrality, and feminism. The theory must therefore recognize the "hegemony of individualism and essential motherhood, mothers' situations and experiences themselves will be overdetermined and contradictory and thus that feminist accounts of mothering will have to negotiate the "dilemma of difference" (DiQuinzio 28). She notes that "difference feminism appeals to accounts of women's situations and experiences from the perspectives of women themselves ... explaining how and why women experience and perceive the world as they do ... to present a view of the world, or a mode of acquiring knowledge" (69). She calls for the refinement and expansion of embodiment and subjectivity within the context of mothering. Scholarship on motherhood should ideally address the impossibility of individualist subjectivity, politics of mothering, identity-based challenges, and resistance to motherhood and individualism.

Unique Contributions of the Volume

This current edited volume captures the stories and experiences of mothers with emerging adults. Although the contributions also resonate with the coeditors' experiences of struggling against normative motherhood, these global contributors bring several unique themes to the discussion.

Social and Psychological Patterns and Relationships

These patterns and relationships are primarily addressed by Catherine Ma in her chapter "AITA: Navigating between Chinese and American Dating Belief Systems across Two Generations and Two Cultures." She speaks to the complex impact of young dating relationships in Chinese American children's lives and the sense of helplessness it introduces for immigrant Chinese mothers within the United States. In her chapter "Enduring Love: Maternal Experiences of Child-to-Mother Abuse," Laura Rite unpacks the issue of enduring love in the constructions of mother-child relations, identities, and tensions while considering the potential for abuse. Rite unpacks these issues by exploring the diverse impact of role construction and experiences on the socio-psychological, emotional, and relational experiences of mothers and daughters.

Non-proximate Mothering

One aspect of mothering rarely explored within the matricentric feminist literature is the concept of non-proximate mothering. Given that normative motherhood frameworks focus on mothering young children, authors in this volume ask the critical question of how mothering frameworks are altered in the latter part of our mothering arc, especially when children go to college or university. How do our mothering, normative motherhood, and maternal thinking become impacted from a distance? In their chapter "In Her Reflection: The Effect of Daughters' Educational Pursuits and Career Exploration on Maternal Career Aspirations and Roles," Lisa H. Rosen and colleagues examine mothers of first-year college students and how their processing of possible career paths affect the mothers who are now mothering non-proximately. Maya E. Bhave's creative essay "Ellipsis: Making Sense of Non-Proximate Mothering" introduces the concept of non-proximate mothering and explores how mothers enter a new type of motherhood in the latter period of their mothering arcs, which she calls "liminal motherhood." In these latter years of mothering, Bhave argues, mothers attempt to fill their new void and keep in touch with male and female children through various patterns she calls "e-mothering." Through this medium of technology, she examines the changing landscape of her motherhood with emerging adults.

Cross-Cultural Mothering

Cross-cultural mothering also emerges as an important point of examination. This is addressed by Irene Rocha Kalil and Martha Silvia Martinez-Silveira from Brazil in their chapter "Challenges of Being a Mother to Adolescents in Brazil: A Review of the Indexed Literature." They provide a useful metasynthesis of the mothering scholarship on Brazilian mothers with teenagers and the treatment of issues related to maternal health. Through their critical review, they discuss the scope of knowledge on adolescent experience in Brazil and its relevance for addressing issues of maternal health and relations and the broader scholarship on motherhood. Similarly, Talia Esnard and Faith Flavius's chapter "Working through Adolescence and Motherhood: A Socio-Poetic and Evocative Caribbean-Centered Reflection" addresses the tensions for adolescent daughters and mothers within the Caribbean. Through their reflection on adolescence as an experience and a perception, they demonstrate how mothers and daughters can think and work through adolescence as a critical period of transition through which both mothers and daughters are affected. Both chapters highlight the need to consider cross-contextual experiences and practices within maternal scholarship.

Maternal Expectations versus Reality

A central theme within the creative pieces is maternal expectations versus the reality of motherhood. Catherine Ma in her chapter "AITA: Navigating Between Chinese and American Dating Belief Systems Across Two Generations and Two Cultures" explores the distinction between expectation and maternal reality, specifically as it relates to the cultural values of the family and those of the choices and actions of teenagers. Carmen G. Farrell's piece "Motherhood Transitions: Menopause, Teenagers, Gender Identity, and Disability" on neurodiversity addresses her expectations of motherhood versus the reality of raising children with diverse personalities. Josée Bergeron in "A Métis Maternal Response to Teenage Nature Disconnection and Ecoapathy" writes about maternal responses to nature disconnection and ecoanxiety, and Vanessa Marr's creative piece "Healing the Blame and Shame in Motherhood: Tokens of Resistance" captures the challenges of dissonance, maternal regret, blame, healing, and resistance.

Both Teresa Cavanaugh Donkin and Victoria Bailey touch on the emotional aspects of mothering. In "Outsmarting Giants," Donkin writes about the sadness she feels about her children getting older, the grief of her eldest leaving home, the unpredictability of her younger teen's emotions, and her evolving role as a mother. Similarly, Bailey's poetry explores the mixed emotions and grief of her eldest leaving home and the eternal maternal, her term for how one is always a mother even when the child has grown and is no longer living at home.

Wendy Thompson and Kae Solomon's chapters explore pain within intergenerational maternal relationships. Thompson's "On Tiger Mothering" speaks to the complexities of generational wounds and trauma in Asian immigrant families. Her vignettes also capture the mother-daughter team journey. The author, who was raised in a disciplined family structure, now has to grapple with tiger mother parenting and the rupture created in her shifting, multiracial family. Like Thompson, Solomon's chapter, "Mothering: The Voices in My Head," captures how intergenerational trauma has shaped and affected four generations of women in her family. Committed to mothering differently and with more education and outside support available, Solomon speaks of how she remained both buoyed and dismayed watching her teenage daughter navigate through these inherited burdens.

Some Concluding Thoughts

Motherhood scholarship has historically explored diverse concepts related to how motherhood is understood, framed, and practised and how it informs the lives and experiences of mothers globally. Much of this work, however, has not focussed on the experiences of mothers of emerging adults. Through our explorations of empirical and creative pieces, this volume contributes significantly to advancing motherhood studies. It expands the literature on maternal experiences by examining the relationship between mothers and emerging adults. It analyzes new and underexplored concepts, such as liminal motherhood and matrescence. The collection also touches on sensitive or tabooed topics, such as narcissism, abuse, anger, and resentment. This focus on emerging adulthood and motherhood represents our contribution to a still growing body of motherhood scholarship.

Works Cited

Arnett, Jeffrey Jensen. "Emerging Adulthood: A Theory of Development from the Late Teens Through the Twenties." *American Psychologist*, vol. 55, no. 5, 2000, pp. 469–80.

Bailey, Alison. "Mothering, Diversity, and Peace Politics." *Hypatia*, vol. 9, no. 2, 1994, pp. 188–98.

Brown, Solveig. "Intensive Mothering as an Adaptive Response to Our Cultural Environment." *Intensive Mothering: The Cultural Contradiction of Modern Motherhood*. Edited by Linda R. Ennis. Demeter Press, 2014, pp. 27–36.

Confortini, Catia, and Abigail E. Ruane. "Sara Ruddick Maternal Thinking as Weaving Epistemology for Justpeace." *Journal of International Political Theory*, vol. 10, no. 1, 2014, pp. 70–93.

DiQuinzio, Patrice. *The Impossibility of Motherhood: Feminism, Individualism, And the Problem of Mothering*. Routledge, 1999.

Douglas, Susan J., and Meredith Michaels. *The Mommy Myth: The Idealization of Motherhood and How It Has Undermined Women*. Free Press, 2004.

Ennis, Linda Rose. *Intensive Mothering: The Cultural Contradictions of Modern Motherhood*. Demeter Press, 2014.

Francis-Connolly, Elizabeth, and Katherine Sytniak. "Mothering Work and Emerging Adult Children." *Work*, vol. 50, no. 3, 2015, pp. 465–72.

Glenn, Evelyn Nakano. "Social Construction of Mothering: A Thematic Overview." *Mothering: Ideology, Experience and Agency*. Edited by Evelyn N. Glenn, et al. Routledge, 1994, pp. 1–29.

Green, Fiona Joy. "Feminist Mothering: Challenging Gender Inequality by Resisting the Institution of Motherhood and Raising Children to Be Critical Agents of Social Change." *Socialist Studies*, vol. 1, no. 1, 2009, pp. 83–99.

Green, Fiona Joy. "Feminist Mothers: Successfully Negotiating the Tension Between Motherhood as 'Institution' and 'Experience.'" *From Motherhood to Mothering: The Legacy of Adrienne Rich's 'Of Woman Born'*. Edited by Andrea O'Reilly. State University of New York Press, 2004, pp. 125–36.

Hays, Sharon. *The Cultural Contradictions of Motherhood*. Yale University Press, 1996.

Hibbs, B. Janet, and Anthony Rostain. *You're Not Done Yet: Parenting Young Adults in an Age of Uncertainty*. St. Martin's Press, 2024.

Huisman, Kim, and Elizabeth Joy. "The Cultural Contradictions of Motherhood Revisited: Continuities and Changes." *Intensive Mothering: The Cultural Contradiction of Modern Motherhood*. Edited by Linda R. Ennis. Demeter Press, 2014, pp. 86–103.

Jeremiah, Emily. "Murderous Mothers: Adrienne Rich's *Of Woman Born* and Toni Morrison's *Beloved*." *From Motherhood to Mothering: The Legacy of Adrienne Rich's 'Of Woman Born'*. Edited by Andrea O'Reilly. State University of New York Press, 2004, pp. 57–71.

Keller, Jean. "Rethinking Ruddick and the Ethnocentrism Critique of 'Maternal Thinking.'" *Hypatia*, vol. 25, no. 4, 2010, pp. 834–51.

Khanna, Ranjana. "Reflections on Sara Ruddick's Maternal Thinking." *WSQ: Women's Studies Quarterly*, vol. 37, no. 3–4, 2009, pp. 302–04.

LeMoyne, Terri, and Tom Buchanan. "Does 'Hovering' Matter? Helicopter Parenting and its Effect on Well-being." *Sociological Spectrum*, vol. 31, no. 4, 2011, pp. 399–418.

Liss, Miriam, and Holly H. Schiffrin. *Balancing the Big Stuff: Finding Happiness in Work, Family, and Life*. Rowman and Littlefield, 2017.

Middleton, Amy. "Mothering Under Duress: Examining the Inclusiveness of Feminist Mothering Theory." *Journal of the Association for Research on Mothering*, vol. 8, no. 1, 2006, pp. 72-82.

Milkie, Melissa, et al. "Time Deficits with Children: The Link to Parents' Mental and Physical Health." *Society and Mental Health*, vol. 9, no. 3, 2018, pp. 277-95.

O'Reilly, Andrea. "Between the Baby and the Bathwater: Some Thoughts on a Mother-Centered Theory and Practice of Feminist Mothering." *Journal of the Association for Research on Mothering*, vol. 8, no. 1, 2006, pp. 323-30.

O'Reilly, Andrea. "Feminist Mothering." *Maternal Theory: Essential Readings*. Edited by Andrea O'Reilly. Demeter Press, 2007, pp. 792-821.

O'Reilly, Andrea. *From Motherhood to Mothering: The legacy of Adrienne Rich's Of Woman Born*. State University of New York Press, 2004.

O'Reilly, Andrea. "'I Envision a Future in Which Maternal Thinkers Are Respected and Self-Respecting': The Legacy of Sara Ruddick's Maternal Thinking." *WSQ: Women's Studies Quarterly*, vol. 37, no. 2, 2009, pp. 295-98.

O'Reilly, Andrea. "Matricentric Feminism: A Feminism for Mothers." *Journal of the Motherhood Initiative for Research and Community Involvement*, vol. 10, no. 1 and 2, 2019, pp. 13-26. Retrieved from https://jarm.journals.yorku.ca/index.php/jarm/article/view/40551

O'Reilly, Andrea. *Matricentric Feminism: Theory, Activism, Practice*. Demeter Press, 2016.

O'Reilly, Andrea. *Normative Motherhood: Regulations, Representations and Reclamations*. Demeter Press, 2023.

Padilla Walker, Laura, and Larry Nelson. "Black Hawk Down?: Establishing Helicopter Parenting as a Distinct Construct from Other Forms of Parental Control During Emerging Adulthood." *Journal of Adolescence*, vol. 35, no. 5, 2012, pp. 1177-90.

Rich, Adrienne. *Of Woman Born: Motherhood as Experience and Institution*. W. W. Norton and Company, 1976.

Robinson, Fiona. "Discourses of Motherhood and Women's Health: Maternal Thinking as Feminist Politics." *Journal of International Political Theory*, vol. 10, no. 1, 2014, pp. 94-108.

Ruddick, Sara. *Maternal Thinking: Toward a Politics of Peace*. Beacon Press, 1989.

Segrin, Chris, et al. "Parent and Child Traits Associated with Overparenting." *Journal of Social and Clinical Psychology*, vol. 32, no. 6, 2013, pp. 569-95.

Schiffrin, Holly, et al. "Helping or Hovering? The Effects of Helicopter Parenting on College Students' Well-being." *Journal of Child and Family Studies*, vol. 23, 2013, pp. 548-57.

Scholz, Sally J. "Reconceptualizing Work and Building Ruddick's Feminist Solidarity Transnationally." *Politics & Gender*, vol. 11, no. 2, 2015, pp. 382-405.

Silva, Elizabeth Bortolaia. "The Transformation of Mothering." *Good Enough Mothering? Feminist Perspectives on Lone Mothering*. Edited by Elizabeth Bortolaia Silva. Routledge, 1996, pp. 10-36.

Takševa, Tatjana. "How Contemporary Consumerism Shapes Intensive Mothering Practices." *Intensive Mothering: The Cultural Contradiction of Modern Motherhood*. Edited by Linda Rose Ennis. Demeter Press, 2014, pp. 211-32.

Thurer, Shari. *Myths of Motherhood: How Culture Reinvents the Good Mother*. Penguin Books, 1994.

1.

AITA: Navigating between Chinese and American Dating Belief Systems across Two Generations and Two Cultures

Catherine Ma

Growing up as an immigrant in a traditional Chinese household where I dated the one boy who would eventually become my husband, I did not have typical American dating experiences. It was a given that I lived at home until I got married, as my aunts did. I was lucky to have met the man of my dreams, who loved me like no other. With our three American-born children who grew up with more of an Asian American experience, my husband and I were open-minded about the possibility that their dating experiences would differ from ours. I felt lucky that my three children never went through a "terrible twos" phase. They were children who behaved and listened to their immigrant parents and family members. I am grateful I helped raise good kids, and we often had strangers complimenting us on how well behaved they were. Raising young children is not always easy, but it does not compare to raising teenagers and young adults. As they became older and started dating, I was often left blindsided and felt unprepared for discussions regarding first loves, having sex, choosing partners, reacting to red flags, and dealing with broken hearts. As my children ventured into this unknown territory, it made me look at my own dating experiences as a Chinese immigrant girl growing up influenced by American culture and an even deeper look at how my beliefs of dating and love affect my adolescent and young adult children. I am constantly navigating between two cultures that often clash, leaving me to wonder, am I the asshole (AITA) holding onto archaic Asian norms that are irrelevant or even dangerous to the mental health of my Asian American children, or am I being too lenient in allowing my children to acculturate into American culture at the expense of their Chinese roots? This chapter explores how my own dating experiences entrenched in filial piety, shame, Chinese cultural beliefs, intergenerational trauma, and American culture have shaped the way I navigate through the dating experiences of my young adult children. It was not an easy chapter to write, as it often forced me to self-reflect, be critical of my mothering practices, and examine the sources of my biases. Still, I want to share my journey into this foreign territory to support other immigrant mothers who find it difficult to understand Chinese and American dating practices as their American-born children become adults.

Methodology

I use a reflective approach to connect my experiences as a Chinese immigrant woman, sharing my mothering experiences in raising my teenage and young adult Chinese American children. I incorporate empirical research on Asian dating into this chapter and reflect on the need to include cultural differences to widen our understanding of dating styles. My reflection is coupled with a critical analysis of how my personal experiences of dating and love may have affected my children's dating relationships. The analytic framing will be from a Chinese mother's perspective, where I navigate my Chinese cultural experiences of dating from my extended family and what I have learned from American culture, including movies that have shaped my definitions of dating and romantic love. As an immigrant Chinese mother, I critically examine how my mothering may have influenced my children's intra- and intercultural experiences of dating and love. Much of this work involves negotiating my role in my children's dating experiences and how their experiences influence how I view myself as a mother. It has been enlightening to see how my views on dating and love can sometimes affect how my children view my intentions and how I struggle to encourage them to have healthier dating habits than I grew up with.

Chinese Dating: That One Guy

One of my clearest adolescent memories was chatting with my dear cousin, who was the same age as me, and expressing in disbelief why we did not have boyfriends. American dating culture normalized that teenage girls should have a boyfriend while in high school. At the time, I felt like an old maid and wondered if I would ever find a boyfriend. This was in stark contrast to my extended Chinese household, where it was the norm for a daughter to live at home until she married. Ironically, this was considered more modern than in my grandparents' day, when one was expected to be arranged by the village matchmaker to be married. Disney's 1998 *Mulan* movie with the matchmaker was not that far-fetched. Although my grandparents always doted on me, I did not feel they loved each other by my American standards of love. My parents' marriage was a step up from my grandparents' as they married more for love instead of being arranged by a matchmaker. Learning about how my parents met may have influenced me more than I thought, as I also married the one boy I met and dated exclusively.

My dad left his home village, Toishan, in China when he was thirteen to find a job to help support his family. He went looking for work in Hong Kong, where my mom was born. He told me it was too expensive to learn how to fix washing machines, but learning how to become a barber was free and included room and board. By happenstance, he chose to train in my grandpa's barber shop, which is how he met my mother. Their dating consisted of going to the movies together, and they were married while in their early twenties. I was born when my mother was twenty-four. When I was twenty-four, I was dating my husband while completing my master's degree.

I also grew up watching my aunts' dating experiences. They all lived at home until they married. I recall seeing their boyfriends (and future husbands), and we would respectfully call them uncle so-and-so. Most of them were nice to us, came over for family dinners, drove family members around, and did the obligatory lifting of us up in the air to show off their strength. I recall my grandparents were happy to see these future sons-in-law in their home during Chinese holidays, except for one. My grandpa did not like this one boyfriend, but he did not stand in their way when he married my aunt, other than the Chinese look of disapproval whenever he was around. In hindsight, my grandpa was correct in his paternal instincts. Seeing my aunts and uncles with their partners was another way I learned about Chinese dating practices as a child. It seemed as though we all dated only one person and eventually married.

I also learned about love from Chinese and American romance movies. I noticed Chinese ones were incredibly tragic, and societal mores often prevented lovers from expressing their true feelings to one another. A Chinese movie that did well in the United States (US) was *Crouching Tiger, Hidden Dragon*, where Michelle Yeoh's character falls in love with her deceased husband's good friend, played by Chow Yun Fat, but she feels she cannot express her feelings to him because of her duty to her dead husband. When Chow Yun Fat's character is about to die, she professes her love to him, only to find out that he feels the same way about her but does not share his feelings for her because she was married to his best friend.

My all-time favourite Chinese movie is *Comrades: Almost a Love Story*, where star-crossed lovers Leon Lai and Maggie Cheung spend the entire movie chasing after different dreams and marrying other people, only to find themselves destined together at the movie's end. Even growing up in the 1970s and renting all the Chinese drama videotapes, a staple in many Chinese households because there were no Asian television channels to watch, those shows often centred on tragic love stories and more star-crossed lovers. My husband enjoys watching these stories of thwarted love while I yell at the characters to tell each other how they feel. I prefer American romantic movies where the boy gets the girl; they are soulmates and live happily ever after.

These types of movies profoundly affected how I viewed dating, romance, kismet, and committed relationships, including marriage. There is still a lot of shame in Asian cultures regarding dating multiple partners, cohabitation, sexual relations before marriage, divorce, and remarriage. Asian cultures often frown on talking openly about these facets of long-term relationships. I admit not always feeling entirely comfortable speaking openly with my children about these topics, but I hope to do better than what I grew up with, even if it makes me uneasy. This seems to be my common theme, leaning into the discomfort until it becomes more tolerable. It is a slow and dreadful process, but it spurred me to find the paltry research on Asian dating habits.

Cultural Differences in Dating Habits

In researching this topic, I found little research on Asian dating habits, but I learned a lot about the correlation between ethnic identity and intraethnic dating or dating within one's ethnic group. I find myself with one foot in each culture regarding dating. On my Westernized foot is the ability to choose our partners based on individualized choice and romance rather than practicalities like earning potential. One of my favourite movies while dating my husband was *The Little Mermaid* because Ariel chose her heart, Prince Eric, despite her father's wishes to marry a merman instead of a fish-eating human. I am headstrong like Ariel, and I fell in love with my husband's looks and how well he treated me, but I also saw that he was a good man who was family centred, which leads me to my Chinese foot, where filial piety is crucial for family harmony. I still want to do what I want, but I also consider my in-laws' and parents' wishes to an extent. The family runs smoother when we all get along and help one another. It was critical for our family's success that I had my mother-in-law caring for our children while my husband and I worked outside of the house. When I was stuck at work, I could count on my sister-in-law or my mother to pick up my kids from school, and when my sister-in-law needed her children to be picked up, the flexibility in my job as a professor made that possible.

I do not find this teamwork to be shared among my white counterparts. It is also sometimes difficult to describe what filial piety means to a non-Asian. I am not saying that all Asians practise filial piety, which combines caring for elders, maintaining a familial order, serving as a moral compass, and providing a support system between parent and child (Bedford and Yeh 100). In addition, being born into a family that only had daughters, filial piety meant something different in my home. I was lucky to have a father and grandfather who loved us equally, if not more, than a son or grandson. I still know many Chinese families where the son is favoured over the daughter. Having the fortune of a more egalitarian family and extended family significantly affected my view of myself as a Chinese woman. I never felt less than a Chinese man, which is rare among Asian women who grew up in patriarchal households.

Filial piety plays a significant role in a typical Asian home that is often hard for non-Asians to understand. It also has its pros and cons. I attribute much of my career success to the familial support of my in-laws and my parents. Childcare is so astronomically expensive in New York

City that without childcare from my family, I would not be able to advance in my career to provide a stable financial home for my children. More current analyses of filial piety find living by today's societal demands makes it difficult to adhere to these traditional norms. Yeh criticizes how this archaic notion can inhibit individual independence, which is necessary to thrive in a Westernized society. With more opportunities for women to become educated and financially independent, they no longer need to be treated in a subservient role that may predispose them to verbal and physical abuse (Yeh 67, 72). These are aspects of filial piety that need to be discussed more openly.

Raising Chinese American children can seem like a double-edged sword: I want my children to feel free to speak their minds and pursue their interests as I have. There are times when I wonder if motherhood would be less aggravating if I had raised my children to be more filial, to listen to their parents' wishes, and to make choices that consider the family's needs instead of one individual. I dare say that some days, I wish my children would listen to what I tell them to do and about whom to choose as a partner and whom not to. Then I reflect on how my happiness would have been hampered if I had listened to my overbearing mother in what she thought was best for me. I reluctantly realize I would have been a miserable accountant instead of my dream job as a psychologist, researcher, and professor.

Although occasionally hurt by my children's seemingly antifilial piety words, I still have the burden of being the responsible adult, the mother, and the psychologist. It feels ironic because I am reading about the burdens of supposedly ungrateful daughters of immigrant families in Erin Khue Ninh's book *Ingratitude*. Reading this text brought up many questions as I reflected on my mothering. Am I perpetuating the same cyclical abuse that I grew up with, as my mother often described me as selfish and ungrateful when I merely wanted to do what I wanted rather than succumb to filial piety? Am I imposing my archaic beliefs about dating onto my children? Do I need to accommodate my children's dating needs more? Why do I have trouble being a permissive parent when I know the benefits of this parenting style lead to positive developmental outcomes for emergent adults (Jensen et al. 519)? These questions race through my mind, making me feel inadequate as a mother. It seems as though once I seemingly master one aspect of mothering, my children begin a new developmental phase, which throws me back into the turmoil of not knowing what to do.

Regarding dating, it is easy to fall in love with the idea of falling in love. Those feelings and emotions from falling in love for the first time are powerful and addictive. In observing the partners my children have chosen, I am reminded of myself when I first fell in love with their father and the slew of mistakes we had made. In my attempt to be a good mother, I try to teach my children so they would not fall into the same pitfalls I had at their age, but maybe that is what growing up is all about—being able to make mistakes and learning from them while you have the support of your family as a safety net.

Treading Precariously as a Closeted-Authoritarian Mother

Being an immigrant mother, I often tread precariously between Chinese and American cultures. Not only must I constantly reflect on my upbringing and the trauma that comes with that, but I also need to constantly pivot on how to raise my children to be physically and mentally healthy. Raising these emergent adults is not for the faint of heart and may be more difficult for immigrant mothers who are unfamiliar with American cultural norms. Chinese people are still viewed as perpetual foreigners regardless of how many generations they have lived in the US (Pew Research Center; Ruiz et al.). That form of racism has made parenting highly stressful for Chinese immigrant parents such as myself and frustrating for my American-born children. Little did I know that the constant reminders that we are not Americans could affect my children's choice of a partner, as assimilation into American culture positively correlates with a preference for partners from the dominant culture (Chan et al. 671). My husband and I have worked hard to instill a strong ethnic identity in our children in our home and to value diversity, but living in a homogenous neighbourhood where the school system has few Asians can affect whom they choose as potential dating partners.

Being a social-personality psychologist has helped me better understand child and adolescent development. Still, little is said about the impact of how my intergenerational trauma can affect the way I raise my American-born children. Being a mother is difficult even in the most idyllic settings, so imagine dealing with intergenerational trauma and a global pandemic where Asians are being assaulted for merely existing.

Mothering young adults is incredibly stressful for me because I try to navigate away from the authoritarian parenting I grew up with. Still, I am sometimes unprepared for my children's independent mindset from growing up in America. With authoritarian parenting, there are clear right and wrong behaviours. Children do as they are told, or there will be unpleasant consequences. As a psychologist, I know this type of parenting leads to obedient children who are often afraid of their parents and grow up to be unhappy adults. On the flip side, authoritative parenting involves parents listening to their children with both parties involved in decision-making. This bilateral parenting style makes children independent, confident, generous, communicative, and happy adults. Michaeline Jensen et al. found that authoritative and permissive parenting styles were more likely to result in positive emergent adult developmental outcomes, especially indulgent parenting (520). This provides evidence that parenting styles need to meet the ever-changing needs of children as they mature and exercise their assertiveness. The Chinese mother in me, who is a closet authoritarian, is often frustrated when my children disagree with my wishes and say to me that they are not a child, can make their own decisions, I need to respect their boundaries, and a slew of other things that make me cringe. I have disagreed with my children's choice of a partner, but as young adults experiencing their first love, they do not see the red flags I do, making it doubly challenging to walk the fine line between a good mother and a meddling busybody. I do have to admit that I may have forgotten how it felt to be knee-deep into your first love.

My husband and I met in 1989 on a blind date, and we did not want to meet each other. I recall my mother asking my older sister if she knew of any nice boys for me, and my sister knew a funny Chinese boy who lived in the same dorm as her. I was busy working that fateful Columbus Day weekend when colleges let out for the long break, but I begrudgingly agreed to meet him. I was outside walking my dog when the ugliest blue car pulled up to my house, and the tallest and most handsome Chinese young man stepped out of it. We doubled-dated with my sister and her boyfriend over dim sum in Manhattan's Chinatown. Afterwards, we watched a Chinese movie alone at the Sung Sing Theater in Chinatown before stopping for a late lunch at the South Street seaport. It was love at first sight, and I eventually transferred to my sister's college in the middle of my sophomore year. He was the only boy I dated and had everything

I looked for. He was kind, funny, tall, athletic, good to his family, and loved me. I was enamored and drunk on this first love. He felt the same, and we quickly became college sweethearts. I was unprepared for the stir I caused when I transferred to his college, as a slew of Chinese girls felt I had thwarted their plans to date my boyfriend. Soon, the dirty looks, crank calls on my phone, vicious rumors, and lies about my reputation came about. No Chinese girl wished to befriend me because I was seen as the enemy who popped up to steal their potential suitor. When the movie *Crazy Rich Asians* came out, and Rachel Chu, the love interest of Nicholas Young, was pranked and bullied by all the Chinese women who wanted to become Mrs. Young, it reminded me of what I had gone through in college as I dated my husband. I was fortunate my husband did not listen to the lies spread about me by his so-called female friends and always stood by me when his friends tried to interfere in our relationship. I was immature and insecure about our relationship and what he saw in me. In remembering my naivete and insecurities, I should give my children more grace as they make mistakes in their dating relationships. With the heaviness of trying to be a good enough mother, I have forgotten a lot about how things were when I was an adolescent navigating the complexities of love.

Growing up in a traditional Chinese home, dating was often frowned upon. I recall telling my mother exactly what was planned as I went on a date with my boyfriend, now my husband. I explained we were going out for dinner around 8:00 p.m. and seeing a movie afterward. With most movies lasting around two hours, I would get home around elevenish at night. When my boyfriend dropped me off at home, my mom stayed up to yell at me for coming home late. It made absolutely no sense for her to humiliate me in front of my boyfriend when I gave her an exact timeline of what we had planned and a reasonable time we would return home. She knew who I was with and how he was honourable. Even my boyfriend commented how strange and unnecessary it was for my mother to behave like that before him.

My husband had a much different dating experience in his household, which was even more traditional, but his ease could easily be attributed to being male. His family and extended family were happy to see him dating me, especially his mom. I would address her formally in Chinese, but after a short while, she told me we did not have to be so formal and to call her Auntie. His grandpa was thrilled when he learned I was working on my doctorate. My husband had never brought any girls home to meet his family, so for him to take me was a big deal. Soon, I was eating dinner with his family, and he would use his chopsticks to put food from the family-style dishes in my rice bowl, which was a sign of love. When he came to my house for holidays with my extended family, my aunts were in awe of such a handsome, tall Chinese boy with big eyes. Chinese people rarely see tall men, and my boyfriend was six feet tall, athletic, and had double-lined eyes, which is considered a desirable trait among Asians as it makes their eyes look bigger. It was like I hit the dating jackpot with my husband, who was handsome, kind, athletic, funny, tall, catered to my every need, treated me and my family with respect, and was utterly devoted to me. All the doubt I had, wondering with my cousin why we did not have boyfriends, quickly dissipated. I only wish my children would meet a partner just like their dad.

I did not realize how my dating experiences with my husband were like finding a needle in a haystack until my children started dating. Fortunately, their first loves, who were more of a nightmare, did not last. I also found myself unprepared to handle their broken hearts, other than to ask if they wanted me to fly up to their colleges to take care of them and offer to beat down their ex-loves. I find myself filled with rage when my children are hurt, and my first motherly instinct is to externalize my anger, but I realize that my children do not want me to beat up anyone for them. From a psychological perspective, my mama bear instincts stem from my inner child who never felt protected enough by the adults around me, so I tend to overcompensate with my children. Again, I am slowly learning that my children do not need the same protection as I did, and I need to listen more instead of assuming what they need or want. In feeling uncomfortable with their choices in life, I have leaned into the discomfort to decipher why I think this way. In doing so, I am reminded of how traditional Chinese culture has a long history of patriarchy.

In living in the US, many of these values do not serve me as a Chinese woman who is well educated, works in and outside of her home, takes care of her children and elders in her family, and embraces traditional Chinese and American feminist values. Sometimes, it is scary to go against the cultural norms you have grown up with, and in raising your children to be bicultural, one has to constantly negotiate what is considered to be Chinese enough or too American. Fostering a strong ethnic identity is critical in accepting the many ways to be Chinese. When one is confident in who they are, they will be more likely to attract a loving and caring partner who is just as assured. This may be the goal I have been searching for as an immigrant mother to my Chinese American children. In trying to build my children's confidence as they are dating, I remind them of their positive attributes, the value of self-respect, and the importance of making responsible decisions. They know they always have the support of their loving parents. It takes a lot of faith as parents to believe that what you have taught your children stays in the back of their minds and that they will make good decisions as they fly farther away from their homes into the real world. As good parents, we talked to our children about drug use, bullying, how to stand up for oneself, and how to keep safe from child predators, but we did not spend as much time talking about the emotional entanglements in dating and falling in love, which I am sure they question AITA.

AITA: The Impact of My Dating Experiences on My Children

In trying to find a way to deal with the stress of dealing with my children's dating choices, I decided to turn to acupuncture. My acupuncturist often noted that my jaw muscles were frequently tense from having to be silent throughout the dating ordeals of my children. Parenting teenagers and young adults is the most stressful period of my life as a mother. You often need to hold your tongue when they say some of the most egregious statements or make choices you would never make. Ironically, keeping the communication lines open has much to do with keeping my mouth shut. I feel teenagers often judge their parents harshly and rarely take into account the trauma their parents have endured growing up as immigrants, trying not to commit the same mistakes they grew up with. Unfortunately, I find the burden of keeping the peace weighs heavily on me, and my acupuncturist sees the stress in my upper body as she pulls the stagnant chi from my neck and shoulders. Jokingly, she would remind me to tell my husband that she was not beating me as the releasing chi looked like bruises on my upper back. After a year of acupuncture, she told me that I had gotten a lot better with my musculoskeletal body.

We often talk about our children at my biweekly sessions, as she also has a son who is dating and close in age to my son. Being Chinese, she understands the cultural nuances of raising a Chinese American son and the struggles we face as mothers to balance bicultural values. We often share our experiences dealing with our sons' dating experiences, trying not to interfere as much as possible. Sharing our collective maternal advice is essential because my generation often did not have much dating experience. Many of us dated one boyfriend, whom we eventually married. This does not offer much experiential advice when our Chinese American children become old enough to date, and conflict may brew when your children's choices differ from yours. It is also doubly hard not to judge their choices as wrong when they are based on generational and cultural differences. I simply want my children to find loving partners who respect them and their families.

As a Chinese immigrant mother, I believe family has a critical cultural value. Having a partner who respects the role of family is crucial for harmony in many Chinese families. One is not just marrying their partner but also their extended family. This is not something many Americans understand because individualist culture emphasizes independence and agency, where the nuclear family is the crux of their value system. For many Chinese families, the extended family is the centre, and having an agreeable family situation is critical for its collective success (Wang and Xia 115). The differences between these two cultures can be oppositional and the source of contention between immigrant parents and their American-born children. It can also have significant effects on dating and ethnic identity. Michele Chan et al. found that a strong ethnic identity correlated with Asian teens choosing dating partners of the same ethnic group (676). Their study also found a positive correlation between higher levels of closeness to parents and a greater likelihood of dating from the same ethnic group (281).

When my son chose to date a girl who was not Asian, it made me feel as though I had failed him in instilling a strong Chinese identity and made me question the closeness of our mother-son bond. I thought we had a good relationship with our children and instilled in them a solid Chinese identity as their father is a descendant of the Song dynasty, making our children heirs of a powerful dynasty. I have often told our children they need to be comfortable with their Chineseness, for that is what people will see first in them. I also discussed the importance of standing up for oneself and breaking barriers, as I am my department's first Chinese full professor. American society tends to blame mothers, and in many ways, Asian cultures are even worse. Sadly, I seem to have internalized that maternal guilt. It does not matter how many accolades I have earned; any negativity involving my children often leads me to question whether I am a good enough mother, even though I know that the hormonal changes during adolescence are influential at this stage of their development.

Love during adolescence is a powerful drug as their raging hormones are altering their brain and bodies. As immigrant parents, we never really discussed the emotional parts of falling in love, which seems to be a cultural norm. My children know I only dated their father. I recall my husband telling the children that relationships in college take up a lot of time, which is not always good because you need to focus on studying and getting the most out of your college years. I was initially hurt hearing his statement, but in hindsight, we did waste a lot of time together that could have been spent studying and planning for our futures. I do not regret enjoying those infatuation years, but looking back, I see how we could have made better use of our time studying while still having fun. Because we learned from our mistakes, we have tried to steer our children to focus more on studying while still being able to have fun at college, and for the most part, they are more studious than we were at their age. The pitfalls of being a first-generation college student are another obstacle many immigrants are trying to figure out.

Unfortunately, with first love, there can also be first heartache. I was unprepared for the feelings of bittersweetness in me. I cannot show any happiness when a breakup occurs with a partner that I do not like, but it also pains me to see my children brokenhearted. Throughout this painful stage, I have learned how to be supportive yet quiet—to discreetly discard tokens of love lost and help them engage in family activities again. Never underestimate the love of a spoiled pug in healing a broken heart. When heartache arrives, I also need to acknowledge this is a part of adulting and share how proud I am of them for navigating this painful period of their lives. I have since learned to keep conversations short with my children because they do not want their mom psychoanalyzing their every turn. It is still hard not to take their sometimes hurtful words spoken in haste to me personally, but I am learning to listen more and talk less. They say hindsight is 20/20, and in retrospect, I should have included a conversation about positive and harmful relationships when we talked about drug and alcohol use. We should have included what to look for in a partner, centred the discussion on the importance of red flags, reiterated how loving parents have their children's best interests at heart, allowed more open conversations about dating, and encouraged questions about dating and long-term commitments. I shall take this as a sign to create better communication channels with my children.

Conclusion

Being a mother during adolescence and young adulthood is a precarious time. My children are busy trying to find their way in the world, and as their mother, I am trying to teach them as much as I can during this pivotal developmental period. Sometimes, I feel they are sliding off the side of a cliff, and I can barely hold onto them to impart all the wisdom they need to land safely. They are getting to a point where they do not wish to stay with their parents but are spending more time with their peers, which can influence them in ways I may disagree with. During this precarity in development, parents can feel they are running out of time, and the world seems to have a greater influence on their children. The world has gotten so much bigger and more problematic. Raising children during this time seems much more complicated than when I was growing up. I cannot fathom the political issues weighing heavily on many of us, from women losing the fundamental right to govern their bodies to the increasing gun violence in the school system. How does a mother protect her children during these troubling times? We must take our children's lead by staying close to them, listening more, and working jointly to help figure out this changing world around them.

I still have much to learn in parenting my children, who are growing into young adults. I need to say less and listen more to them. I need to give them space to make mistakes and let them know I am always here to support their decisions, even if I disagree. I had a funny conversation with my son about memes on Chinese parenting. We both enjoyed the movie *Shang-Chi and the Legend of the Ten Rings*, which is about a Chinese family. There is a meme on Asian parenting where a friend asks, "What's the most unrealistic part of being Asian in Shang-Chi?" and the response is a picture of Shang-Chi's mom telling him as a child how proud she is of him (@VinceLicas). The only time my mother told me she was proud of me was at my doctoral graduation. I have a picture of that occasion with a shocked look on my face.

In researching and writing this chapter, I have learned a lot about young love and have worked on being more supportive of my children's decision-making, taking their concerns seriously, centring the discussions on the behaviours and not the individual, not pushing them into a corner with ultimatums, and including their input without my judgmental motherly ways. Love is respect. Maybe one day, when my children become parents and raise their own teenagers and young adults, they will come across this chapter and realize how difficult this adjustment period is, not just for their soon-to-be adult children but also for their mamas. I hope they will know I was trying my best to run alongside them and catch up to them on this wild new journey to figure it out just as they were.

If and when my children become parents, I hope they will see with more clarity that I was not purposefully trying to be problematic and give me more grace in navigating all the internal and external chaos of being an immigrant mother trying to raise her American-born children in the best way she knew how at that moment in time. I also need to give myself more grace as I mother these beautiful beings on the cusp of adulthood without a roadmap, often stumbling in the dark and pivoting as quickly as possible. If each generation's success is to do better than the previous one, I feel confident I have played a part in my children's growing successes. I hope this chapter widens the perspective on young adult dating practices and offers some tools to help Asian mothers navigate this new stage of development. I conclude by sharing my wish for my children and yours. I wish for our children to learn to love themselves first so they can see and hear with clarity what they deserve: a loving partner who supports their growth as individuals, someone who loves them for who they are at the moment but also loves the person they are growing into, a person who dreams big with them and helps them achieve those dreams, and, lastly, a caring soul who travels with them as they live their best authentic lives.

Works Cited

Bedford, Olwen, and Yeh Kuang-Hui. "The History and the Future of the Psychology of Filial Piety: Chinese Norms to Contextualized Personality Construct." *Frontiers in Psychology*, vol. 10, no. 100, 2019, pp. 1–11.

Chan, Michele, et al. "Correlates of Ethnicity Related Dating Preferences Among Asian American Adolescents Across the High School Years." *Journal of Research on Adolescence*, vol. 30, no. 3, 2020, pp. 669–86.

Jensen, Michaeline, et al. "Parenting Styles in Emerging Adulthood." *Youth*, vol. 4, no. 2, 2024, pp. 509–24.

Ninh, Erin Khuê. *Ingratitude: The Debt-Bound Daughter in Asian American Literature*. NYU Press, 2011.

Ruiz, Neil, et al. "Asian Americans and the 'Forever Foreigner' Stereotype." *Pew Research Center*. 30 Nov. 2023, https://www.pewresearch.org/race-and-ethnicity/2023/11/30/asian-americans-and-the-forever-foreigner-stereotype/. Accessed 11 Mar. 2025.

Vince Licas [@vincelicas]. "Friend: "whats the most unrealistic part of being Asian in Shang-Chi?" Me:" X, 26 Nov. 2021, https://x.com/VinceLicas/status/1464405920792793090. Accessed 11 Mar. 2025.

Wang, Dan, and Yan Xia. "Couple Relationships in China." *Couple Relationships in a Global Context: Understanding Love and Intimacy Across Cultures*. Edited by Angela Abela et al. Springer, 2020, pp. 107–24.

Yeh, Kuang-Hui. "The Beneficial and Harmful Effects of Filial Piety: An Integrative Analysis." *Progress in Asian Social Psychology: Conceptual and Empirical Contributions*. Edited by Kuo-Shu Yang, et al. Praeger, 2003, pp. 67–82.

2.

Enduring Love: Maternal Experiences of Child-to-Mother Abuse

Laura Rite

In recent decades, much attention has been given to domestic and sexual violence against women, regarded by feminists as a "continuum of violence" (Kelly 46). However, many forms of gendered violence remain understudied, and the abuse of a mother by her child is believed to be one of the most hidden and underrecognized (Holt, "Researching Parent Abuse" 289; Holt and Lewis 792; Jackson 321). Frequently explored under the terminology "child-to-parent abuse" (CPA), Henry Harbin and Dennis Madden first called it "battered parent syndrome" (1288), who drew on their clinical experience with families to identify the prevalence of children physically abusing their parents. As with intimate partner violence, psychological threats, financial exploitation, and even sexual harassment can be used by children to gain control (Baker 225; Eckstein 367; Kennair and Mellor 204), and mothers are overwhelmingly recognized as the primary targets of such abuse (Simmons et al. 34). Although there is now growing evidence on the issue, it remains one of the most underrecognized and underreported maternal experiences, one steeped in shame and stigma forcing victim-survivors to keep the abuse hidden. This chapter and the research that it draws upon uses the term "child-to-mother abuse" (CMA), seeks to highlight the gendered nature of the harm, and explores maternal experiences within abusive mother-child relationships. This chapter aims to provide an overview of CMA while seeking to uncover some of the intricate dynamics shaping the mothering experiences of those navigating abuse from their teenage and young adult children.

Background

CMA refers to "a pattern of behaviour that uses verbal, financial, physical, or emotional means to practice power and exert control over a [mother]" (Holt, "Adolescent-to-Parent Abuse" 1). Although this chapter adopts the term due to its broad scope and reference to power dynamics, many countries lack a legal definition for such harm. Gender-neutral terminology, such as CPA, is more commonly adopted, and several different terms can also be found across the literature, including "youth-to-parent violence and aggression," "adolescent violence towards parents," and "parental abuse." Despite the use of the word "child," children of any age can perpetrate CMA; most commonly, the child behaving abusively is between twelve and eighteen. For some families, the abuse continues once the child has become an adult. Although abuse from adult children remains highly underresearched, teenagers and young adults abusing children is well documented. The words "child" and "mother" are used here to emphasize the relationship between the parties involved and its gendered nature, which is fundamental to this harm. Those subjected to this form of abuse can be biological mothers, stepmothers, adoptive and foster mothers, or other female caregivers who live with the child. Although to date the literature has concentrated primarily on biological parents, several studies have explored the experiences of adoptive parents—such as Julie Selwyn and Sarah Meakings, who identified it in their sample of 390 adoptive families (1228)—CPA was the primary reason for adoption disruption.

Prevalence

Even though frontline professionals and researchers have identified adolescent children abusing their mothers as a significant social issue, there is a dearth of robust and reliable data to evidence its prevalence (Moulds et al. 233; Walsh and Krienert 563). Prevalence estimates for CMA vary significantly depending upon the definition adopted, the type of study, and the research methodology used. These discrepancies, coupled with CMA's hidden and secretive nature, mean that finding accurate and reliable data is increasingly challenging. Much of the prevalence literature comes from North America, alongside a collection of papers from Australia, France, and Spain, and draws on data from different sources including police reports, youth justice data, and community studies. In the United States, population studies using randomized probability sampling provide the most substantial image of CPA's prevalence (Agnew and Huguley 706; Ulman and Straus 47), although much of this data is over thirty years old and focusses on physical abuse towards parents. Data from these studies identify prevalence rates of between 5 and 11 per cent for physical abuse (Agnew and Huguley 706; Peek et al. 1054). However, most employ self-reported data, and these figures may reflect an underreporting of abuse.

In the United Kingdom (UK), Kevin Browne and Catherine Hamilton's 1998 study is regularly cited as evidence of the "lifetime prevalence" of CPA (Baker 238), in which 469 university students completed questionnaires about their childhood and tactics used to handle conflict. Overall, 14.5 per cent of the students disclosed using violence towards their parents, and 3.8 per cent reported using significant violence in the last year. More recently, an analysis was conducted on the Crime Survey for England and Wales from 2011 to 2020, which identifies that CPA constituted 1.2 per cent of all violent crimes reported in the survey (Brennan et al. 88). However, it also highlights that around 43 per cent of families experiencing CPA did not report it to the police, so relying on criminal justice data is likely to underestimate the scale of the problem.

Methodology

The findings presented here are part of a larger piece of doctoral research aiming to explore the gendered nature of CMA and how professionals address it in the UK. The study specifically centres on amplifying the voices of mother victim-survivors, focussing on their lived experiences of abuse by their children and their interactions with support services. A constructivist grounded theory approach was employed, developed by Kathy Charmaz ("Grounded Theory" 30), which builds on the original methodology by Bar Glaser and Anselm Strauss (2–6). Grounded theory is particularly valuable in contexts where there is limited existing knowledge (Bryant and Charmaz 1–28). Despite an increasing body of literature on CMA, there remains a dearth of studies seeking to understand mothers' lived experiences of abuse (Burck et al. 13).

Data for the study was gathered through a qualitative methodology, involving in-depth interviews with victim-survivors, professionals, and experts in the field of CMA. Mothers were primarily recruited with the support of gatekeeper organizations who disseminated recruitment posters to relevant mothers. Interviews were conducted remotely over videoconference software (Microsoft Teams and Zoom) and lasted ninety to 120 minutes. Each interview was recorded with the participant's consent and transcribed as part of the grounded theory analytical process. Twenty mothers participated in the study, alongside four professionals and three experts. Twelve of these mothers were subjected to abuse from their teenage and adult children, and it is these mothers' narratives that are presented here. Interviews explored mothers' experiences of abuse from their children, other forms of gender violence, and their help-seeking journeys.

Data Analysis

Data analysis was conducted simultaneously with sampling and data collection, following the grounded theory methodology (Tie et al. 3). After each interview, verbatim transcription was performed using audio recordings. Analysis began with line-by-line coding, often using gerunds as recommended by Charmaz (*Constructing Grounded Theory* 49). This initial coding stage involved comparing each transcript and grouping similar codes into categories. The second stage, focussed coding (Charmaz *Constructing Grounded Theory* 57), involved refining and condensing the initial codes to explain key elements of the data. These codes were continuously compared against the entire dataset and other codes to ensure they accurately captured victim-survivors' experiences. The final stage, theoretical coding (A. Bryant and K. Charmaz 362), identified relationships between categories through constantly comparing initial and focussed codes, leading to the development of core categories. Theoretical saturation was achieved when no new categories emerged from the data.

Ethical Considerations

Ethical approval was obtained from the University's Humanities & Social Sciences Research Ethics Committee. Before each interview, the researcher explained the study's purpose and reminded participants of their right to withdraw from the interview or decline to answer any question. Informed consent was obtained from all participants before the interviews commenced. All data have been pseudonymized, and any identifying details have been removed.

Theoretical Framework

CMA is a highly complex issue intersecting with multiple areas of concern, including but not limited to violence against women, youth crime, and child protection. As a result, numerous competing approaches exist to understand the phenomenon. Given the multifaceted nature of this issue, it felt inappropriate to rely on a singular perspective, and although a feminist orientation strongly informs this study, this perspective alone does not adequately aid in a comprehensive understanding of such a complex harm. Consequently, a multiconcept framework was adopted that draws on four core theoretical perspectives to support the enquiry into the ranges of ways mothers may experience and make sense of CMA: feminist theory and theories related to the social construction of motherhood, ideologies of childhood, and social learning. Most relevant to the findings presented here are how the ideologies surrounding motherhood and how motherhood is socially constructed have led to the ideal archetype of the good mother (Garwood 19; Tardy 435) and harsh judgment of those who do not fulfil the expectations associated with it (Strega et al. 707). To gain a deeper understanding of how this form of abuse affects mother victim-survivors, it is crucial to reflect on the various ways through which motherhood is socially constructed and how ideals of good motherhood may have been internalized by both victim-survivors and professionals

Findings: CMA Experiences

Guilt, Shame, and Blame

When asked to describe their experiences of CMA, mothers invariably began to discuss the ways the abuse had affected them and their lives. Although how their mental and physical health had been negatively affected were prevalent in their accounts, mothers' descriptions of the specific impact of being subjected to abuse from their children was particularly striking. Across their narratives, mothers spoke at length about the feelings of embarrassment and shame they experienced when their child displayed abusive behaviour in a way that was visible to the outside world. Although not all participants used the word "shame," every mother described a desire to hide the abuse from those outside of the immediate family. Mothers were acutely aware of how their children's behaviour would be perceived, and the need to prevent others from becoming aware was intricately tied to how their mothering abilities would be viewed and judged. Victim-survivors felt their children's abuse was a direct reflection of them and their capabilities as mothers, with many specifically referencing the social culture of holding parents responsible for their children's behaviour: "I'm very embarrassed, um, about his behaviour and whilst I say it's his behaviour yeah, I know it's because I think there is still this... 'blame the parents' mentality... and so I would almost say I feel ashamed" (mother of adult son).

Mothers of teenagers and young adults often experienced particularly intense feelings of shame, especially when friends or family members witnessed their abuse. There was a sense for these mothers that their children's behaviour could no longer be excused by their age. For mothers of younger children, their narratives were regularly filled with descriptions of how the abusive behaviours were minimized or dismissed, particularly at the start of the abuse, as such behaviour was viewed as normal for children of that age. However, for those whose children continued (or started) behaving abusively into their teenage and young adult years, it was evident that the behaviour was automatically considered less acceptable. Mothers reflected that their children's behaviours became more visible to those outside of the family unit as they got older, which exposed them to further shame and embarrassment: "[I feel] shame, yes, especially in public, you know, my god, when your kids kick off in public, and you just wanna walk away, and, you know, you just want a paper bag over your head and to be like, 'No it's not me; they're not my children.' Yeah, it's definite shame, yeah" (mother of young adult son and daughter). A mother of a young adult son shared the following: "But look at the way everybody's looking at me because he is my son; therefore, I am responsible for his behaviour. Oh, the shame, oh my gosh, that was awful, awful.... I still feel this shame inside and I don't think I'll ever get rid of it."

It was clear that mothers not only felt the weight of responsibility for their children's behaviour, but also of its visibility, particularly when the abuse occurred in view of others. As one mother articulated above, it is not just the way that their children behave that creates this feeling of shame, but also a pre-emption that they are going to be blamed for the abuse. This suggests that mothers are aware of ingrained cultures of mother blaming even before they are subjected to such judgment, and that the fear alone of being held responsible for their children's abusive behaviour is enough to cause deep feelings of shame and a need to hide the abuse. This isolation furthered feelings of embarrassment, often negatively impacting mothers' perception of themselves, their abilities, and their mothering identity.

Impact on Mothering Identity

Experiencing abuse from their child had a series of significant effects on victim-survivors' identities as mothers. Several mothers referred to how their children had intentionally and directly targeted their mothering identity, through verbal abuse such as "when things are difficult... they will say you're not my mum" (Mother of three teenage sons). However, for most mothers the impact on their mothering identities was a more indirect consequence of CMA, and there was unanimous agreement that the mother-child relationship was permanently changed. For all mothers, the abuse that they were subjected to placed strain on their relationships with their children, often affecting their bond not only with the child displaying the abusive behaviours but also with any siblings. There is a dichotomy present for many of these mothers in which they both love their children yet at the same time also experience a range of negative emotions, including fear, disappointment and, at times, intense dislike. This dichotomy subverts the maternal emotions which are expected and accepted, and so mothers often report further shame and embarrassment because of feeling this way. In their interviews, mothers described a sense of disbelief that the child they had raised could cause them such pain and suffering, something directly contradicting what they had believed children could be capable of. In the quote below, one mother of a teenage son explained how she struggled to recognize her son in light of his behaviour, and she reveals the fracture that the abuse had created between them: "It was awful. It was like he was possessed by somebody else. He was not a child that I recognized as somebody I could have given birth to 'cause I'm not like that. My sisters and brothers are not like that. None of my family is like that. And it was... I just didn't recognize him."

For some, this distance affected their identities as their children's mother to the extent that several described feeling that they no longer had a maternal relationship with their children. Since they felt unable to fulfill the responsibilities of good mothers and, most crucially, control their child's behaviour, mothers felt the abuse was preventing them from being able to mother in the way that they wanted to, effectively stripping them of their mothering identity. In the quotations below, it is striking how one mother describes feeling that her son belongs to someone else, suggesting that an element of maternal identity is having ownership of one's child and, in a sense, ownership of their actions:

> This is gonna sound like a strange phrase, and it's not meant to sound how it does, but I don't feel like I even own [child's name] anymore. I feel like he belongs to someone else. (mother of teenage son)

> To be honest, I don't want him to call me mum. Umm I I I wish he would just call me [name]. I don't want to be his mum anymore. (mother of young adult son)

As the mothers describe in the quotations above, this level of detachment from their sons felt significant and may have also served as a coping mechanism to enable them to manage their abusive situations. It is important to also reflect here on the level of shame that often accompanied these feelings and the courage it took for mothers to disclose them within the interview. Societal stories of motherhood are dominated by descriptions of unconditional maternal love, setting an expectation this is something that all mothers should and do experience with their children, regardless of circumstances (Garwood 21; Takševa 153). Although, as will be explored, most of the mothers interviewed continued to express maternal love and responsibility for their children despite the abuse, this was often experienced simultaneously with feelings of fear, grief and, for some mothers, hatred: "I went through stages where I hated her" (mother of teenage daughter). Mothers were highly conscious that they are not supposed to hate their children, which further affected their mothering identities and, for some, the belief they were not good mothers, leading to intensified feelings of shame.

Narratives of Responsibility: Motherhood as Sacrifice

As mothers described the many ways their experiences of abuse affected them and their mothering identity, the notion of maternal responsibility emerged as a central theme, with this responsibility taking several different forms. Mothers appeared quick to label themselves as at least partially responsible for their children's abusive behaviours, with self-blame often accompanying the feelings of shame explored earlier. Mothers grappling with this self-blame believed that if they had been better mothers, or been able to mother differently, their children would not have been behaving abusively. These feelings of guilt and self-blame were not fully rationalized explanations of the abuse but rather a reflection of the social and cultural expectations and responsibilities placed on women to be good mothers:

> I felt at times guilt, should I be doing something more, because I should be able to fix this. (mother of teenage sons)

> Um. I feel like it's just, uh, how I'll be perceived as such cause ummm, I'm supposed to be the nurturer, and I'm supposed to like umm to know how to handle my own child, you know? (mother of teenage children)

Both mothers highlight how self-blame can manifest from the internalized expectation that mothers should be able to handle their child and use their mothering skills to stop or prevent their child from displaying unwanted and socially unacceptable behaviours. For many of the mothers interviewed, however, no matter how hard they tried and despite the various techniques adopted, they could not stop their child from behaving abusively, perceived by some as further evidence of their failure to meet the expectations of good motherhood.

Not only did mothers feel responsible for the abuse they were experiencing, but their accounts were often filled with narratives around the responsibility they feel for their children, particularly about protecting them. The desire, or need, to protect their children was considered by many mothers a part of their maternal role, and this often meant protecting them from criminalization or police involvement. For all mothers interviewed, there was a sense that motherhood and, importantly, good motherhood was accompanied by a responsibility to love and support their children unconditionally, regardless of their behaviour, and even at the mothers' expense. For many, pursuing criminal charges against their children was not something they felt willing or able to do, regardless of the severity of the abuse they experienced:

> And I refused to make a statement 'cause I said he needs help, I don't, I don't want my child to be a criminal. He needs help. (mother of young adult son and daughter)

> I don't want my son criminalized from the fact that I've given them information. (mother of teenage son)

Criminalizing their children was presented by the mothers interviewed as a permanent reaction to an impermanent problem. Despite the harm the abuse was causing them, most mothers wanted to protect their children from these consequences. This desire to protect their children from criminalization was particularly significant for those mothering teenagers and young adults, where the fears of police involvement became particularly acute. For these mothers, the likelihood of their reports to police being taken seriously and progressing to criminal charges posed a significant barrier to seeking this form of support. Effectively, most mothers were willing to sacrifice themselves and allow themselves to be subjected to violence and abuse to protect their children's future. By remaining silent about their abuse to protect their children, the mothers could not seek or receive any support for themselves, and for most families, this meant the abusive behaviours continued. Mothers felt that it was their responsibility to protect their children, and this is what good mothers would do. One mother specifically described her maternal responsibility as the reason behind her decision never to contact the police regarding her young adult's abusive behaviours: "Not once did I think about phoning the police, not once. Yeah, it's the maternal responsibility and the morals within the maternal role. I would never contemplate ringing the police."

For this mother, the decision to protect her son and keep the abuse secret was tied to her moral responsibilities as a mother. This mother made numerous references to these moral responsibilities throughout her interview and continuously reenforced the notion that regardless of how her son's abuse had escalated, she would not have contacted the police. Motherhood, for many interviewed, was synonymous with acts of self-sacrifice for their children, and regardless of the abuse they were subjected to, all mothers interviewed expressed the continued sense of maternal responsibility to love and protect their children at all costs.

Discussion

The study sought to capture the lived experiences of mothers affected by CMA and foreground the voices of those who have remained hidden in the existing literature: mothers who have been subjected to abuse from their children. CMA remains an underrecognized and underresearched form of abuse (Holt, "Researching Parent Abuse" 289; Hunter and Nixon 211), and although a body of evidence has developed in this area, research focussed specifically on the experiences of mothers remains lacking (Burck et al. 13). Empirical research can, therefore, further develop the field and enable a deeper and more comprehensive understanding of CMA as a social issue.

Being abused by one's child affects mothers in a host of different ways, from contributing to poor mental health, financial instability or job loss, to the physical consequences of being subjected to violence and abuse (Herring 199; Holt, "Adolescent-to-Parent Abuse" 492). However, something that appears frequently across the literature on CMA and was also highly prevalent in the narratives of mothers interviewed for this study was the sense of shame associated with their abuse. CMA is a social issue that remains deeply stigmatized due in part to the societal assumption that mothers are responsible for the actions of their children. Amanda Holt describes CPA as a "double stigma" (Holt, "The Terrorist in My Home" 454; Holt and Retford 365), the stigma of being the victim of abuse within their home and the stigma of parenting a problematic child. This double stigma is arguably highly gendered. Mothers may also experience additional stigmatization for failing to stop or prevent their child from behaving abusively, as this may be perceived as a further indication of mothering failure (Brule and Eckstein 198).

Across their interviews, all mothers in this study displayed a tendency to blame themselves and express feelings of guilt for their children's abuse (Jackson 327; Peck et al. 7; Williams et al. 601). As they attempted to make sense of their abuse, the mothers' narratives were often filled with feelings of deep embarrassment and shame, which were multifaceted and influenced by many elements associated with their abuse. Most commonly, mothers felt their children's behaviour was an indicator of their proficiency and competency as mothers. They were concerned about how this abuse would be interpreted by others, regardless of whether they believed their mothering was to blame for it. The shame associated with CMA is highly gendered, as it is intricately linked to ideologies of motherhood and associated social expectations. The visibility of their children's abuse, be that to their motherhood peers, or professionals, was something that deeply troubled mothers, and there was an overwhelming sense of fear of their family's situation being discovered. In this way, the performative nature of the good mother ideology becomes apparent (DeGroot and Vik 43; Orton-Johnson 7) as mothers felt forced to keep their abuse hidden rather than allow their reputations as mothers to become tarnished. In his writing on stigma, Erving Goffman describes stigmatization as the process of living with a "spoiled identity" (31). The mothers felt their identities as good mothers had been damaged by the stigma or the double stigma of CMA (Holt, "The Terrorist in My Home" 454; Holt and Retford 365). Aware of their "spoiled identities," mothers expressed a desperate need to rectify their image and prove themselves to be good mothers despite the behaviour of their children while also wrestling with the reality they could not mother in a way they wanted.

The abuse from their children and the subsequent shame and guilt that mothers experienced also had a significant impact on their mothering identities and the mother-child relationship. Mothers subjected to CMA are continuously challenged to reconcile the multiple roles they play; they are the mother and thus feel responsible for loving and protecting their children while also being the victim of their children's abuse. Many mothers described complex feelings towards their children, which often involved intense dislike, and these experiences and emotions directly disrupt societal stories around motherhood and the unconditional love mothers are supposed to feel for their children. In recent decades, motherhood scholars have sought to reclaim the concept of "maternal ambivalence," the mixture of positive and negative thoughts and feelings that mothers can have towards their children (Takševa 154). Although originally framed as potentially damaging to a child's development, maternal ambivalence has more recently been recognized as a natural phenomenon that may be experienced across motherhood journeys (Takševa 153; Raphael-Leff 1). Despite this, the idealized image of unconditional maternal love remains dominant and expected, and feelings of ambivalence towards one's child, even if only fleeting, are often accompanied by shame and guilt (Davies and Welch 418). This maternal ambivalence is compounded further for those living with CMA, and mothers are left feeling deeply ashamed, not only about the abuse they are subjected to but for the way it makes them feel about their children. For some, the distance between themselves and their children and the maternal ambivalence created by the abuse affected their identities significantly. Several mothers described feeling their child was no longer theirs and they did not have a maternal relationship with them, a feeling that may be further compounded for those mothering teenage or young adult children, who may already be experiencing feelings of distance or separation from their children as they entered adolescence.

Alongside discourse of responsibility for the abusive behaviours, mothers' accounts were filled with narratives around the responsibility they feel for their children, particularly with protecting them. The desire, or need, to protect their children was considered by many mothers a part of their maternal responsibility, and this often meant protecting them from criminalization or police involvement. Across the literature, the involvement of the police and engagement with the criminal justice system is presented as something that many mothers will try to avoid to prevent their children from suffering the potentially long-term consequences of their abusive behaviour. In a study by Rosemary Paterson et al., the mothers interviewed said involving the police was a betrayal of their roles as mothers and reporting their children to the police would be betraying them (98). Many of the mothers in Jo Howard and Naomi Rottem's (54) report viewed contacting the police as a viable option if their children's abuse escalated in severity, although they were also reluctant to do this. For many, it was also unlikely they would press charges or pursue a criminal conviction, and, thus, the sense of maternal responsibility to protect their children often created a significant barrier to support. The intersectional barriers the victim-survivors from different social identities face may further exacerbate the challenges of accessing appropriate support. Institutional racism against people from racialized minority backgrounds within the criminal justice system is well documented, and mothers from minority groups often feel less able to trust the police to support them adequately (Femi-Ajao et al. 22; Tam et al. 528). Crucially, mothers from minority groups may feel less able to contact the emergency services for fear of discriminatory practices or harsher responses to their children (Hulley et al. 1004; Nowakowski-Sims and Rowe 273).

Conclusion

Accounts from mothers subjected to abuse from their children demonstrate the multifaceted nature of the harm, and the wide-reaching impact it can have on mothers' identities, their sense of self, and their relationship with their children. This chapter has provided an overview of CMA before drawing on the author's emerging doctoral research to explore mothers' lived experiences of CMA. Mothers' narratives revealed the guilt, shame, and self-blame they felt due to their abuse, and the idea that their children's behaviour reflected upon them as mother was a prevalent theme. For those with teenage and young adult children, the shame associated with their abuse was compounded by the inability to excuse such behaviour due to the children's age and their increased visibility. Mothers wrestled with the notion of maternal responsibility towards their children, often resulting in their refusing to report the abuse to protect their child. As they described their experiences of abuse, mothers regularly referred to the archetype of the good mother and how they were burdened by the social expectations accompanying this ideal. These expectations, often internalized by the mothers themselves, compounded the impact of the shame and stigma of CMA and left mothers further isolated in their abuse. These findings highlight the need for further awareness of CMA to enable the deconstruction of the stigma associated with the harm and empower impacted families to reach out for support.

Works Cited

Agnew, Robert, and Sandra Huguley. "Adolescent Violence Toward Parents." *Journal of Marriage and Family*, vol. 51, no. 3, 1989, pp. 699–711.

Baker, Victoria. "Adolescent-to-Parent Violence and Abuse." *Working with Domestic Violence and Abuse across the Lifecourse: Understanding Good Practice*. Edited by Ravi Thiara and Lorraine Radford. Jessica Kingsley Publishers, 2021, pp. 222–51.

Brennan, Iaian, et al. *Comprehensive Needs Assessment of Child/Adolescent to Parent Violence and Abuse in London*. London's Violence Reduction Unit, 2022.

Browne, Kevin, and Catherine Hamilton. "Physical Violence Between

Young Adults and Their Parents: Associations with a History of Child Maltreatment." *Journal of Family Violence*, vol. 13, no. 1, 1998, pp. 59–79.

Brule, Nancy, and Jessica Eckstein. "'Am I Really a Bad Parent?': Adolescent-to-Parent Abuse (AtPa) Identity and the Stigma Management Communication (SMC) Model." *Journal of Family Communication*, vol. 16, no. 3, 2016, pp. 198–215.

Bryant, Anthony, and Kathy Charmaz. "Grounded Theory Research: Methods and Practices." *The Sage Handbook of Grounded Theory*. Edited by Anthony Bryant and Kathy Charmaz. SAGE Publications, 2007, pp. 1–28.

Bryant, Anthony, and Kathy Charmaz. *The Sage Handbook of Grounded Theory*. SAGE Publications, 2007.

Burck, David, et al. "Silenced Mothers: Exploring Definitions of Adolescent-to-Parent Violence and Implications for Practice." *Advances in Social Work and Welfare Education*, vol. 21, no. 1, 2019, pp. 7–18.

Charmaz, Kathy. *Constructing Grounded Theory*. 2nd ed. SAGE Publications, 2014.

Charmaz, Kathy. "Grounded Theory." *Rethinking Methods in Psychology*. Edited by Jonathan Smith, et al. SAGE Publications, 1995, pp. 27–49.

Davies, Bronwyn, and D'arne Welch. "Motherhood and Feminism: Are They Compatible? The Ambivalence of Mothering." *The Australian and New Zealand Journal of Sociology*, vol. 22, no. 3, 1986, pp. 411–26.

DeGroot, Jocelyn, and Tennley Vik. "'Fake Smile. Everything Is under Control': The Flawless Performance of Motherhood." *Western Journal of Communication*, vol. 85, no. 1, 2021, pp. 42–60.

Eckstein, Nancy. "Emergent Issues in Families Experiencing Adolescent to Parent Abuse." *Western Journal of Communication*, vol. 68, no. 4, 2004, pp. 365–88.

Femi-Ajao, Omolade, et al. "A Qualitative Systematic Review of Published Work on Disclosure and Help-Seeking for Domestic Violence and Abuse Among Women from Ethnic Minority Populations in the UK." *Ethnicity and Health*, vol. 25, no. 5, 2020, pp. 732–46.

Garwood, Eliza. "Regulating Motherhood: A Foucauldian Analysis of the Social Construction of the Mother." *The New Birmingham Review*, vol. 1, no. 1, 2014, pp. 19–28.

Glaser, Bar, and Anselm Strauss. *The Discovery of Grounded Theory: Strategies for Qualitative Research.* Aldine Publishing, 1967.

Goffman, Erving. *Stigma: Notes on the Management of Spoiled Identity.* Englewood Cliffs, 1963.

Harbin, Henry, and Dennis Madden. "Battered Parents: A New Syndrome." *American Journal of Psychiatry*, vol. 136, no. 10, 1979, pp. 1288-91.

Herring, Jonathan. "The Abuse of Parents by Children." *Domestic Abuse and Human Rights.* Edited by Jonathan Herring. Intersentia, 2020, pp. 195-214.

Holt, Amanda. "Adolescent-to-Parent Abuse as a Form of 'Domestic Violence': A Conceptual Review." *Trauma, Violence, and Abuse*, vol. 17, no. 5, 2016, pp. 490-99.

Holt, Amanda. "Researching Parent Abuse: A Critical Review of the Methods." *Social Policy and Society*, vol. 11, no. 2, 2012, pp. 289-98.

Holt, Amanda. "'The Terrorist in My Home': Teenagers' Violence Towards Parents—Constructions of Parent Experiences in Public Online Message Boards." *Child and Family Social Work*, vol. 16, no. 4, 2011, pp. 454-63.

Holt, Amanda, and Sam Lewis. "Constituting Child-to-Parent Violence: Lessons from England and Wales." *The British Journal of Criminology*, vol. 61, no. 3, 2021, pp. 792-811.

Holt, Amanda, and Simon Retford. "Practitioner Accounts of Responding to Parent Abuse—A Case Study in Ad Hoc Delivery, Perverse Outcomes and a Policy Silence." *Child & Family Social Work*, vol. 18, no. 3, 2013, pp. 365-74.

Howard, Jo, and Naomi Rottem. *It All Starts at Home: Male Adolescent Violence to Mothers.* Melbourne Inner South Community Health Service, 2008.

Hulley, Joanne, et al. "Intimate Partner Violence and Barriers to Help-Seeking among Black, Asian, Minority Ethnic and Immigrant Women: A Qualitative Metasynthesis of Global Research." *Trauma Violence Abuse*, vol. 24, no. 2, 2023, pp. 1001-15.

Hunter, Caroline, and Judy Nixon. "Introduction: Exploring Parent Abuse—Building Knowledge Across Disciplines." *Social Policy and Society*, vol. 11, no. 2, 2012, pp. 211-15.

Jackson, Debra. "Broadening Constructions of Family Violence: Mothers' Perspectives of Aggression from Their Children." *Child and Family Social Work*, vol. 8, no. 1, 2003, pp. 321–29.

Kelly, Liz. "The Continuum of Sexual Violence." *Women, Violence and Social Control*. Edited by Jalna Hanmer and Mary Maynard. Humanity Press, 1987, pp. 46–60.

Kennair, Nicola, and David Mellor. "Parent Abuse: A Review." *Child Psychiatry and Human Development*, vol. 38, no. 3, 2007, pp. 203–19.

Moulds, Lauren, et al. "Adolescent Violence Towards Parents—Prevalence and Characteristics Using Australian Police Data." *Australian and New Zealand Journal of Criminology*, vol. 52, no. 2, 2019, pp. 231–49.

Nowakowski-Sims, Eva, and Amanda Rowe. "The Relationship between Childhood Adversity, Attachment, and Internalizing Behaviors in a Diversion Program for Child-to-Mother Violence." *Child Abuse and Neglect*, vol. 72, no. 1, 2017, pp. 266–75.

Orton-Johnson, Kate. "Mummy Blogs and Representations of Motherhood: "Bad Mummies" and Their Readers." *Social Media + Society*, vol. 3, no. 2, 2017, pp. 1–10.

Paterson, Rosemary, et al. "Adolescent Violence Towards Parents: Maintaining Family Connections When the Going Gets Tough." *Australian and New Zealand Journal of Family Therapy*, vol. 23, no. 2, 2002, pp. 90–100.

Peck, Allison, et al. "Young Person–to–Mother Violence: An Integrative Review of Evidence from Australia and New Zealand." *Australian Social Work*, vol. 76, no. 2, 2021, pp. 245–58.

Peek, Charles W, et al. "Teenage Violence toward Parents: A Neglected Dimension of Family Violence." *Journal of Marriage and Family*, vol. 47, no. 4, 1985, pp. 1051–58.

Raphael-Leff, Joan. "Healthy Maternal Ambivalence." *Psycho-analytic Psychotherapy in South Africa*, vol. 18, no. 2, 2010, pp. 57–73.

Selwyn, Julie, and Sarah Meakings. "Adolescent-to-Parent Violence in Adoptive Families." *The British Journal of Social Work*, vol. 46, no. 5, 2016, pp. 1224–40.

Simmons, Melanie, et al. "Sixty Years of Child-to-Parent Abuse Research: What We Know and Where to Go." *Aggression and Violent Behavior*, vol. 38, 2018, pp. 31–52.

Strega, Susan, et al. "Connecting Father Absence and Mother Blame in Child Welfare Policies and Practice." *Children and Youth Services Review*, vol. 30, no. 7, 2008, pp. 705–16.

Takševa, Tatjana. "Mother Love, Maternal Ambivalence, and the Possibility of Empowered Mothering." *Hypatia*, vol. 32, no. 1, 2017, pp. 152–68.

Tam, Dora, et al. "Racial Minority Women and Criminal Justice Responses to Domestic Violence." *Journal of Family Violence*, vol. 31, no. 4, 2016, pp. 527–38.

Tardy, Rebecca. "'But I Am a Good Mom': The Social Construction of Motherhood through Health-Care Conversations." *Journal of Contemporary Ethnography*, vol. 29, no. 4, 2000, pp. 433–73.

Tie, Ylona Chun, et al. "Grounded Theory Research: A Design Framework for Novice Researchers." *SAGE Open Medicine*, vol. 7, no. 3, 2019, pp. 1–8.

Ulman, Arina, and Murray Straus. "Violence by Children Against Mothers in Relation to Violence between Parents and Corporal Punishment by Parents." *Journal of Comparative Family Studies*, vol. 34, no. 1, 2003, pp. 41–60.

Walsh, Jeffrey, and Jessie Krienert. "Child-Parent Violence: An Empirical Analysis of Offender, Victim, and Event Characteristics in a National Sample of Reported Incidents." *Journal of Family Violence*, vol. 22, no. 7, 2007, pp. 563–74.

Williams, Megan, et al. "'It's Like He Just Goes Off, BOOM!': Mothers and Grandmothers Make Sense of Child-to-Parent Violence." *Child and Family Social Work*, vol. 22, no. 2, 2016, pp. 597–606.

3.

In Her Reflection: The Effect of Daughters' Educational Pursuits and Career Exploration on Maternal Career Aspirations and Roles

Lisa H. Rosen, Linda J. Rubin, Isabella Iven, Maritza Marquez, Savannah Dali, and Dante Jackson

Influences on career aspirations and vocational identity development have been analyzed through many lenses. Prior research has established the importance of career exploration for young adults (Jiang), particularly emphasizing the influence of mothers on their children's career decision-making (Chifamba; Whiston and Keller). However, there is a dearth of literature on the inverse: how young adult children's career exploration influences their mothers.

Research examining how children influence maternal career trajectories largely focusses on young children. The expectation of having children can affect maternal career development even before starting a family. Depending on a woman's age and current career outlook, women planning to have children may work fewer hours, gravitate towards more family-friendly occupations with flexible schedules, and earn less than women without children (Kahn). Those who become mothers are often unofficially assigned as the primary managers of the household and are limited within the workspace through the reinforcement of gender stereotypes (Ciciolla and Suniya). Although family-friendly jobs facilitate working mothers' professional experiences, wage penalties still affect women (Fuller and Hirsh).

Maternal theorists Andrea O'Reilly and Sharon Hays have previously highlighted the phenomenon of intensive mothering, or parental scripts surrounding child-centred mothering wherein the mother is primarily responsible for their children's life success. Prior research on intensive mothering suggests the expectations placed upon mothers to devote significant time, labour, and energy towards childrearing do not disappear or dampen in the face of workforce demands, which can affect women's career decisions and advancement (Hays; O'Reilly). The concept of the "second shift" underscores such effects: Mothers are expected to work their paid jobs in addition to engaging in unpaid labour in the home (e.g., cooking, cleaning, and childcare), creating a double burden (Dugan and Barnes-Farrell; Hochschild and Machung).

Together with the societal notions surrounding working mothers, the intersectionality of individuals' different identities creates unique lived experiences. For instance, working single mothers often have to navigate all aspects of the household as the only parental figure (Dugan and Barnes-Farrell). Research suggests mothers who feel more pressure towards perfect mothering have difficulty with work-life balance and may have lower career ambitions (Meeussen and Van Laar). With greater household responsibilities and the pressure of intensive mothering norms, single mothers are disproportionately affected by the systems of inequality affecting motherhood and careers (Dharani and Balamurugan). Immigrant mothers in the United States (US) similarly face many barriers to success, including education level, language, and race (Fitzsimmons et al.). Due to the intersectionality of maternal identities, this chapter acknowledges the diverse experiences of the mothers of young adults interviewed.

The current study focusses on the mothers of first-year college students, as the transition to college is associated with major changes for both daughters and their mothers. First-year students often engage in important aspects of career exploration, such as choosing their major and working in jobs outside of school, which affect the trajectory of their educational and vocational journeys (Hey et al.). Mothers report changes in parent-child dynamics during their child's first year of university

(Harper et al.). This qualitative study examined a unique aspect of parenting young adults: how daughters leaving for college and engaging in career exploration affect mothers' reflections on their career trajectories and maternal roles. This chapter addresses the literature gap on daughters' influence on their mothers' career decision-making in the workforce and the second shift at home. In this study, mother-daughter dyads were interviewed about their experiences with career development and vocational identity. A thematic analysis of the recorded interviews was conducted according to the guidelines established by qualitative researchers Virginia Braun and Victoria Clarke in 2006. Building from prior research on how mothers affect their daughters' conceptions of careers, this chapter focusses on the inverse experience: how daughters' career exploration influences their mothers.

Methodology

Participants

Participants included sixty-four mother-daughter dyads recruited from introductory psychology classes at a Hispanic-serving institution in the Southwestern US, which is primarily for women. To participate, daughters needed to identify as women between eighteen and nineteen whose mothers had been employed during the past two years. Daughters agreed to be interviewed simultaneously with their mothers and have these interviews recorded for later transcription.

Demographic responses from the mothers are found in the table on the next page. Because participants could skip questions if they preferred, not all participants answered every question. For the daughters' group, the mean age was 18.45 years (SD = 0.50), with all participants between eighteen and nineteen.

Table 1. Participant Demographics—Mothers

Age Range

35–40: 9 (17.3%)
41–45: 10 (19.2%)
46–50: 18 (34.6%)
51–55: 11 (21.2%)
56–60: 3 (5.8%)
61–65: 1 (1.9%)

Race/Ethnicity

White: 12 (18.8%)
Black or African American: 16 (25.0%)
Hispanic or Latino: 26 (40.1%)
Asian or Asian American: 4 (6.3%)
Other: 1 (1.6%)
Missing: 5 (7.8%)

Highest Education Level

Some grade school: 2 (3.1%)
Some high school: 5 (7.8%)
High school diploma or GED: 14 (21.9%)
Some college or two-year degree: 17 (26.6%)
Four-year college graduate: 10 (15.6%)
Some school beyond college: 3 (4.7%)
Graduate or professional degree: 8 (12.5%)
Missing: 5 (7.8%)

Personal Annual Income

$0: 2 (3.1%)
$1 to $9,999: 1 (1.6%)
$10,000 to $24,999: 7 (10.9%)
$25,000 to $49,999: 19 (29.7%)
$50,000 to $74,999: 8 (12.5%)
$75,000 to $99,999: 6 (9.4%)
$100,000 to $149,999: 7 (10.9%)
$150,000 and greater: 4 (6.3%)
Prefer not to answer: 2 (3.1%)
Missing: 8 (12.5%)

Total Household Income

$0: 0 (0.0%)
$1-$9,999: 1 (1.6%)
$10,000 to $24,999: 5 (7.8%)
$25,000 to $49,999: 10 (15.6%)
$50,000 to $74,999: 10 (15.6%)
$75,000 to $99,999: 7 (10.9%)
$100,000 to $149,999: 7 (10.9%)
$150,000 and greater: 12 (18.8%)
Prefer not to answer: 5 (7.8%)
Missing: 7 (10.9%)

Procedures

Daughters signed up to complete the study via a departmental research pool to gain course credit. They were directed to an external link, which allowed them to sign up for an online interview with their mother. Before beginning the interview, the mothers and daughters completed a demographic survey consisting of questions about their age, race, education level, relationship status, income, and employment status. Structured interviews were conducted by trained researchers who posed open-ended questions regarding reciprocal influences between mothers and daughters relating to their experiences with career development, vocational identity, stress, and wellbeing. The mothers were asked the following questions: "Did you find yourself working a second shift?", "How did working a second shift impact your work and motherhood?", "How has your daughter's process of pursuing a degree and leaving for college impacted you and how you see your role as a mother, as well as your role in your career?", "Describe your daughter's process of career exploration.", and "How has this impacted you and how you see your role as a mother, as well as your role in your career?" These five questions were a subset of a larger qualitative study exploring career development. Interviews took place between March 2024 and August 2024.

Data Analysis and Coding

Data analysis was guided by Braun and Clarke's thematic analysis approach to qualitative data. All transcripts were reviewed by four authors, initially providing brief notes throughout the interviews. Next, the authors reviewed their notes across the transcripts and created codes representing patterns of the participants' experience. Lastly, the authors compared their individual codes to establish four main themes encompassing the participants' collective experience. These themes were consistent among each author's interpretation of the interviews, and the results illustrate the mothers' perception of their daughters' educational pursuits and career exploration.

Results

The four themes represent a range of experiences relating to educational and vocational aspirations, familial and gender roles in the home and workplace, and general aspects of well-being.

Theme #1: Mothers sacrificed their career goals by working flexible, underpaying jobs to be more present at home and create a better future for their daughters, but this became less of a priority as their daughters entered adolescence

Prior research has indicated that women with children are more likely to seek jobs with family-friendly hours. This routinely leads to a reduction in pay or mothers working jobs for which they are overqualified (Fuller and Hirsh). Many participants echoed these findings in their interview responses. Take for instance, the experience of one of our participant mothers: "I think it started with, you know, climbing the corporate ladder ... trying to improve and grow and go to the next level with my career, personally, and then it switched once I had kids to what works for the family. So, I stayed home for a while, and then when I went back, I took a completely different type of job just to be on their schedule." This sentiment is highly representative of the responses provided by our sample.

Mothers also noted that these career shifts were often implemented specifically to be more present in their children's lives. Despite these sacrifices, many participants said that as their daughters reached adolescence, they relied on their mothers less. One mother shared: "Now that everybody's getting older and ain't no more babies around the house and things like that, it's now giving me the option to now kind of open myself up for something greater within my career roles." Many mothers reported their children's transition to adolescence affected their work-home dynamic, as they felt more comfortable re-entering the workforce and did not feel as strong of an obligation to remain at home with their children.

In many cases, mothers verbalized an expectation that their career and position in the working world would take a backseat to their role and perceived duties as a mother. Although several mother-daughter dyads discussed the influence of fathers on their daughters' career aspirations, there was no mention in any interview of a father taking on a less lucrative position at work to be home for the family. In this way, there is a unique pressure on women to prioritize childcare and domestic responsibilities at the cost of their career aspirations, with a slight reduction in expectations as their children grow older and enter adolescence.

Theme #2: Mothers described the second shift as their duty or responsibility, with some noting a positive ramification of being able to lead by example and teach their daughters independence

Some mothers viewed the second shift as a normalized necessity. One mother shared: "It wasn't anything new to me to go to work and come home and do my house chores. Because I see it as my responsibility, my duty to do that." Many mothers noted the second shift had not affected their motherhood or work, but some discussed obtaining family-friendly, more flexible jobs to remain at home and work a second shift. Other mothers had redefined their understanding of the second shift and developed individual rationales for their actions. One mother talked about the intersection of her religious identity and view on the second shift:

> So this is where I lean into my faith a little bit. So, you know, as a mother, sometimes you do get resentful, like, "Oh, I'm always picking up the same stuff, or I'm always cleaning. Why is that always just me?" And then, so for me, my faith helped me through all of that, that I'm not doing this solely for my kids' health and wellbeing. That's part of it, but I am also doing it to be a good servant to the Lord.

Several mothers experienced the second shift as a positive experience for themselves and their daughters, with the hope that their daughters would develop into responsible young adults. One participant shared this sentiment:

> I grew up seeing my mother go to work and still be our mother. So, I don't know any other way. And I also feel it was the perfect example for my children because these children are only gonna do what they saw happen. I knew I had to set an example, and I still have to do it now. "Go to work. You've got to go to work. Get back home." And even on my day off, stuff has still got to be done.

As this mother acknowledged, working the second shift exemplified the importance of balancing work and home life and developing skills.

Similarly, another participant spoke about her experience with the second shift, managing her after-work schedule, and how that ultimately led her daughter to become more independent in her afterschool routine. The mother shared:

> Definitely, the second shift was real. You know, just coming home and trying to prepare for dinner and homework. But I would say, like, because of that second shift.... I can admit, I definitely didn't have as much sit-down time as a parent to do homework with my kids. But, you know, so I really try to teach them to be independent, and it's instilled in them that they had to do it.

Although this mother spent limited time with her children, she remained preoccupied with the duties of the second shift, indirectly requiring her daughter to establish a sense of independence in herself. Establishing independence is a key developmental aspect of adolescence, and several mothers expressed wanting their daughters to maintain this independence and responsibility as they went off to college.

Generally, mothers viewed the second shift as a normalized duty continuing throughout their children's development. The evolution of the second shift was unique for each dyad due to their different identities and circumstantial situations. A few mothers did note a shift from previous developmental years to young adulthood. Most mothers expressed sentiments of sadness and pride, but some elaborated more about their parental shift as they reflected on their daughters going away to college. One mother described the process of her daughter leaving:

> But you're not an infant or a toddler or in those ages where I had to be a lot more hands-on. This is more of a time for you to figure out who you are. So as a mom, I have to just kind of step back...let you [be] with friends and recognize that my role is still to be the support and be here for you, but, like, let you explore the world.

Similarly, another participant explained how her daughter going away to college created shifts in her own career:

> It also allowed me to shift careers or shift my roles with work. I was working in small clinics that were very rural and not pursuing my leadership skills. It allowed me to take on a role that completely changed my career, really, and so that I could grow into having

this role of working with universities and empowering doctors, really around the entire country. So, actually, her and the empty nest syndrome kind of help boost my career, even though it's hard having her gone.

The daughters transitioning into young adulthood changed some mothers' perceptions of the second shift. Some, however, did not experience the shift of having their daughters leave the family home to attend college because their daughters lived at home and commuted.

Theme #3: Mothers sought to better themselves and provide a positive example for their daughters

Based on the open-ended responses provided by mothers, another positive theme emerged: wanting their daughters to achieve more. Mothers sought ways to better themselves to be seen as a strong example for their daughters. Due to several factors, such as childcare expectations or a lack of postsecondary education, some mothers held work positions or had chosen career paths that did not align with their interests. These mothers described growing alongside their daughters and directing them towards a more successful future. One mother stated: "I'm saying, well, dang, if my daughter can come out of high school and do this, then I know I have the availability and the ... strongness to go ahead and move forward to do what I have to do as well. So, it does make me push harder to even want even better for myself than what I already had and played beforehand." As their daughters graduated from high school and moved on to pursue a college degree, these mothers reported a reciprocal desire to do more for themselves as well.

Mothers who did obtain careers they enjoyed and valued strove to be the best version of themselves and encouraged their daughters to follow their example. One mother speaking to her daughter said:

> I would think that I inspire you to be a working woman. As you see me working all the time, you see me travelling for work, you see me working nights, weekends, doesn't matter what it is…. I want you to be able to step in my shoes in the future and be that independent person. Like, I've never depended on anyone. And I would hope to think that has been inspiring to you. To be able to do that, never depend on anyone, you know? You should be able to stand on your own two feet.

Mothers, both those who had achieved their personal career goals and those who had to take a step back, expressed they were affected by their daughters' choices and they acquired an internal motivation of self-improvement for the sake of their daughters' future development. Similarly, some mothers shared that they wanted to set a positive example for their daughters in terms of seeking better educational opportunities and that the experience of raising their daughters pushed them to explore these opportunities for themselves. One participant said:

> I was influenced by my mother, who had no education at all, not even a high school education. So, I, early on in my career, I chose a career that was better suited, just kind of a traditional field as a nurse, and wanted to make sure that I had an established education and career for my children. [Daughter's name] was my youngest of four, and my only daughter. So around the time that she came along, I started considering other career paths and just trying to find something that I was more passionate about and that challenged me. So, I did inter-veterinary medicine later in life, and entered veterinary school later in life, and have just always kind of tried to set the example for her that through education and being strong, we can accomplish anything that we want and still balance family and relationships, and just improve ourselves daily. And I try to be an example of that to her every day.

However, societal barriers, such as language differences or financial factors, impaired some participants' ability to improve themselves. Some mothers worked to provide financial support or positive messaging surrounding education to encourage their daughters to do what they could not. One mother told her daughter: "Well, I have always told you that the only thing that you will have is your future. It is not for you to help us, but for yourself, so you can keep on going. We have given you advice, and I have influenced you, but you are the one who decides things." As their daughters began to engage in career development during adolescence and emerging adulthood, these mothers wanted their daughters to succeed beyond what they had accomplished and to be more successful and educated. Mothers shared that their decision to better themselves developed from wanting to see their daughters succeed beyond what they could accomplish.

Theme #4: Mothers allowed their daughters to explore career choices freely

Mothers provided their daughters with the opportunity to freely explore their career choices throughout their childhood and adolescence. The interviewed daughters represented a vast array of chosen college majors, but several mothers said they pushed their daughters to explore their options on their own rather than the mothers providing direct input or explicit direction. This is evident in what one participant shared about her daughter: "She had choices. I think she has mentioned that I never thought she would go into nursing. I remember [saying], 'You don't want to be a lawyer?' Because she was very argumentative. You make money, you know? You'd make a good lawyer. And we gave her all these options." This mother's career was in nursing, yet she discussed her daughter having the option to pursue other occupations, even when her daughter's choice did not align with her expectations. Another mother shared a similar sentiment, that her daughter had full autonomy in her career choice as long as it made her happy: "I don't know that [I] would necessarily be influencing [my daughter], besides just being supportive. I really want my kids to do what they want in life to make them happy." Along with mothers encouraging their daughters' autonomy, the bidirectional influence between the mother and daughter became clearer throughout the interviews.

Some mothers acknowledged the indirect influence their career had on their daughter's decision to pursue a similar path. Many of the mother/daughter dyads interviewed were both involved in the healthcare field, particularly nursing. However, many mothers also expressed the influence their daughters' career choices had on their own parenting and career, demonstrating a reciprocal effect. One mother mentioned, "Having [daughter's name] has always been an inspiration to me. Having [her] is just making me work hard." This quote provides insight into the relationship between mothers and daughters, and how integral daughters' choices are in shaping their mothers' outlook on careers.

Cultural Considerations

Finally, many mothers who participated in the interview process were immigrants, and they discussed unique experiences of coming to the Southwestern US and working, living, and raising a family there. These mothers discussed the lack of opportunities for women in their home countries, and many of them shared that their own mother was a homemaker who was not able to or allowed to work outside of the home.

One participant from Eastern Europe shared: "My mother only completed fourth grade. And I think as a result ... life was really tough for her, and my upbringing as well. But I think because of that, because of the hardships ... that drove me to accomplish something greater. I am one of twelve [children], but I am the first one in my family to get a college degree." Another participant, from Africa, spoke about the limitations placed on her own mother growing up: "You know, back home in Africa, women just get married at her age.... This is why she wants us to have the thing she didn't get, which is education." Echoing this sentiment, many immigrant mothers stated it is important to them their daughters have more educational and vocational opportunities than previous generations of women in their families. One mother, from Latin America, shared: "I don't have a career, just [being a] housekeeper, so it's something like…as a Hispanic person, I had to work [so] I can support the family, [so] I can support my daughter, [so] she can have a future, a better future."

All participants discussed their perspectives on being working mothers, but the diverse experiences of immigrant mothers and their insights on family, education, and career opportunities were especially noteworthy. Immigrant women in the US face unique challenges when seeking to improve not only their lives but the lives of their families, especially their daughters. Many of these participants did not or could not attend college, so their daughters' current journey of reaching emerging adulthood and pursuing higher education presents a novel and meaningful perspective. Interviews with this subset of mothers not only reinforced other themes found across other participants but also provided new ideas for further research examining the effects of work-life balance, the second shift, and reciprocal career influences on immigrant mothers and their daughters.

Discussion

Exploring aspects of mother-daughter relationships through the lens of career development revealed four main themes.

1. Mothers who sacrificed their career goals believed their duties as a mother superseded their career aspirations, which resulted in providing a better future for their daughters. This sense of duty came at the expense of working underpaid jobs because they more often had flexible hours. This perspective began to shift as their daughters reached adolescence.

2. Mothers described the second shift as their duty rather than an additional burden; they normalized working full-time while still maintaining household responsibilities. Some mothers did express resentment about engaging in their second shift due to overwhelming responsibilities. However, through individualized redefining, mothers frequently described working a second shift as an opportunity to show their daughters how to approach a work-life balance. The mothers explained that leading by example had been passed down through generations of women in their families; it helped their daughters develop independence during adolescence and emerging adulthood.

3. Mothers sought self-improvement to encourage and set a positive example for their daughters. Through internal motivation, mothers described working towards new opportunities (e.g., educational and vocational) to better themselves. Many mothers noted how their daughters' development, as they reached their adolescent years, inspired this desire for personal growth.

4. Some mothers allowed their daughters to explore career alternatives freely, indicating their primary concern was their daughters' happiness. However, several mothers also noted their influence on their daughters' career path.

Our findings further suggest that mothers are actively influencing their daughters' career choices (Chifamba; Whiston and Keller). The mothers interviewed spoke primarily about the positive experiences of motherhood and work, specifically viewing the second shift as a way of establishing independence and responsibility in their daughters and sacrificing to provide their daughters with greater career and educational opportunities.

Daughters progressed in their career development as their mothers either intentionally or unintentionally transmitted beliefs surrounding work-life balance and family responsibility. Thus, previous findings that intensive mothering aids in forming daughters' career self-efficacy and career aspirations were supported (Mao et al.; Nauta and Kokaly).

The mothers' reports in the current study add needed data and perspective to a developing conversation around mothers facing a new phase of life as their daughters step out into the world. Despite the challenges faced by mothers in their careers, participants overwhelmingly reported being proud of their daughters' career aspirations and educational achievements as their daughters left the safety of the nest to pursue a college degree. Mothers expressed the care they devoted to their daughters and their sacrifices helped build a strong bond with their daughters. In their own words, mothers said they did not regret paying club fees, getting up early to drive to soccer games, or doing the laundry so their daughters could focus on studying. Intensive mothering is a process stemming from the mother's approach to parenting but considering the bidirectional influences within the mother-daughter dyad. This study suggests further implications, including the impact of daughters' career aspirations on their mothers' career development. This work builds on the child effects model of development (Bell and Harper) and shows adolescents and emerging adults continue to influence their mothers in important ways.

Normalizing mothers in the workforce and leadership positions presents a new dynamic affecting the relationship between a mother and her children (Armstrong; Ennis). Many mothers in the current study voiced they were willing to delay their career goals to provide stable lifestyles for their daughters. Intensive adolescent parenting is a frequent result of such sacrifice; mothers often feel they alone are responsible for attending to their daughters' needs (Ennis). Participants frequently reported engaging in intensive mothering and emphasized preparing their daughters for their future career aspirations, which they helped develop by supporting or placing daughters in school organizations, sports, or lessons. Opportunities of this nature are seen as evolving from middle-class influence and perspective where cultural values dictated a primary goal of obtaining a well-paying job through higher education. Yet an observable shift has taken place as the burden of achieving said goal now falls not just to middle-class parents but to all mothers tasked with the second shift as they manage their children's future career aspirations and household duties (Ennis).

In considering the themes identified, it is important to note our sample's demographics. There was a discrepancy between personal income and total household income reported by mothers. The most common reported personal income range was $25,000 to $49,000, compared to the most common total income range of $150,000 or more, implying their partners provide a significant portion of the family's income. Previous literature has long suggested the motherhood wage penalty presents less lucrative career opportunities and higher wage gaps for mothers (Cukrowska-Torzewska and Matysiak).

The majority of the participants in the study identified as racial and ethnic minorities, with most identifying as Hispanic or Latino. Prior research supports the finding that Latina mothers prioritize family-centred, collectivistic parenting over individualistic parenting (Nomaguchi et al.). The daughters viewed their mothers' mothering as generally positive, relating it to emerging developmental responsibilities. Black, Latina, and Asian mothers describe intensive mothering as a self-sacrifice, and many participants indicated wanting to provide a better life for their daughters through their self-improvement (Nomaguchi et al.).

Our findings highlight an understudied aspect of adolescent mothering by providing perspective on how a daughter's vocational development affects a mother's career trajectories and maternal roles. Past studies have only examined the development of vocational exploration in adolescents, with a focus on family characteristics (e.g., family structure or SES) while neglecting the bidirectionality of vocational exploration development between adolescents and mothers (Gagnon et al.) This unique perspective on adolescent mothering helps further expand the literature, providing a deeper understanding of the maternal notions and career impacts on mothers' experiences as they navigate their adolescents' vocational exploration. As many mothers noted, their maternal expectations lowered when their children entered adolescent developmental years, but this lessening provided them with more time to focus on their long-awaited career goals.

Furthermore, even within our results, there is a duality in the singular experiences of participants that add to the intensive mothering framework. The majority of the academic literature surrounding intensive mothering depicts experiences as those placing women in demanding situations based on gender (Lamar et al.; Verniers et al.); however, a collection from our participants' testimonies highlights a new, profound meaning within their maternal labours. For instance, mothers described their experiences of second shift with positivity as it taught their daughters independence beyond the household and in their vocational exploration experiences. These findings support work highlighting a more modern, reflective spectrum of motherhood (Ennis; Lankes).

A primary limitation of the current study was that recruitment was limited to participants who were working mothers of daughters currently enrolled in college. The majority of the daughters interviewed were pursuing careers in health science occupations (e.g., nursing) due to recruitment from lower-level psychology courses. As such, current findings may not be generalizable to mothers of daughters pursuing other areas of study. Future research should examine mothers whose daughters are pursuing a broader range of career options and mothers whose daughters are not attending college.

Prior scholarship establishes that mothers influence the career decisions of their daughters (Armstrong). The idea that emerging adult daughters' career exploration in college can impact the career decision-making of their mothers presents a novel perspective. Further, the multi-dimensional intersection of career, parenting, race, and gender has a meaningful impact on mothers and daughters and deserves further attention. Documenting mothers' and daughters' intersectional experiences is important in an increasingly diverse world. As a fuller picture of the complexities of this dyad is understood, policies and programs designed to support mothers and daughters as they navigate this increasingly complex world will need to evolve as well.

Authors' Note

This work was part of a larger project, *Passing the Torch: How Mothers' Leadership Ambitions Affect the Next Generation,* supported by the Jane Nelson Institute for Women's Leadership (JNIWL Award 3989).

Works Cited

Armstrong, Jill. *Like Mother, Like Daughter? How Career Women Influence Their Daughters' Ambitions.* Policy Press, 2017.

Bell, Richard, and Lawrence Harper. *Child Effects on Adults*. Routledge, 1977.

Braun, Virginia, and Victoria Clarke. "Conceptual and Design Thinking for Thematic Analysis." *Qualitative Psychology*, vol. 9, no. 3, 2022, pp. 3–26.

Camilleri, Marisabelle, and Damian Spiteri. "Work-Life Balance, Upward Career Mobility and Further Education: the Case for Working Mothers." *International Journal of Management, Knowledge and Learning*, vol. 10, 2021, pp. 305–21.

Carr, Deborah. "'My Daughter Has a Career; I Just Raised Babies': The Psychological Consequences of Women's Intergenerational Social Comparisons." *Social Psychology*, vol. 67, no. 2, pp. 132–54.

Chifamba, Constance. "An Analysis of How Parents Influence their Children's Career Decisions." *International Journal of Innovative Science and Research Technology*, vol. 4, no. 12, 2019, pp. 1207–13.

Ciciolla, Lucia, and Suniya Luthar. "Invisible Household Labor and Ramifications for Adjustment: Mothers as Captains of Households." *Sex Roles*, vol. 81, no. 7, 2019, pp. 467–86.

Cukrowska-Torzewska, Ewa, and Anna Matysiak. "The Motherhood Wage Penalty: A Meta-Analysis." *Social Science Research*, vol. 88–89, 2020, pp. 1–19.

Dharani, Muthu, and Janarthanan Balamurugan. "The Financial Hardships of Single Mothers: A Review of Two Decades." *Multidisciplinary Reviews*, vol. 7, no. 8, 2024, pp. 1–6.

Dugan, Alicia, and Janet Barnes-Farrell. "Working Mothers' Second Shift, Personal Resources, and Self-Care." *Community, Work, and Family*, vol. 23, no. 1, 2018, pp. 62–79.

Ennis, Linda Rose. *Intensive Mothering: The Cultural Contradictions of Modern Motherhood*. Demeter Press, 2014.

Fitzsimmons, Stacey, et al. "Intersectional Arithmetic: How Gender, Race and Mother Tongue Combine to Impact Immigrants' Work Outcomes." *Journal of World Business*, vol. 55, no. 1, 2020, pp. 1–12.

Fuller, Sylvia, and C. Elizabeth Hirsh. "'Family-Friendly' Jobs and Motherhood Pay Penalties: The Impact of Flexible Work Arrangements Across the Educational Spectrum." *Work and Occupations*, vol. 46, no. 1, 2019, pp. 3–44.

Gagnon, Émilie, et al. "Developmental Trajectories of Vocational Exploration from Adolescence to Early Adulthood: The Role of Parental Need Supporting Behaviors." *Journal of Vocational Behavior*, vol. 115, no. 2, 2019, p. 1–14.

Harper, Casandra Elena, et al. "Parents and Families of First-Generation College Students Experience Their Own College Transition." *Journal of Higher Education*, vol. 91, no. 4, 2019, pp. 540–564.

Hays, Sharon. *The Cultural Contradictions of Motherhood*. Yale University Press, 1998.

Hey, William, Kristine Calderon, and Denise Seabert. "Student Work Issues: Implications for College Transition and Retention." *Journal of College Orientation, Transition, and Retention*, vol. 10, no. 2, 2003, pp. 35–41.

Hochschild, Arlie, and Anne Machung. *The Second Shift: Working Families and the Revolution at Home*. 2nd ed. Penguin Books, 2012.

Jiang, Zhao, et al. "Career Exploration: A Review and Future Research Agenda." *Journal of Vocational Behavior*, vol. 110, 2019, pp. 338–56.

Kahn, Joan, et al. "The Motherhood Penalty at Midlife: Long-Term Effects of Children on Women's Careers." *Journal of Marriage and Family*, vol. 76, no. 1, 2014, pp. 56–72.

Lamar, Margaret, et al. "Helping Working Mothers Face the Challenges of an Intensive Mothering Culture." *Journal of Mental Health Counseling*, vol. 41, no. 3, 2019, pp. 203–20.

Lankes, Jane. "Negotiating Impossible Ideals: Latent Classes of Intensive Mothering in the United States." *Gender & Society*, vol. 36, no. 5, 2022, pp. 677–703.

Mao, Ching-Hua, et al. "The Role of the Mother-Daughter Relationship in Taiwanese College Students' Career Self-Efficacy." *Social Behavior and Personality*, vol. 40, no. 9, 2012, pp. 1511–21.

Meeussen, Loes, and Colette Van Laar. "Feeling Pressure to Be a Perfect Mother Relates to Parental Burnout and Career Ambitions." *Frontiers in Psychology*, vol. 9, 2018, pp. 1–13.

Nauta, Margaret, and Michelle Kokalay. "Assessing Role Model Influences on Students' Academic and Vocational Decisions." *Journal of Career Assessment*, vol. 9, no. 1, 2001, pp. 81–99.

Nomaguchi, Kei, et al. "Beyond Intensive Mothering: Racial/Ethnic Variation in Maternal Time with Children." *Social Science Research*, vol. 119, 2024, pp. 1–20.

O'Reilly, Andrea. *Twenty-first Century Motherhood: Experience, Identity, Policy, Agency*. Columbia University Press, 2010.

Verniers, Catherine, et al. "Intensive Mothering and the Perpetuation of Gender Inequality: Evidence from a Mixed Methods Research." *Acta Psychologica*, vol. 227, no. 1, 2022, pp. 1–14.

Whiston, Susan, and Brianna Keller. "The Influences of the Family of Origin on Career Development: A Review and Analysis." *The Counseling Psychologist*, vol. 32, no. 4, 2004, pp. 493–568.

4.

Ellipsis: Making Sense of Non-Proximate Mothering[1]

Maya E. Bhave

I watch the dots bubble up, flicker, and then vanish ... I know they were there a second ago, but now nothing—just a blank line on our text chat on my iPhone. Three fleeting black dots that carry so much gravity. Gone. My stomach drops, and my mind starts racing. What were they going to say? What were they going to share? The blank line stares back at me, as if to say, "You don't get to know." This is the new world of liminal motherhood I find myself in, this threshold and transition between being young and becoming older for my kids and me.[1] "I'm still their mom. I'm still their mom," the echoed refrain pops into my head, one I had heard in a research interview from a mom whose son, a recent college graduate, was getting married. She spoke spiritedly about still wanting to be connected to her firstborn child, now a young adult. Her comment—a yearning to know she mattered somehow and somewhere in this new transitional world—is one I can all too easily relate to now my adult sons are twenty-one and twenty-six.

This new spatial location and uncertain certainty often knock me off kilter and make me feel imbalanced. You see, the old mothering space, the one from the early part of my mothering arc, the normative mom space of years gone by, seemingly made more sense. I knew who I was and what my roles were. The space in which I dictated all meal schedules, oversaw academic progress, threw myself into shaping family vacations, and organized travel to, and from, every athletic training, game/match or summer camp before they could drive. Before that rite of passage, they relied on, needed, and depended upon me. In this maternal space, I planned the meals and made sure there was enough food at any time, given they seemed to eat constantly. Only an hour after dinner, I could hear the rummaging in our kitchen, the swoosh of the large fridge door opening, and the subsequent clinking of items in the fridge, nudging my concentration, as one of my sons uttered, "I just want protein." It seemed, at times, there were never enough meals or snacks to keep them fully satiated. Ironically, their search for more, their hunt for morsel contentedness left me feeling at peace. I had done my job. I knew I had done enough. I was good enough, at least in the cooking department. It was the same in my role as overseer of athletic events. I had even become team manager on my older son's soccer team, so I had crucial, detailed information. I knew every hotel reservation, game time, and field location long before other parents. I had mapped out the drive times (thank goodness for GPS), best places for large team dinners (thank you *Yelp* reviews), and the exact timing everyone needed to leave the hotel to get to the respective fields on any given day for an adequate warm-up before gametime. I had planned out every detail and subsequently felt in control and capable and confident as a mom.

My maternal practice was clear. Unknowingly at the time, I followed Sara Ruddick's line of maternal thinking in which mothers engage in active attention focused on growth, preservation, and social acceptability. I did that. I wanted my kids to be happy, healthy, and well adjusted. I used to say that. But what exactly is happy and well adjusted? Back then, it meant organize, schedule, and implement. There was maternal clarity, even if coupled with emotional bumps and learning curves in the journey. Motherhood had its ups and downs, its good and bad days or weeks. Yet in those early years of mothering, I was not waiting in a grey transition area, attempting to make sense of flickering, disappearing dots.

I was the one who seemingly connected all the pieces and points. I arranged and marshaled the everyday life minutiae, the details and specifics that made up my sons' days and weeks. When my kids were younger, this hectic, overly filled schedule seemed to give me purpose, a plan, and an identity. If we weren't travelling to soccer or tennis matches, I found myself with a household of boys watching movies and playing ping pong in our finished basement. The dents in the walls still match the outline of the ping pong paddles, but I did not care; it meant I knew where they were. They were just one staircase away, a surety I knew and valued. This knowledge seemed to soothe my soul and made me feel I had oversight and guidance; in fact, those normative motherhood tenets of naturalization, idealization, privatization, expertization, and intensification were strong and in place. I bought into the notion that my family's physical and emotional state was intact because I saw myself crafting, assembling, nurturing it one meal and activity at a time. So, I had no problem cooking up a storm for ten sixteen-year-olds at a moment's notice, as it led me to believe I was buttressing and shoring up the family foundation. I spent many a Sunday afternoon finding and subsequently cleaning up the wayward crumbs and detritus after a Saturday night sleepover, with those young teenage boys waking and dispersing well after noon. The crumbs—greasy, orange tortilla chip bits and inky, *Oreo* shards, like the black texting dots—gave me what I believed was discernment accompanied with certitude. Or so I continued to believe.

Now, that messy yet absolute world is no longer. Now, I live in this liminal space in which e-mothering, not food or social interaction, is our main medium. It is a muted world where the laundry piles are small, the well-ordered and unsullied beds and bedrooms never change, and the counter spaces remain vacant and crumb free. This liminal space of motherhood is punctuated by hours of silent sureness and wistful longing.

The wistful part is that I, surprisingly, miss the frenzied days of chaos and noise. I need the fetid sneakers piled in the mudroom and the sweaty, grimy tennis and soccer shirts chucked carelessly on their carpeted bedroom floors and nowhere near the laundry room, just ten feet away. These messes drove me mad, pushing my obsessive nature to the edge. Yet now there is nothing but unfamiliar, ordered quiet. This wistfulness, however, is punctuated by fleeting snippets of joy. This elation based upon their emerging adulthood, who they have become.

I marvel at their tall, grown bodies, devoid of chubby cheeks or mischievous smiles. I beam at their capability, maturity, and successes. These days when I bump into a young mother with a small toddler, I stare for far too long, my eyes narrowing in a tense focus, desperately trying to remember my two at that young age. Sure, I can look at the multitude of pictures lining the living room sideboard and my office desk, yet I honestly have a hard time remembering those early years. So much like a sunny fall November day in Vermont, my trace of maternal joy changes in an instant, suddenly becoming dim, given my maternal ruminations and questions about myself and the passing of years.

I hang on tightly to those three little black dots. When they pop up,

I smile, feel a little lighter, and have a long-distance sense of connection. Their reaching out means something and offers me a gift of settledness and happiness. Yet I am still a non-proximate mother, physically and emotionally.

I think of my sons often, yet my thinking does not translate into knowing. What is it about this concept of knowing that we moms want so much? Why for eighteen years did we perseverate over every detail? Every yearly lunchbox (until lunch boxes, I was told, were no longer cool)? Every summer camp (until it was obvious what their respective sports were, and they did not need that camp)? Every school class decision? And every piece of clothing, sporting equipment, and every grade? Why did we want to check in on them? What was it that such check-ins gave us?

It gave me a feeling of control, investment, and the belief that what I did for my children mattered. I bought into those entrenched feelings of normative motherhood, and suddenly the foundation of what matters dissipated, seemingly overnight. So, I search now for signs and snippets of evidence that my concern, control, and choices still impact. But now those signs are hard to see. Now, I am the one blindfolded, as they were at their six-year-old birthday parties. Before the treasure hunts, the chocolate cake, and the oodles of nerf guns, movie theatre gift cards, and remote-control car gifts, there was the pin the tail on the donkey. At the time, it seemed fun, funny, and a necessary party event. Blindfold the child and let them wander aimlessly against the living room wall, hoping they would not hit the target. Why did we make children do that? Looking back, I wonder why that seemed so funny and appropriate.

I now feel like I am that child, feeling my way against a wall that feels tenuous and unstable, like a moving target. This liminal space of motherhood makes me feel like a six-year-old child: clumsy, bungling, and always slightly nervous and unsure of what is beyond my fingertips in the dark. As mothers of young, emerging adults, we find ourselves in this new space, which in many ways holds such potential yet feels simultaneously fraught with uncertainty, loss, and a unique type of maternal grief.

To any outsider, both of my kids are incredibly successful, and, yes, I know that and believe that. I see them scaffolding their lives socially, financially, and academically. Yet, it is me that feels, at times, like I have nothing to hold on to. Ironically, as they build up their lives, my maternal scaffolding is being disassembled year after year, as they find their paths. Is this new maternal questioning about my worth, value, and identity? Maybe, yes, if I'm honest. Yet there is more lurking under my latent thoughts. I realize it is about knowing not only myself but them. As a different mother shared in a research interview, "If I don't see my kids, I don't know what's going on with them."

So, maybe it is not only about eyes on, about seeing them; maybe it is about hopeful guarantees and reliability. It is about really trusting ourselves as women and ultimately as mothers with a new identity in this latter period of our mothering arc. It is a new period, marked with celebrative pride and joy but coupled with sadness for what is no more. For so long, we bought into the confining notion of normative motherhood. We argued that we as mothers mattered and that our private spaces allowed us to feel in control. In that safe, private place, we knew how we structured the world and what that meant. Our maternal thinking, strategies, and intensive parenting added up to us knowing who we were and how, and where, our children were. Yet now that expertization and intensification are gone—just like our children. Our mother role within the nuclear family has been transformed, just as our little toddlers—those bouncy, smiley, sweet, and busy kids—have grown into fully fledged, muscled men. At times, I shake my head at the transformation of them and me. In this new homeland, the maternal questions (the ones moms do not want to admit) creep in. Will I matter? In what way and for how long? And will I still know how my kids are?

Some days, the silent dissonance regarding my adult children is deafening. It is not that I do not believe in them, trust them, or know that they will succeed—they will. But it is the dissonance of what happens to my maternal role now that lingers. What does it look like amid these shifts and transitions? What does it mean to parent a young adult who is not only twice your size and thus physically different from who they were but also emotionally different? How do you now do the intricate dance of support and listening non-proximately?

This new world feels like a New England County fair tilt a whirl. I am pinned to the wall, slightly nervous, until the old, rusty looking machine spins up on its side, and then I am just downright terrified that I might look stupid, idiotic, a woman who might swear out loud, pee my pants, or vomit in public. All things that "good moms" do not do. So, I dance, quietly and steadily. I reach out casually to my kids—"how are things?" My vagueness allows a persona who is not intensely intrusive, and I hope to get a quick response in reply. Those return words—"good, good nothing new" and "fine not much going on"—all speak positively to me. At least it is not "terrible, horrible, no good." So, why does just a tiny bit of text bring me so much joy? No tragedy equals fine to me and is a reassuring balm. The few reassuring words help me to realize that I may not see them most days, but they are intact and secure. I may not have daily updates, conversations, or quick passes in the kitchen, but here is what I have learned in the last few years as a non-proximate mom: The dots were never about the unknown. The dots were never about uncertainty or instability or not connecting. The dots and their flickering disappearance are not about me; they are about solidity, certainty, and groundedness. The distance, periods of silence, and space are not always negative, even though I do not love it at times. But it is about growth, for them and me. My kids have taught me that yes, we might disagree at times. We are from different generations for goodness sake. And they have learned they can and will persevere. They have been taught that.

So, I see the dots bubble up and disappear. And once again, I am reminded that the dots are not an ellipsis, those spaces of unknown echoing a problem. The fact that the dots disappear is my kids saying, "It's okay. I've got this. I've got this." I need to trust in the disappearing dots.

Endnotes

1. This essay is a brief introduction to the concept of liminal motherhood explored in depth in my forthcoming book *Mothering College-Aged Children: Strategies and Patterns of Maternal Influence, Investment and Sustained Social Bonds.*

5.

Challenges of Being a Mother to Adolescents in Brazil: A Review of the Indexed Literature

Irene Rocha Kalil and Martha Silvia Martinez-Silveira[1]

Introduction

With the creation in the nineteenth century of gynecology—the science dedicated to the knowledge of the female body that has no corresponding science for the male body (Vieira)—a deep medicalization of the woman's body took place. Gynecology pointed out the differences and particularities of female physiology and formulated "a whole set of theories and practices, assumptions, theses, behavioral norms, seeking to tame women's bodies, desires and sensibilities" (Matos 15). An idea of feminine nature was then forged, which determined the existence of standards of behaviour based on women's biological condition (Vieira), especially their ability to gestate and give birth. In this context, motherhood is the central axis on which female identity is supposed to be erected.

As Philippe Ariès points out, from the second half of the eighteenth century in Europe, "a gradual movement of the family household towards the modern sentimental family" (235) can be observed, centred on the child and for which the affection between parents and children becomes the basis of the entire family's reality. In this direction, a new conformation of family is forged, "with the State gaining progressive legal, moral and physical prevalence over the woman" (Kalil 53).

Through what psychologist and philosopher Valeska Zanello calls the "maternal device"—defined as the "naturalization of the ability to care (in general) in women, resulting precisely from this mixture (fairly recent, with the advent of capitalism) between procreation and motherhood" (149)—women experience a physical and mental overload with care activities.

According to the report *Time to Care: Unpaid and Underpaid Care Work and the Global Inequality Crisis* (Lawson et al.), women all over the world "are responsible for more than three-quarters of unpaid care and comprise two-thirds of the workforce engaged in paid care activities" (10). The report also points out that for an equal human economy, it is paramount to "fully address the role of unpaid and underpaid care work. Building a more egalitarian world will only be possible with fundamental changes in the way this work is carried out and appreciated" (15).

As pointed out by Helena Hirata and Danièle Kergoat, the sexual division of labour "is characterized by the priority attribution of women to the reproductive sphere whereas men are assigned to the productive sphere" ("Atualidade da divisão sexual" 23). Thus, men perform functions with strong added social value (political, religious, military, etc.), whereas women are responsible for domestic work, which encompasses caring for the home and offspring, tacitly separating what is man's work and what is woman's work. This separation, as stressed by the authors, remains current, and is not only a separation but a hierarchy in which a man's work is worth more than a woman's.

However, many women also work in the paid labour market, which generates even more work for those who also perform care work. This situation, which became more obvious from the two years of social isolation imposed by the COVID-19 pandemic, remains, in our opinion, largely uninvestigated and even more so unremedied socially.

Motherhood, in this context, is a condition that significantly accentuates the potential female overload. This is especially the case when motherhood is considered a natural function of women, "the crucial experience of femininity" (Badinter 71), which should be exercised in a totalizing (Wolf) or intensified (Hays) manner—"a kind of 'moral code' that exhorts mothers to perfect all dimensions of their children's lives, starting in the gestation" (Kalil 36).

Although the interfaces between gender, communication, and health are manifold and expanding daily, we believe new perspectives on old issues are needed. One of them is motherhood itself, which is not limited to the approaches already worked on so far but involves discussions about career, sexual division of labour and feminization of care, and physical and psychological illnesses due to overworking in managing domestic and family life, among other problems lingering in most societies.

Recently, in Brazil, we witnessed the emergence of the Maio Furta-Cor Campaign, which is dedicated to "raising awareness of the population to the cause of maternal mental health" (par 3) because it recognizes that there is still "a strong social stigma around themes related to mental health and, when it extends to the maternal field, this stigma is even stronger" (par 2). Cases of depression and anxiety, in addition to suicides, have been increasing among mothers. However, we are paying little attention to the factors contributing to this suffering.

Faced with this gap, this study discusses the relationship between the maternal condition of teenage daughters and sons and mental health, recognizing the challenges of maternal care in the contemporary context, in which working mothers feel a lack in their work and family lives but believe that they should "be 100% in each and every one of these activities" (Iaconelli 77). Our premise is that maternal health is more often treated from a biomedical perspective, prioritizing the body's pain and in a specific period of motherhood: pregnancy, childbirth, and puerperium. This period does affect the psyche and health of women, but it does not exhaust the challenges they experience while mothering.

Being a mother to an adolescent in Brazil is affected by several markers of difference, such as race and class. Using the theoretical-methodological framework of intersectionality as a guideline, which allows us to "see the collision of structures, the simultaneous interaction of identity avenues" (Akotirene 14), shows these identities affect motherhood in an articulated fashion. With that, we assume that, if white women from the most privileged socioeconomic strata, with the biggest support network, experience motherhood as an extremely challenging task, Brown, Black, and Indigenous women and those from the lower socioeconomic strata face considerably greater hurdles in their exercise of motherhood, such as the fear Black mothers have of burying "their children victimized by necropolitics, which confessionally and militarily kill and let die" (Akotirene 16).

Although maternal health is a more widely discussed topic in the literature, the mental health of mothers, especially of teenagers, remains a seldom explored subject, whose nuances require better investigation. In this sense, this chapter seeks to map out, based on the indexed scientific literature, the main problems affecting mothers of Brazilian adolescents and influencing their mental health and their carework.

Methods

The study is an exploratory review of indexed literature and seeks to learn about the main challenges of being a mother of adolescents in Brazil and its implications for their mental health. In this sense, the review selected studies addressing the mental aspects of mothers in the challenge of raising their teenage children currently in this country. The study designs considered for inclusion were experimental or observational studies, including cohort, case-control, and cross-sectional studies. Qualitative studies were also considered for selection. Only articles published in English, Portuguese, or Spanish were included. Duplicate articles and those not qualified as original were excluded.

A search strategy was carried out covering the concepts "mothers of adolescents" and "mental health" (See Appendix I). The strategy was adapted for each database. Given that the keyword search for these concepts yielded abundant results of studies more focussed on the theme from the biomedical standpoint of the mother or adolescent only, we used the following criteria: The article should contain some of the terms related to the mother concept, adolescents, and mental health (i.e., it should mention all three concepts in its title and/or abstract, as well as in the keywords and subject headings).

In our search, performed in February 2024, the following sources were used: Medline/PubMed, the main health database, Web of Science (Clarivate), a multidisciplinary database and Lilacs, the Latin American and Caribbean literature database. Complementarily, a search was carried out in the SciElo Electronic Library, which coalesces most journals from Brazil and other Latin American countries, as well as the verification of the list of references of all included articles to identify additional studies that the electronic searches might have failed to find.

Two independent reviewers read the titles and abstracts of the studies to select the literature according to the review's inclusion criteria.

Potentially relevant studies were read and assessed in full. The data of each selected article were extracted by the reviewers using a data extraction tool developed by the authors, including specific details about the characteristics of the studies, such as author, year, location, study design, population, main subject, and main conclusions.

During data selection and extraction, it was noticed that few studies specifically addressed the subject of our research—that is, the mental health of women as a result of their role as mothers of adolescents. However, information about the mother, such as educational level, quality of life, and race, were identified in several studies as determining factors for the behaviour and mental health of adolescents. For this reason, they were selected for this study to broaden the approach to the theme.

Based on the data found, we sought to build a categorical analysis of the literature inspired by Laurence Bardin, according to which the categories are a "kind of significant drawers or headings that allow the classification of the constitutive elements for the signification of the message" (37), being, therefore, an appropriate taxonomic method to introduce order to elements in apparent disorder. For Bardin, "categorization has as its first objective (in the same way as documentary analysis) to provide, by condensation, a simplified representation of the raw data" (119).

To classify the main subject, the specific themes of each article were identified and then grouped into broader categories that could handle more comprehensive challenges, working from the perspective of the categorical analysis proposed by Bardin. The same synthesis effort was made concerning the main conclusions of the studies. We extracted and summarized the main issues of adolescents, their risk factors and protective factors, as well as the main issues of mothers, their risk or complicating factors, and the protective, mitigating or facilitating factors.[2]

Results

We obtained 162 single articles (after excluding duplicates) from the database search, plus thirty-three articles in the complementary search, totalling 195 (see Figure 1). By reading the titles and abstracts, we selected all those addressing the inclusion criteria, totalling forty-one articles (see Appendix II).

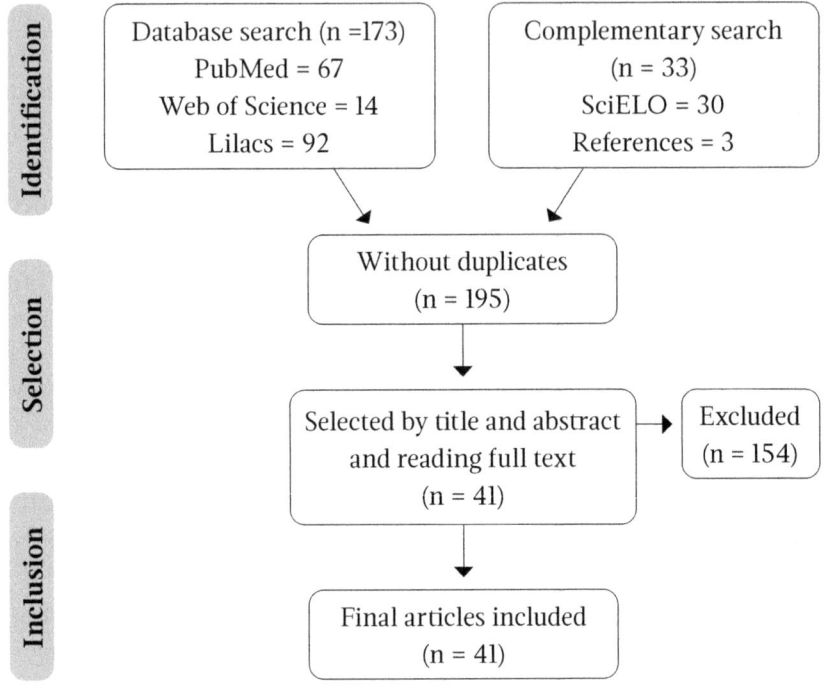

Figure 1. Selecting Process Flowchart.
Source: Own authorship adapted from Moher.

Regarding the main authorship of the studies, five are authored by Deborah Carvalho Malta and two by Flávia Carvalho Malta Mello, who is an author of the same research group as Deborah Carvalho Malta, totalling seven articles; five are authored by Isabel Altenfelder Santos Bordin and one by Cristiane Seixas Duarte, who is an author of the same research group as Isabel Altenfelder Santos Bordin, totalling six articles. The other 28 articles have someone with only one article in scope as the first author.

As for the year of publication, nine articles (about 22 per cent of the total) were published between 2000 and 2010; twenty-four (almost 59 per cent) between 2011 and 2019; and eight articles (just over 19 per cent) from 2020 on. In the first eleven-year period, only one more article was published than the last period considered, which stands out for the number of articles found, thereby hinting at an upward trend in research on the theme from 2020 to 2024.

Concerning the region of the country represented in the study (where the data come from), fourteen are from states of the southeast region of Brazil (about 34 per cent); ten are from states in the south region (just over 24 per cent); four are from states in the northeast region (almost 10 per cent); one is from the north region; and twelve are nationwide studies (almost 30 per cent). There are no articles specific to the Midwest region. A concentration of studies can be observed in the south and southeast regions, the richest in the country, although the articles, for the most part, point out that the data were collected in the poorer areas of cities to evaluate the health issues of the most vulnerable populace.

In the classification of type or study design, the majority (thirty-one, or about 76 per cent) are cross-sectional studies. The main characteristic of this type of study design is the analysis of surveys or medical-hospital documentation located in a given time and place. Thus, a snippet of the reality on the studied phenomenon is acquired, such as a photograph (Hochman 3) or more appropriately a cross-section of reality. The advantage of these studies is that data are collected only once, and multiple results can be studied. The largest issue with these studies is that they do not differentiate cause and effect from simple association (Mann 57). This is also evident from our result, as at least nine studies are based on the results of a large nationwide study (*Pesquisa Nacional de Saúde dos Escolares* [PeNSE]).

Among the other studies, four are cohorts, which are also observational studies of the analytical and longitudinal type, meaning that there is a long-term follow-up; data can be collected at various times. Cohorts can be either prospective or retrospective (Hochman 5). The last five studies are of the qualitative variety, such as focus groups and interviews, in addition to an inquiry.

Regarding the population or data source, thirty-one articles collected information from adolescents; eight articles collected information from mothers; one article collected information from mothers and fathers; and one article collected information from adolescents and school managers. We added up all studies that collected information from or about adolescents (thirty-two, around 76 per cent of the scope) and all those that collected information from or about mothers (nine, around 22 per cent of the scope).

Below is a list of the main issues (in decreasing order of number of times mentioned in the articles) and their risk and protective factors for adolescents and their mothers, as summarized in Tables 1 and 2 respectively.

Table 1. Top Issues of Adolescents and Their Risk and Protective Factors

Top issues of adolescents	Risk or complicating factors	Protective, mitigating, or facilitating factors
Mental Health Articles 3, 5, 8, 10, 11, 12, 15, 26, 31, 32, 33, 34, 3	**For common mental disorder** Female gender Age fifteen and over Higher socioeconomic status Mother's level of education is lower Mother is bipolar Alcoholic parents **For perception of being fat/ dissatisfaction with body image** Tobacco consumption Sedentary behaviour Intrafamily violence Assistance gaps	**For common mental disorder** Exposure to unpaid work **For teens living with alcoholic parents** Mother's level of education is higher **For teens who do not live with alcoholic parents** Living in families classified as nuclear **For external problems** Having a husband or partner residing with them (this is a protective factor for adolescents but not for children)
	For internal problems (peer and emotional relationships) Female gender Age eleven through seventeen Obesity in boys Mother with depression and anxiety Mother has a job (if resulting in poor parenting practices) Social vulnerability	
	For external problems (antisocial behaviour, hyperactivity, aggression, and behaviour problems) Female gender Severe physical punishment Parental psychopathology Absent father Mother with depression and anxiety (only for teens not exposed to severe punishment) Severe punishment (only for teens not exposed to mothers with depression and anxiety) Mother is unemployed (among low-income teens) **For teens living with alcoholic parents** Mother's level of education is low	

CHALLENGES OF BEING A MOTHER TO ADOLESCENTS IN BRAZIL

Top issues of adolescents	Risk or complicating factors	Protective, mitigating, or facilitating factors
Mental Health (cont) Articles 3, 5, 8, 10, 11, 12, 15, 26, 31, 32, 33, 34, 3	For teens who do not live with alcoholic parents Female gender Father's level of education is higher (seldom at home) Belonging to the nonnuclear model family	
Consumption of licit/illicit drugs Articles 1, 4, 9, 13, 19, 22, 25, 28, 29, 30, 39	**For alcohol consumption** Age fifteen and over Gender female Gender male Race/colour white Influence of friendships Tobacco and other drug use Having had sexual intercourse Higher socioeconomic status Higher level of education of the mother or guardian Missing school without parents knowing Alcohol consumption by the mother External behaviour problems (e.g., hyperactivity) Psychosocial stress Family disengaged in raising and educating children Fewer meals in the company of parents Enabling parents Parents smoke **For consumption of tobacco and other drugs** Gender Female Non-white race/color Going to private school Going to schools not as concerned with promoting health History of failing in school Positive score for psychic morbidity Influence of friendships Need for acceptance and belonging Not living with parents Mother's level of education is lower Alcohol consumption by the mother Family using drugs Mother's age under twenty or around thirty-five	Mother's level of education is higher Going to private school Had rigid social isolation (pandemic) Physical activity Dialogue with the family (mainly with the mother) Structured family Socioeducational activities Authoritative parenting style (high levels of control and affection) Quality of life Occasional physical punishments Limits Good education Joy in the family relationship Parental control of companies Self-esteem Never suffered intrafamily violence Personal and family scenarios favorable to the promotion of health **For alcohol and tobacco consumption** Schools with lifeskill programs, full-time classes, reinforcement sessions about alcohol and other drug use in the curriculum, better peer relationships, and greater parental participation in school **For homeless youth** Female gender Age between nine and eleven School attendance Parental affection and bonding Been on the streets for less than a year Being on the streets with a family member Never suffered intrafamily violence Reduced exposure to street culture Not sleeping on the street

table continued next page

Top issues of adolescents	Risk or complicating factors	Protective, mitigating, or facilitating factors
Consumption of licit/illicit drugs (cont) Articles 1, 4, 9, 13, 19, 22, 25, 28, 29, 30, 39	External (e.g., hyperactivity and conduct problems) and internal (e.g., peer and emotional relationship problems) mental problems Passive smoking Parents smoke Residents of the south and southeast regions Sleep issues Social vulnerability Living near areas where drugs are sold and used Family disengaged in raising and educating children Negative relationship with parents Having fewer meals in the company of parents Internet use without parental supervision Broken home Intrafamily violence Mother has a job Nonauthoritative (mostly negligent) fathers and mothers Lack or excess of financial resources of providers Practising bullying, mainly verbal Being homeless	
Intrafamily violence (e.g., severe physical punishment, psychological aggression, and sexual abuse) Articles 2, 7, 8, 11, 14, 17, 20	For severe physical punishment Female gender Age thirteen Race/colour Black, Asian, brown Mother's level of education is lower Mother's age is lower Mother has depression Dangerous alcohol consumption by the mother Going to a private school Exposure to paid work Relational factors in intrafamily and school life Family interactions Psychoactive substance use Violence in the school environment Maternal experience of severe punishment in childhood Intrafamily/marital violence	For intrafamily violence Female gender Age between sixteen and seventeen years old Mother's age is higher Mother's level of education is higher (college/university degree) Parents are aware of what teens do in their free time Parents monitor school activities Parents respect the adolescent's internal world and its concrete objects Parents who understand the adolescent's problems Family supervision **For psychological aggression** Mother's level of education is higher Higher socioeconomic status

CHALLENGES OF BEING A MOTHER TO ADOLESCENTS IN BRAZIL

Top issues of adolescents	Risk or complicating factors	Protective, mitigating, or facilitating factors
Intrafamily violence (e.g., severe physical punishment, psychological aggression, and sexual abuse (cont) Articles 2, 7, 8, 11, 14, 17, 20	**For psychological aggression** Mother's level of education is lower Social vulnerability Not having a partner **For sexual abuse** Minor (childhood)	**For sexual abuse** Family support Protective action of mother Help from third parties in making decisions Sending daughters to live away from home Specialized care and adequate support of the victim and the mother
Bullying Articles 19, 21, 23, 37	**To be bullied:** Male gender Ages thirteen and under Race/colour Black and Asian Insomnia Mother has a job Exposure to paid work Studying in public school Mother's level of education is lower Broken home Intrafamily violence Missing school without parents knowing **To be the bully:** Male gender Consumption of licit or illicit drugs Tobacco consumption Alcohol consumption Insomnia Going to private school Mother's level of education is higher Trying drugs Having had sexual intercourse Living with parents Parents are employed Intrafamily violence Missing school without parents knowing	**To be bullied:** Age fourteen, fifteen, and sixteen Mother's level of education is higher Family supervision Parents are aware of what teens do in their free time **To be the bully:** Family supervision
Sexual behaviour Article 27	Male gender (boys have more sex with and without protection) Older age (both protected and unprotected sexual activity increases with age)	**For unprotected sex** Race/colour white Going to private school Receiving sexual and reproductive health information at school Mother's level of education is higher

table continued next page

Top issues of adolescents	Risk or complicating factors	Protective, mitigating, or facilitating factors
Sexual behaviour (cont) Article 27	For unprotected sex Race/colour Black, Indigenous, or Asian Studying in public school Mother's level of education is lower Exposure to paid work Social vulnerability Consumption of licit or illicit drugs Lack of guidance on contraception in school Residing in the north region Practising bullying, mainly verbal	
Internet addiction Article 41	Conflicts and disagreements between parents and children (mainly with the mother) Conflict between parents Parents control and oversee behaviour	Mother educates and provides emotional support
Poor health self-assessment Article 18	Female gender Age fifteen and over Race/colour Asian, brown, or Indigenous Mother's socioeconomic status is lower Mother's level of education is lower Dissatisfaction with body image Loneliness/lack of friends Insomnia Asthma Missing classes for health reasons Not living with at least one parent Not having meals with parents Not eating breakfast Recent use of tobacco and alcohol Consumption of carbonated soft drinks Trying drugs Having had sexual intercourse	
Consumption of prescribed drugs Article 38	Female gender (study included use of hormonal contraceptives) Age Seventeen and over Mother's level of education is lower Family habit of taking prescribed drugs (especially mothers)	

Table 2. Top Issues of Mothers and Their Risk and Protective Factors

Top issues of the mother	Risk or complicating factors	Protective, mitigating, or facilitating factors
Maternal mental health Articles 14, 16, 26, 35, 40	**For posttraumatic stress** COVID-19 pandemic Greater maternal age Residing in the north region of the country (authors believe that it may be related to economic, cultural, and informational differences between regions) Preexistence of neuropsychiatric diseases Medication use Less satisfaction with their own life **For suffering with the experience of motherhood** Inequalities between experiences of motherhood and fatherhood Centrality of motherhood in women's lives Denial of self and prioritization of others Feeling of incompleteness and torn in their desires Maternal overload Struggling to impose limits on children Independence of children as they grow up Intrafamily sexual abuse of their daughters (because some were also victimized by intrafamily sexual abuse in childhood or adolescence)	Seeking help for one's children can provide help and an ear for mothers Specialized care and adequate support are important for mothers whose daughters have been sexually abused by family members
Fears about drug use by their children (middle class and high education families) Article 39	Sensationalistic and dramatic treatment of the media and disinformation of society Contact with drugs through the influence of friends Contact with drugs through environmental influence Marginality/crime Addiction Hospitalization/treatment Overdose	Dialogue with children Search for guidance

table continued next page

Top issues of the mother	Risk or complicating factors	Protective, mitigating, or facilitating factors
Acknowledging mental issues in children and/or seeking help Articles 6, 16, 26	Social vulnerability Lack of support network Feminization of care, even in cases where women are responsible for the family's income Lack of good quality healthcare services Long wait times for care service Stigma and fear of being judged because of the child's problem Unappreciation of mental suffering as a sufficient reason to seek help, as well as its consequences in the future	**For acknowledgement** Male gender of the adolescent Concomitance of different types of issues (e.g., hyperactivity, emotional problems, and behaviour problems) Only emotional problems Interfering with school performance Interfering with friendships Parental distress and stress Maternal anxiety and depression **To seek help** Male gender of the adolescent Absent father Maternal overload Severity of symptoms

Discussion

This is a relatively recent field. Its oldest article is from 2004, which denotes the period from which the mental health of adolescents or mothers of adolescents begins to be studied. The largest concentration of articles is found in the intermediate period (lasting nine years), a situation we believe will change in the next few years. Brazilian research on adolescent health, encompassing mental health variables, is recent, as is research on the mental health of their mothers.

A small concentration of researchers has dedicated themselves to the theme of mental health related to motherhood and adolescents, since almost 32 per cent of the articles were written by only two groups of authors, whereas the rest is divided among twenty-eight different authors.

Of the forty-one articles found, only nine had mothers (or mothers and fathers) as data sources; the remaining thirty-two were dedicated to collecting and/or analyzing data on adolescents, which allows us to infer that most of the studies deal with issues affecting the adolescents' mental health or that are affected by it.

However, the data's source is not the only element to be considered because a few articles, although the source of data is the mother, have the teenager as their main interest. This is the case in Elias Barbosa Oliveira et al., in which the goal is to understand the importance of family in preventing drug use among children and adolescents, and in

Joana Azevêdo Lima and Maria de Fátima Pereira Alberto, whose interest is supporting girls who are victims of intrafamily sexual abuse and their mothers, some of whom were also victims of intrafamily sexual abuse in their infancy and adolescence. In contrast, Camila Junqueira Muylaert et al., despite their data source being adolescents, are interested in the caregiver, who is generally the mother (or, in some cases, the grandmother).

As for the main problems related to adolescents, we identified eight categories: mental health, use of licit or illicit narcotics, intrafamily violence, bullying, sexual behavior, internet addiction, poor health self-assessment, and consumption of prescription drugs. These last four topics are covered in only one article each.

Our adolescent results show the risk factors vary for the different problems found. Regarding age, older teens are vulnerable to most of the issues listed, except for intrafamily violence and bullying, which usually affect children and adolescents of up to thirteen years old. In the category of consumption of licit or illicit narcotics, the social class marker is more evident. Although being white and having a mother with a higher level of education and socioeconomic status are risk factors for the consumption of alcohol, nonwhite teens whose mothers have a lower level of education, who are in situations of higher social vulnerability and who are living near places where drugs are sold and consumed—which in Brazil is usually the case in poorer areas and the slums—are more prone to the consumption of tobacco and other drugs.

The gender marker is almost deterministic. Females are more prone to suffer from any one or all of these categories: mental health problems, consumption of licit or illicit drugs, intrafamily violence, poor health assessment, and consumption of prescription drugs. Male teens are more exposed than females only to bullying (both as bullied and the bully) and unprotected sex. A further nuance appearing in some of these articles is that of body perception: adolescents who feel fat or are dissatisfied with their bodies have a higher risk for common mental disorders and emotional and relationship problems with their peers.

Concerning race/colour and socioeconomic status, nonwhite adolescents (e.g., Black, Asian, Brown, and Indigenous people) are more subject to problems, such as the consumption of tobacco and other drugs, severe physical punishment, bullying, unprotected sex, and poor health assessment. Such problems are also more common among adolescents living in conditions of social vulnerability, who are exposed to paid work and whose mothers have less education. However, white adolescents with a higher socioeconomic level are more prone to problems such as common mental disorders and alcohol consumption and, in the case of males, to bullying.

The variables about the mother highlighted in the articles reviewed are presented either as risk factors or as protective or facilitating factors. Younger mothers whose education level is low, are employed (work outside the household), and have mental health conditions, such as depression, anxiety and bipolar disorder, appear as risk factors for several problems. Having a mother with a lower education level, for example, contributes to mental health problems, tobacco and other drug use, intrafamily violence, bullying, unprotected sex, poor health self-assessment, and use of prescription drugs. Furthermore, issues related to the family are evident, such as social vulnerability, broken homes, families neglecting the upbringing and education of their children, consumption of licit or illicit drugs by parents, and intrafamily violence, which are risk factors for adolescents.

Among the maternal variables seen as protective factors for the problems affecting adolescents, having a mother with a higher level of education and who acts in a protective and emotionally supportive manner was mentioned with greater recurrence. Regarding the characteristics of families exhibiting a protective effect, we can highlight nuclear and structured families and authoritative nonviolent parents who use dialogue and affection and monitor school activities, what their children do in their free time, and whose company they keep.

For the few studies about the mental health of mothers or caregivers of adolescents, the subjects addressed were organized into three categories: maternal mental health, fears about drug use by children, and recognition of mental health issues in children or seeking help, or both. This demonstrates that, to a large extent, such issues mirror those considered problematic for adolescents, such as problems related to mental health and the use of licit or illicit drugs.

In the category addressing fears about drug use by their children, data were collected from middle-class and highly educated mothers and fathers about their most common fears and the measures they take to confront them in the country's largest city, São Paulo. In this sense, more particular issues brought up by mothers that may affect their mental health are not observed.

In maternal mental health and acknowledging mental issues in children and/or seeking help categories, the gender influence in the caregiving experience is manifest, demonstrating how persistent inequalities between expectations, social discourses, and lived experiences of motherhood and fatherhood are risk factors for mental illness and maternal vulnerability. This process demonstrates the maintenance of the sexual division of labor, a concept that emerges from the perception of the workload, performed in a free and socially invisible way by women, not for their benefit, but for others, "always in the name of nature, love and maternal duty" (Hirata and Kergoat, "Novas Configurações da Divisão Sexual").

Maternal overworking, capable of making the mother fall ill, does not seem to happen only among mothers with a lower socioeconomic status, although we acknowledge that lacking a support network and good quality healthcare services is more prevalent among families with a higher degree of social vulnerability. The feminization of care, however, is a widespread characteristic in Brazilian society, affecting women of all social classes, as suggested by the data. Mothers with higher education were more affected by posttraumatic stress due to the COVID-19 pandemic (Slompo).

The centrality of motherhood in women's lives, generating effects such as self-denial, overworking, and a sense of incompleteness due to the abdication of their desires, is not only related to poor women, but facilitates a hegemonic motherhood model that preaches caregiving as a natural function of the mother, who must prioritize the needs of her children to the detriment of her own (Kalil 73).

Conclusions

Our exploratory study sought to learn what the indexed scientific literature says about mental health issues of mothers to teenagers in Brazil. What we found, for the most part, were works related to the troubles that affect adolescents, which is more a testament to the indirect challenges facing the mothers of teens than an actual answer to the questions brought about by the study.

In this sense, the review of these articles partially fulfilled the study's purpose, as a strategy to collect data allowing both researchers and public policymakers to understand the needs and define the priorities regarding the mental health of Brazilian adolescents by identifying the main issues affecting people in this age group and their risk and protective factors.

However, we consider that even though most studies did not focus on the mother's perspective, reviewing the literature proved useful in two different ways. These studies highlight issues affecting mothers of adolescents and map out the main mental health issues faced by Brazilian adolescents in the first decades of the twenty-first century. It is no less important to note that, according to the studies reviewed, sociodemographic conditions and maternal behaviours are directly linked to greater prevention of teenagers having these problems. This situation is a burden put on the mother of an adolescent, corroborating the idea of total or intensified motherhood (Hays; Wolf). This burden is a contributing factor for stress and mental distress among mothers.

In light of the foregoing, we deem it necessary and urgent to carry out new studies, especially of qualitative ones, whose main focus is the mental health of mothers of adolescents in Brazil. These studies, done from an intersectional perspective—by the articulation between markers such as race, social class, age and region—can improve public policies aimed at these mothers.

Endnotes

1. All Portuguese-English translations are our own.
2. This stage was supported by journalism student Walber de Jesus Geronimo, a research intern at the Laboratory of Communication and Health of the Institute of Scientific and Technological Communication and Information in Health of Oswaldo Cruz Foundation (Fiocruz), under the supervision of the first author.

Works Cited

Akotirene, Carla. *Interseccionalidade* [*Intersectionality*]. Polen Livros, 2019.

Ariès, Philippe. *História Social da Criança e da Família* [*Centuries of Childhood: A Social History of Family Life*]. LTC Editora, 1981.

Barbosa de Oliveira, Elias, et al. "A Importância da Família na Prevenção do Uso de Drogas Entre Crianças e Adolescentes: Papel Materno" ["The Importance of the Family in Prevention of Drug Use among Children and Adolescents"] *SMAD. Revista Eletrônica Saúde Mental*

Álcool e Drogas, vol. 4, no. 2, 2008, pp. 1–16.

Bardin, Laurence. Análise de Conteúdo [Content of Analysis]. Edições 70, 1977.

Hays, Sharon. Contradições Culturais da Maternidade [The Cultural Contradictions of Motherhood]. Translated by Maria Jose Silveira. Gryphus Editora, 1998.

Hirata, Helena, and Danièle Kergoat. "Atualidade da Divisão Sexual e Centralidade do Trabalho das Mulheres" ["Update of the Sexual Division and Centrality of Women's Work"]. Revista de Ciências Sociais, vol. 1, no. 53, 2021, pp. 22–34.

Hirata, Helena, and Danièle Kergoat. "Novas Configurações da Divisão Sexual do Trabalho" ["New Configurations of the Sexual Division of Labour"]. Cadernos de Pesquisa, vol. 37, no. 132, 2007, pp. 595–609.

Hochman, Bernardo, et al. "Desenhos de Pesquisa." ["Research Designs"]. Acta Cirúrgica Brasileira, vol. 20, no. 2, 2005, pp. 2–9.

Iaconelli, Vera. Criar Filhos no Século XXI [Raising Children in the Twenty-First Century]. Editora Contexto, 2019.

Kalil, Irene Rocha. De Silêncio e Som: A Produção de Sentidos nos Discursos Oficiais de Promoção e Orientação ao Aleitamento Materno Brasileiros. [Of Silence and Sound: The Production of Meanings in Official Discourses on the Promotion of Guidance of Brazilian Breastfeeding]. 2015. Instituto de Comunicação e Informação Científica e Tecnológica em Saúde, Fundação Oswaldo Cruz, dissertation.

Lawson, Max, et al. Tempo de Cuidar: O Trabalho de Cuidado Não Remunerado e Mal Pago e a Crise Global da Desigualdade [Time to Care: Unpaid and Underpaid Work and the Crises of Global Inequality Report]. Oxfam Internacional, 2020, https://www.oxfam.org.br/forum-economico-de-davos/tempo-de-cuidar/. Accessed 13 Mar. 2025.

Lima, Joana Azevêdo, and Maria de Fátima Pereira Alberto. "Urgências Psicológicas no Cuidado às Mães em Casos de Abuso Sexual Intrafamiliar." ["Psychological Urgencies in the Care of Mothers in Cases of Intrafamilial Sexual Abuse"]. Estudos de Psicologia, vol. 21, no. 3, 2016, pp. 337–47

Maio Furta-Cor. "Saúde Mental Materna Importa" Minas Gerais, 2024, www.maiofurtacor.com.br. Accessed 22 Oct. 2024.

Mann, Christopher. "Observational Research Methods: Research Design

II: Cohort, Cross Sectional, and Case-Control Studies." *Emergencies Medical Journal*, vol. 20, no. 1, 2003, pp. 54–60.

Moher, David, et al. "Preferred Reporting Items for Systematic Reviews and Meta-Analyses: The PRISMA Statement." *PLoS Medicine*, vol. 6, no. 7, 2009, pp. 1–8.

Muylaert, Camila Junqueira, et al. "Relações de Gênero Entre Familiares Cuidadores de Crianças e Adolescentes de Serviços de Saúde Mental." ["Gender Relations Among Family Caregivers of Children and Adolescents in Mental Health Services"]. *Physis*, vol. 25, no. 1, 2015, pp. 41–58.

Santos de Matos, and Maria Izilda. "Corpo: Âncora de Emoções: Trajetórias, Desafios e Perspectivas" ["Body: Anchor of Emotions: Trajectories, Challenges and Perspectives"]. *Opsis*, vol. 7, no. 8, 2007, pp. 11–32.

Slompo, Nayara Ribeiro, et al. "Factors Associated with Symptoms of Posttraumatic Stress in Mothers During the Covid-19 Pandemic." *Maternal and Child Health Journal*, vol. 27, no. 9, 2023, pp. 1559–69.

Vieira, Elizabeth Meloni. *A Medicalização Do Corpo Feminino* [*The Medicalization of the Female Body*]. Editoria Fiocruz, 2002.

Wolf, Joan. "Is Breast Really Best? Risk and Total Motherhood in the National Breastfeeding Awareness Campaign." *Journal of Health, Politics, Policy and Law*, vol. 32, no. 4, 2007, pp. 595–636.

Zanello, Valeska. *Saúde Mental, Gênero e Dispositivos: Cultura e Processos de Subjetivação* [*Mental Health, Gender and Devices: Culture and Subjectivation Processes*]. Appris Editora, 2018.

Appendix I: Search Strategies

Database	Search Strategies
Medline/PubMed	#1 ("maternal Health" [Mesh] OR "mothers" [MESH] OR "motherhood" [TIAB] OR "parenthood" [TIAB] OR "mother child" [TIAB:~4] OR "mother infant" [TIAB:~4])
	#2 ("mental health" [Mesh] OR "mental health" [TIAB] OR "psychic suffering" [TIAB:~4] OR "mental disorders" OR "mental suffering" OR "mental illness" OR "women suffering" [TIAB:~4] OR "mothers suffering"[TIAB:~3])
	#3 ("adolescent" [MESH] OR "adolesce"* [TIAB] OR "young adult" [MESH] OR "teen"* [TIAB] OR "young"[TIAB] OR "parent-adolescent dyad"* OR "parent-adolescent relationship"*)
	#4 ("BRAZIL"* OR "BRASIL")
	#5 #1 AND #2 AND #3 AND #4
Lilacs (BVS) and SciELO	("maternidade" OR "mães" OR "maternal" OR "mãe-bebê" OR "parentalidade") AND ("saúde mental" OR "sofrimento em mulheres" OR "transtornos mentais" OR "saúde da gestante" OR "sofrimento psíquico") AND "Brasil"* AND ("adolescente"* OR "jovem")
Web of Science (Clarivate)	1. TS=("maternal" OR "mother"* OR "parenthood" OR ["women" OR "mother"] NEAR/4 ["child" OR "adolescent"*])
	2. TS=("mental health" OR "mental suffering" OR "mental illness")
	3. TS=("psychic NEAR/4 Suffer*) OR "mental disorders")
	4. TS=(["women" OR "woman" OR "mother"] NEAR/3 ["suffer"*] NEAR/4 ["adolescent"*])
	5. #2 OR #3 OR #4
	6. ALL=("BRASIL" OR "BRAZIL")
	7. ALL=("adolescent"* OR "young adult")
	8. #1 AND #5 AND #6 AND #7

Appendix II: References of Articles Comprising the Scope

Almeida, Camila Souza de, et al. "Factors Associated to Alcohol Use by Adolescents." *Texto & Contexto-Enfermagem*, vol. 30, 2021, pp. e20190008–e08, doi:10.1590/1980-265x-tce-2019-0008.

Antunes, Juliana Teixeira, et al. "Fatores de Risco e Proteção Relacionados à Violência Intrafamiliar Contra os Adolescentes Brasileiros." *Revista Brasileira de Epidemiologia*, vol. 23, 2020, p. e200003., doi:10.1590/1980-549720200003.supl.1.

Assunção, Maria Cecília Formoso, et al. "Tornar-se Obeso na Adolescência Pode Trazer Consequências à Saúde Mental?" *Cadernos de Saúde Pública*, vol. 29, no. 9, 2013, pp. 1859–66, doi:10.1590/S0102-311X2013001300024.

Benchaya, Mariana C., et al. "Pais Não Autoritativos e o Impacto no Uso de Drogas: A Percepção dos Filhos Adolescentes." *Jornal de Pediatria*, vol. 87, no. 3, 2011, pp. 238–44, doi:10.1590/S0021-75572011000300010.

Bordin, I. A., et al. "Lifetime Paid Work and Mental Health Problems among Poor Urban 9-to-13-Year-Old Children in Brazil." *Scientific World Journal*, vol. 2013, p. 815218, doi: 10.1155/2013/815218.

Bordin, I. A., et al. "Maternal Recognition of Child Mental Health Problems in Two Brazilian Cities." *Brazilian Journal of Psychiatry*, vol. 40, no. 1, 2018, pp. 63–71, doi:10.1590/1516-4446-2016-1957.

Bordin, I. A., et al. "Severe Physical Punishment and Mental Health Problems in an Economically Disadvantaged Population of Children and Adolescents." *Brazilian Journal of Psychiatry*, vol. 28, no. 4, 2006, pp. 290–96, doi:10.1590/s1516-44462006000400008.

Bordin, I. A., et al. "Severe Physical Punishment: Risk of Mental Health Problems for Poor Urban Children in Brazil." *Bulletin of the World Health Organization*, vol. 87, no. 5, 2009, pp. 336–44, doi:10.2471/blt.07.043125.

Cartana, Maria do Horto Fontoura. "'Às Vezes Eles Vão': Compreendendo Qualidade de Vida e Promoção da Saúde Sob a Ótica de uma Mãe de Pré-Adolescentes." *Revista Latino-Americana de Enfermagem*, vol. 13, no. spe2, 2005, pp. 1177–84, doi:10.1590/S0104-11692005000800012.

Carvalho, Priscila Diniz de, et al. "Condutas de Risco à Saúde e Indicadores de Estresse Psicossocial em Adolescentes Estudantes do Ensino Médio." *Cadernos de Saúde* Pública, vol. 27, no. 11, 2011, pp. 2095–105, doi:10.1590/S0102-311X2011001100003.

Curto, B. M., et al. "Environmental Factors Associated with Adolescent Antisocial Behavior in a Poor Urban Community in Brazil." *Social Psychiatry and Psychiatric Epidemiology*, vol. 46, no. 12, 2011, pp. 1221–31, doi:10.1007/s00127-010-0291-2.

Duarte, C. S., et al. "The Child Mental Health Treatment Gap in an Urban Low-Income Setting: Multisectoral Service Use and Correlates." *Psychiatric Services*, vol. 73, no. 1, 2022, pp. 32–38, doi:10.1176/appi.ps.202000742.

Freire, Nicolau Maués Serra, et al. "Avaliação da Multifatorialidade para Dependência Química entre Infantes e Adolescentes no Estado do Rio de Janeiro." *Semina: Ciências Biológicas e da Saúde*, vol. 31, no. 1, 2010, pp. 83–92.

Gebara, C. F., et al. "Psychosocial Factors Associated with Mother-Child Violence: A Household Survey." *Social Psychiatry and Psychiatric Epidemiology*, vol. 52, no. 1, 2017, pp. 77–86, doi:10.1007/s00127-016-1298-0.

Gonçalves, H., et al. "Maternal Depression and Anxiety Predicts the Pattern of Offspring Symptoms During their Transition to Adulthood." *Psychological Medicine*, vol. 46, no. 2, 2016, pp. 415–24, doi:10.1017/s0033291715001956.

Langaro, Fabíola, and Zuleica Pretto. "Experiências de Parentalidade como Fatores Geradores de Sofrimento em Mulheres." *Fractal: Revista de Psicologia*, vol. 27, no. 2, 2015, pp. 130–38, doi:10.1590/1984-0292/453.

Lima, Joana Azevêdo, and Maria de Fátima Pereira Alberto. "Urgências Psicológicas no Cuidado às Mães em Casos de Abuso Sexual Intrafamiliar." *Estudos de Psicologia*, vol. 21, no. 3, 2016, pp. 337–47, doi:10.5935/1678-4669.20160032.

Malta, Deborah Carvalho, et al. "Características Associadas à Autoavaliação Ruim do Estado de Saúde em Adolescentes Brasileiros, Pesquisa Nacional de Saúde do Escolar, 2015." *Revista Brasileira de Epidemiologia*, vol. 21, no. supl. 1, 2018, pp. e180018–e18, doi:10.1590/1980-549720180018.supl.1.

Malta, Deborah Carvalho, et al. "Exposição ao Álcool entre Escolares e Fatores Associados." *Revista de Saúde Pública*, vol. 48, no. 1, 2014, pp. 52–62, doi:10.1590/S0034-8910.2014048004563.

Malta, Deborah Carvalho, et al. "Fatores Associados aos Episódios de Agressão Familiar entre Adolescentes, Resultados da Pesquisa Nacional de Saúde do Escolar (Pense)." *Ciência & Saúde Coletiva*, vol. 24, 2019, 1287–1298, doi: 10.1590/1413-81232018244.15552017.

Malta, Deborah Carvalho, et al. "Prevalência de Bullying e Fatores Associados em Escolares Brasileiros, 2015." *Ciência & Saúde Coletiva*, vol. 24, no. 4, 2019, pp. 1359–68, doi:10.1590/1413-81232018244.15492017.

Malta, Deborah Carvalho, et al. "Smoking among Brazilian Adolescents During the Covid-19 Pandemic: A Cross-Sectional Study." *Sao Paulo Medical Journal*, vol. 141, no. 6, 2023, p. 8, doi:10.1590/1516-3180.2022.0424.R1.30032023.

Mello, Flávia Carvalho Malta, et al. "A Prática de Bullying entre Escolares Brasileiros e Fatores Associados, Pesquisa Nacional de Saúde do Escolar 2015." *Ciência & Saúde Coletiva*, vol. 22, no. 9, 2017, pp. 2939–48, doi:10.1590/1413-81232017229.12762017.

Mello, Flávia Carvalho Malta, et al. "Bullying e Fatores Associados em Adolescentes da Região Sudeste Segundo a Pesquisa Nacional de Saúde do Escolar." *Revista Brasileira de Epidemiologia*, vol. 19, no.4, 2016, pp. 866–77, doi: 10.1590/1980-5497201600040015.

Moura, Yone Gonçalves de, et al. "Drug Use among Street Children and Adolescents: What Helps?" *Cadernos de Saúde Pública*, vol. 28, no. 7, 2012, pp. 1371–80, doi:10.1590/S0102-311X2012000700015.

Muylaert, Camila Junqueira et al. "Relações de Gênero entre Familiares Cuidadores de Crianças e Adolescentes de Serviços de Saúde Mental." *Physis*, vol. 25, no. 1, 2015, pp. 41–58, doi:10.1590/S0103-73312015000100004.

Oliveira-Campos, Maryane, et al. "Sexual Behavior among Brazilian Adolescents, National Adolescent School-Based Health Survey (Pense 2012)." *Revista Brasileira de Epidemiologia*, vol. 17, no. supl. 1, 2014, pp. 116–30, doi:10.1590/1809-4503201400050010.

Oliveira, Elias Barbosa de, et al. "A Importância da Família na Prevenção do Uso de Drogas entre Crianças e Adolescentes: Papel Materno."

SMAD, *Revista Eletrônica de Saúde Mental, Álcool e Drogas*, vol. 4, no. 2, 2008, pp. 1–16.

Oliveira, Luciano Machado Ferreira Tenório de, et al. "Influence of Parental Smoking on the Use of Alcohol and Illicit Drugs among Adolescents." *Einstein*, vol. 17, no. 1, 2019, pp. eAO4377–eAO77, doi:10.31744/einstein_journal/2019ao4377.

Paz, Fernanda Marques, et al. "School Health Promotion and Use of Drugs among Students in Southern Brazil." *Revista de Saúde Pública*, vol. 52, 2018, pp. 1-11, doi:10.11606/s1518-8787.2018052000311.

Pereira, Vagna Cristina Leite da Silva, et al. "Sofrimento Psíquico em Adolescentes Associado ao Alcoolismo Familiar: Possíveis Fatores de Risco." *Revista Eletrônica de Enfermagem*, vol. 17, no. 2, 2015, pp. 178–85, doi:10.5216/ree.v17i2.24396.

Petresco, S, et al. "The Prevalence of Psychopathology in Offspring of Bipolar Women from a Brazilian Tertiary Center." *Brazilian Journal of Psychiatry*, vol. 31, no. 3, 2009, pp. 240–46, doi:10.1590/s1516-4446 2009000300009.

Pinheiro, Karen Amaral Tavares, et al. "Common Mental Disorders in Adolescents: A Population Based Cross-Sectional Study." *Brazilian Journal of Psychiatry*, vol. 29, no. 3, 2007, pp. 241–45, http://www.scielo.br/scielo.php?script=sci_arttext&pid=S1516-44462007000 300009. Accessed 13 Mar. 2025.

Poton, W. L., et al. "Problemas de comportamento internalizantes e externalizantes e uso de substâncias na adolescência." *Cadernos de Saude Pública*, vol. 34, no. 9, 2018, p. e00205917, doi:10.1590/0102-311x 00205917.

Régio, L., et al. "The Care Provided to Black-Skinned Children and Adolescents with Mental Health Problems in the Intersection between Gender and Race." *Revista Latino-Americana de Enfermagem*, vol. 31, 2023, p. e3941, doi:10.1590/1518-8345.6058.3941.

Ribeiro, Isabel Batista da Silva, et al. "Common Mental Disorders and Socioeconomic Status in Adolescents of Erica." *Revista de Saúde Pública*, vol. 54, 2020, pp. 01–09, doi:10.11606/s1518-8787.2020 054001197.

Santos, Renata Ferreira dos, and Eliseu Verly Junior. "Bullying e Associação de Comportamentos de Risco entre Adolescentes da Região Norte: Um Estudo a Partir da Pesquisa Nacional de Saúde do Escolar,

2015." *Desidades*, vol. 29, 2021, pp. 217–31.

Silva, Clécio H. da, and Elsa R. J. Giugliani. "Consumo de Medicamentos em Adolescentes Escolares: Uma Preocupação." *Jornal de Pediatria*, vol. 80, no. 4, 2004, pp. 326–32.

Silva, Eroy Aparecida da, et al. "Drogas na Adolescência: Temores e Reações dos Pais." *Psicologia Teoria e Prática*, vol. 8, no. 1, 2006, pp. 41–54.

Slompo, N.R., et al. "Factors Associated with Symptoms of Posttraumatic Stress in Mothers During the Covid-19 Pandemic." *Maternal and Child Health Journal*, vol. 27, no. 9, 2023, pp. 1559–69, doi:10.1007/s10995-023-03723-3.

Terres-Trindade, Michele, and Clarisse Pereira Mosmann. "Discriminant Profile of Young Internet Dependents: The Role of Family Relationships." *Paidéia*, vol. 25, no. 62, 2015, pp. 353–62, doi:10.1590/1982-43272562201509.

6.

Working through Adolescence and Motherhood: A Sociopoetic and Evocative Caribbean-Centred Reflection

Talia Esnard and Faith Flavius

Adolescence[1] represents a significant period of neurological and social changes (Coleman), which collectively affect the nature and dynamics of the relationships that emerging adults share with peers, family, and romantic partners (Giordano). These developmental milestones have been linked to shifting periods of growth and adaptation (Brown and Prinstein), with growing social sensitivities shaping how adolescents understand themselves with others (Crone and Fuligni, 2020). Some notable concerns are the changing nature of adolescent relationships, the type of social networks they branch into, and the nature of the interrelationships that follow (Collins and Laursen). These transitional periods have also introduced some curiosity about what Sarah-Jayne Blakemore has termed the "social brain," with attention to how brain regions process these relational networks and, relatedly, how adolescents situate themselves within the social world during this transitional period. These insights also point to the relative significance of the cognitive functions that dramatically change during adolescence, with increasing tendencies for social processing (Blakemore and Mills). For the most part, this impacts not just how tasks and situations are processed to impact social action but also how parent-child conflicts emerge and are moderated (Laursen et al.).

Although studies have explored the adolescent period, few have interrogated and appreciated the changes taking place in the lives of mothers (Jones). From one perspective, Lucy Jones argues for the importance of understanding matrescence as one of the most significant transformations occurring outside adolescence. Through her work, she makes visible the experiences mothers undergo, such as matriphagy,[2] birth trauma, and emotional and physiological changes. Other studies have shown that the neurological and social metamorphosis experienced within this maternal process remains relatively similar to those occurring in adolescence but with a persistent silence within academic scholarship and beyond (Jones; Orchard et al.). From another perspective, Edwina R. Orchard et al. in their work *Matrescence: Lifetime Impact of Motherhood on Cognition and the Brain,* argue that although "the developmental changes of childhood, adolescence, and aging are the subject of intense study, the impact of motherhood as a life stage in humans remains poorly understood" (303). In this work, matrescence emerges as a neurocognitive developmental stage that differently unfolds into motherhood and later life. In this representation, motherhood extends neurological, psychological, and social changes with different moral, spiritual, ecological, and existential realities associated with this period (Athan). These transitions also raise questions related to maternal distress (Athan and Reel; Copeland and Harbaugh; Maxwell et al.), the interpersonal contexts of adolescent development (Collins and Laursen), and the impact on how mothers and daughters are empowered within this process (O'Reilly, "Mothering against Motherhood").

This focus on daughters and the connections to their mothers (O'Reilly, "Mothering against Motherhood"; Rich) and the ambivalent relationship that unfolds (Serbin and Karp) represents a crucial yet underexplored area within the field of motherhood studies. This element of social neuroscience is an increasingly explored area, but without extensive connections to maternal-adolescent relationships (Branje). The chapter seeks to address these gaps but in the context of the Caribbean. The aim therefore is to explore how these developmental changes may affect the relational encounters between daughters and mothers during these critical periods of change. This chapter also presents sociologically and historically situated constructions of children, adolescents, women, and mothers to allow for a more contextual framing of mother-daughter experiences and their relational engagements. As the chapter argues, working through adolescence and motherhood is negotiated within historical and sociocultural constructions that define the parameters for attachments, relations, and wellbeing. This type of exploration is particularly important for overcoming the silenced experiences of mothers and daughters from the Global South, where these experiences are still being scrutinized through northern-centric standpoints (Pillay et al.).

Making the Case for Mother-Daughter Interrogations

Motherhood has been represented within the Global North literature as a major period of transformation with significant changes that affect how mothers self-identify and negotiate their relationship with their children. Although these works do not capture the experiences of mothers in the Global South and specifically in the Caribbean, the foundational work of Adrienne Rich, Sara Ruddick, and Andrea O'Reilly offers critical insights and starting points for advancing maternal scholarship.

In her early work, Adrienne Rich discusses how mothers work within the gaze of others and the broader constructions or framings of motherhood. Sara Ruddick likewise acknowledges how mothers become subject to normative white middle-class constructions of motherhood, as well as the standards and values that have been set to define the practice of motherhood. Yet Rich also reminds us of how these expectations and normative framings of motherhood superimpose maternal expectations and role alignments that affect the experiences and relations of mothers and their daughters. She notes that... "Thousands of daughters see their mothers as having taught a compromise and self-hatred they are struggling to win free of, the one through whom the restrictions and degradations of a female existence were perforce transmitted" (235). This feeling becomes one of matrophobia—"the fear not of one's mother or of motherhood but of becoming one's mother" (236). In such cases, Rich sees the "loss of the daughter to the mother, the mother to the daughter, [as] the essential female tragedy" (237). She suggests that many "daughters live in rage at their mothers for having accepted too readily and passively whatever comes... [and in such cases], the mother's self-hatred and low expectations are the binding-rages of the psyche of the daughter (243)." She argues that these tensions have to be situated within a deeper understanding that "few women growing up in patriarchal society can feel mothered enough; [and] the power of our mother, whatever their love for us and their struggles on our behalf, is too restricted ... [and] ... it is the mother through whom patriarchy ... teaches the small female her proper expectations" (Rich 243).

O'Reilly has advanced some of these arguments. In "Mothering against Motherhood," she notes that matrophobia exists through the devaluation of motherhood and fears of maternal inauthenticity, which negatively affects the intimacy, empathy, and connection between mothers and daughters. This treatment of mothers, without considering the gendered expectations and cultural idiosyncrasies that come with these roles, represent critical factors that play into how mothers are perceived and received by their daughters. O'Reilly also explains that during adolescence, Western culture mandates separation of children from parents to create an autonomous and self-propelled individual. This practice typically emerges at the end of adolescence when there is a tendency to promote independence within a growing child (O'Reilly, "Mothering against Motherhood" 163). This level of social awareness and search for autonomy, as a measure of individuality, can produce a negative outcome where mothers are not perceived as approachable to daughters during critical periods of their lives and where the connections become key issues. In such cases, the need to secure the self-worth of daughters becomes quintessential to how they develop within the consciousness of their minds and bodies, and begin to connect to their mothers differently.

Yet O'Reilly's work questions this narrative of unavailability and locates this framing within the patriarchal view of mothering and the inherent decentring of this relationship, which emerges as a direct consequence of the separation during this critical time. Where these dominant values and cultural practices around normative mothering are adopted, these experiences can compromise one's empowerment. The tensions in this case emerge both as inevitable and necessary but relatively underexplored as a social and relational experience within maternal scholarship and certainly beyond the Global North. We attempt to tease through the relevance of these questions by extending the matricentric feminist perspective, which is presented below.

Positioning a Matricentric Caribbean perspective

Although feminist theories offer critical insights into the social construction of motherhood, this remains an unfinished agenda (O'Reilly, *Matricentric Feminism*). We recognize therefore that feminist theorizations have situated the gendered yet diverse ways in which women have been constructed and positioned within sociohistorical and political contexts. Matricentric feminism can decentre narratives related to the selfless mother and child centredness and critique patriarchal representations of mothering (O'Reilly, *Matricentric Feminism*). This matricentric perspective, while not so conceptualized or developed within a Caribbean context, provides an overall framework that can be leveraged to extend existing attempts (by feminist and non-feminist scholars) to reframe understandings of maternal identity, practice, and relations for Black mothers. This is particularly important given that the family systems and dynamics of Black mothers within the Caribbean have been historically denigrated as dysfunctional, atypical, and outside of accepted synchronic structures within early anthropological and Eurocentric research (Esnard, "Towards Matricentric"). Such analytical interrogations allow for important examinations of the stereotypes within existing constructions and representations of Black motherhood and the challenges of working through mother-daughter relations within this social and political complexity.

Through the cocentring of mothers and daughters and exploring this relational element of maternal experience, the work advances a contextual framing of matricentric feminism to situate motherhood studies. This type of context-specific framing is important to push back against historically oppressive and middle-class Western-centric framing that normalizes marriage and intensive mothering practices (Bush). We use this contextual approach to question racialized discourses that are rooted within experiences of slavery and that continue to dehumanize and denigrate Black populations (Bush 71). This is important, for example, to high-light how understandings of care and negligence have been built on Eurocentric framing of matrifocality. Selective evidence is used on marriage and mating patterns among Black mothers in the Caribbean to pigeonhole and misconstrue mother-child attachments and the role of the father (Barrow, "Caribbean Masculinity"; Rowley; Senior). This type of misrepresentation is well documented as a critique of gendered, racialized, and classed representations of the Black family within early research on the Caribbean (Barrow, *Caribbean Masculinity*; Barrow, "Living in Sin"; Esnard). This type of matricentric feminist scholarship is therefore a necessary part of debunking the labels surrounding matrifocal Black Caribbean families that are embedded within historically grounded, functionalist-driven, and social Parsonian reengineering agendas.

There has been some effort to re-represent Caribbean mothers as hardworking, resilient, and socially mobile (Getfield) to situate and counterstory the experiences of Black mothers (Mullings and Mullings-Lewis). One useful starting point has been the recognition of the cultural constructions of matrifocal households which have been nested in analysis of attachments between mothers and daughters. Other narratives demonstrate an absence of normative representations and expectations within maternal attachment, such as a relative lack of involvement of mothers in the social activities of daughters (Evans; Landman). Hyacinth Evans speaks to existing discourses that link a lack of verbal communication and open expression between mothers and daughters to the mothers' ignorance concerning their children's physical and emotional needs. This perceived ignorance is also connected to high levels of frustration for mothers who attempt to process the conflicting values of their children and their aspirations for them. She reframes this representation with attention to the historical and social setting of working-class Black families, the ensuing type of parent-child interaction, and the values and beliefs that were inculcated through these experiences. Christine Barrow (*Families in the Caribbean*) extends this line of thinking to underscore the gendered representations of young girls and women. Barrow speaks to the tendency for mothers to be overprotective of their children, with noted fears (around sexuality and intimacy) that affect how they negotiate the relationship with their children. These experiences have been presented as generational silences, which have been historically linked to religious and cultural taboos (Kerr) that have affected mother-daughter relations but with negative outcomes related to early school dropouts and pregnancies among young girls between fourteen and fifteen (Barrow, *Families in the Caribbean*). Kerr, however, signals the need for deeper interrogations of the adolescent period, the cultural underpinnings of motherhood within this localized space, and the responses of mothers within that transitory period. These remain open and undertheorized areas of exploration for which the chapter addresses.

Situating Evocative Sociopoetic and Evocative Approaches

We use the combination of poetry and sociocultural evocative analysis to understand where we are placed to experience the connections or relationships as mother and daughter. This type of sociopoetic analysis emerges as a postmodern influence where data are presented in poetic form to create meaningful dialogue between the participant and the reader (Richardson). This method allows for cocreators to understand their positionality and location within specific sociocultural dynamics. In this case, we start with a bit on our social locations.

> As an academic mother of three—with her eldest Faith now twenty-one (also as coauthor) and the fraternal twins at ten years—Talia has written about the sociocultural nuances that have affected her experiences of mothering within the academy and her strategies for navigating some of the challenges (See Esnard, "(Re) turning to Motherhood"). Through this reflection, related experiences, and other writings on motherhood within the context of the Caribbean, she works to unpack some of the still yet unveiled aspects and experiences of the Black mother.

> Faith is a final year undergraduate student at the University of the West Indies, double majoring in history and sociology. This unique background has enabled her to assess phenomena and situate them within their nexus of sociohistorical contexts. Moreover, her lens of perception expands to a third dimension with her poetic abilities. Writing poetry for twelve years, Faith attempts to capture the raw emotions of her life and those around her. Together, she crafts the complex contextual realities of Caribbean life with a quill pen.

The use of sociopoetic evocative reflection within this chapter emerges as an extension of our work and interest. This method provides a useful way of communicating imagery, voice, context, and emotions but within the structure and broader parameters of poetry. As a method, this type of poetic representation extends dialogue and disciplines by embracing emotions and relations and examining societal issues. This method can create evocative analyses that can broaden perspectives and understanding using reflective and self-conscious representations (Richardson). This method aligns with other studies that have explored the use of autobiographical poetry, which is analyzed in qualitative research, to address issues of representation and identity formation among adolescents and mothers (Furman et al.; Richardson). This approach is also similar to Rich's autobiographical work through which she centres the "I" within the discussion on mothering. Rich largely uses this approach to emphasize recovery, loss, self-discovery, self-knowledge, and recreating mothering to envision this sense of liberatory practice.

This move into the personal realm is a deliberate way of reframing the experience, narrative, and institution of motherhood as constructed and contested. The subjective representation, with a recognition of the ambiguity and contradictions unfolding within that process (Gergen and Gergen). This representation becomes a way for us to speak through the broader tensions of change and to advance notions and practices of how these can be used to re-represent human relations and connections (Stein), in this case, mother-daughter relations and experiences. We capture this through our dual reflection of the adolescent journey, written within the realm of poetic and discursive expression but with the use of analogies related to a tour of a local swamp (Faith) and a roller coaster ride (Talia) as differing experiences. The reflections therefore represent two voices (mother and daughter) but with different images and representations connecting the journeys of working through adolescence and motherhood within these reflections.

Caroni Swamp[3]

It's 4:30 p.m., and I wobble into the boat like a newborn.

On the entry of the swamp, the sun is aglow.

She holds me with the comforting warmth of my mother's first hug under frigid hospital lights. She glistens on the blue crabs.

The zephyr directs you to the allure of the scarlet ibis against the endless green mangrove peaks and skies.

The debut of the journey; eagerness and curiosity like youth when I was seven,

and every year around then when my mum painted these skies and was my unwavering boat...

Oh to live in such apricity, like the unknowing child behind me.

But then the sun diminuendoes as the boat propels harshly.

I notice the darkness between the life of the mangrove,

the civil war that unleashes itself like a home with an angry wife and avoidant father.

Snakes that hang from trees and purposely prey on the weaker.

The ugly fish that lunge at me and open my weakened reflection in the water to a dirty lens of the swamp below.

I see all the mud.

Why my mother would pinch my chin and tell me to not haste.

I see why she was fearful,

Why she carries some rust from wear

And somehow the tour guide chooses now to recall proposals and those who found love in this penumbra,

What a joke.

Ahead are some stems that form arbours to clearer waters, but I dither.

I used to be an eager child, but now I am the cowardly woman I thought my mother was. Yet I sit censoriously in the front of this boat inclined.

I am angry remembering her vexation on the dock, attempting to burst my bubble and prattling that her paintings were just fairytales to cautiously seal my innocence.

My mother could still be wrong... there's arbours ahead and clearer waters.

I cup my ears from the vociferous chirps I thought she exaggerated.

My anxiety crescendos.

I close my eyes,

leaves fall to my back,

fresh water falls to my lids.

Every branch I bend to circumvent,

every snake I pray is sleeping,

every insect that pushes me further into my seat.

This pernicious solipsism that is ruining the journey.

I wish I could hide behind my mum like the child behind me.
What would she think of my despondence?
What would she say about my myopia?

Then just for a moment, the swamp is placid, and petrichor rains.
The tails of the sky catch the head of the swamp so purposely.

Then it all settles as we arrive at the end.
Can I reconcile these baby blue skies with the terror I just witnessed?
Can I be both a coward and an optimist?
To acknowledge wars and fairytales can collide,
to carry the caution of my mother with the unwavering faith of my youth?
The tour guide reels me in again and surmises the swamp:
To the right at the roots of the enclosing mangrove, occasional vibrant red fleets dot the dull browns.
Here, the scarlet ibises rest; they fight for life, they die and grow.
Above the shrub of green in magnificent blue they soar and go.
"That is the duality of our swamp," he said.

Together, we reflected on the evocative and poetic writings. We both acknowledge the visual imagery that Faith presents to describe her entry into the Caroni Swamp as her entry into adolescence. Faith juxtaposes these two entrances to reflect on the beginning of her life becoming an adolescent and the mixed bag of emotions that follow as she begins to explore all that the future has in store. She comes to the point of having social sensitivities.

This sense of social sensitivity becomes a similar reality but with a different process for Talia, who captures this through her reflection on her daughter's transitory years and the transformations within her thinking and practice.

Getting on the Adolescent Rollercoaster

That already is a problem. As a person, I typically do not like heights. Yet I recognize confronting this is unavoidable in concrete and symbolic ways. The adolescent rollercoaster, or at least how I conceived of this, with sharp curves and steep inclines offered an experience with the latter. As a mother, I have always been one to help my children get onto the rollercoaster ride—but then to look at them from a distance with mixed emotions. I am ready to let them go but with utmost fear and confusion as to how they can enjoy something so frightening. It never ceases to amaze me how risk can be feared and claimed in the same space and time.

I have located this bewilderment over time in personal, social, and historical contexts. I have grown over the years to appreciate that it all depends on the perspective you hold and how you process the situation you face. Yet I know understanding this is never a simple and uncontested process. In the early years of having my children, I parented without a conscious or reflective approach to my practice. As they transitioned into new stages of their lives and new challenges, for all of us, I have also worked to relocate myself outside of a history of traditional parenting where conservatism and social restrictions defined the public experience for young girls and mothers. I recognize the difference and context and the need to directly confront the spaces and histories of my experience not just as a mother but also as a mother who engages in maternal scholarship.

As my children grow into different stages of their development, I have learned to appreciate these differences. I work towards understanding these differences and make sense of the many changes within the landscape and networks defining the experiences of young persons. I take forward the lessons of my children and from the experience of working through adolescence and motherhood with my eldest daughter, Faith. Over the last few years, her journey into adolescence has already taught me a lot. The ride into adolescence was nothing expected and an experience rarely discussed among other mothers or within public spaces. However, it has contained many moments of elevated heartbeats, with scattered thoughts and emotions, as well as many momentous occasions and some not so easy ones. I have had to pause to question the what and why of my experiences and, more importantly, my expectations for certain trajectories, choices, and voices within that mix.

I recognize within these experiences the need to stop, acknowledge, and celebrate the major milestones, but to let her carve her own space, self-definition, and voice. I have learned to appreciate the difference in perspective and acknowledge my perception and construction of this adolescent rollercoaster have been framed by my fears and experiences. Her journey is evolving in different ways and in different time frames. I have also accepted my construction of this adolescent rollercoaster may be perceived and positioned differently by her. She captures her journey in her poetic description of our relationship through the swamp analogy.

Discussion

This work highlights the stages of growth and change that affect the relationship between mothers and daughters. This poetic and discursive reflection captures the dualisms, contradictions, and tensions related to working through simultaneous experiences related to life and death, hope and pessimism, and reservation and openness, all situated within the social landscapes mothers and daughters find themselves in, in our case the swamp. Through these reflections, we symbolically locate our experiences within the description and conversation of natural wetland communities (Juman and Rameswa) and the rollercoaster ride. We also speak to growing discomforts for children who transition into adolescence and for parents who attempt to work through these experiences, and the impact these have on their relationships (Goede et al.; Shearer et al.).

In thinking through the significance of these transitioning periods, our work calls for centring how mothers and adolescents experience these changes and work through them. The work calls for some unpacking and historicizing around how mothers and daughters construct the relationships with their children and the need to protect and safeguard in the process of mothering. Through our reflection, we recognize the weight of considerations for mothers to steer children down the right pathway. This emerges as a representation of the moral values associated with family systems and dynamics in the Caribbean, which have been historically infused within representations of the selfless mother and strong maternal attachments. Of significance here is the work of Erica Lawson, who while researching Caribbean mothers in Canada, highlights caution of Caribbean mothers around issues of intimacy and sexual relations. These practices have been linked to historical experiences and representations of trauma, linked to the legacies of enslavement, the reproductive exploitation of ex-slaves, and the abuse of women and culture of silence that followed. These experiences related to the precautionness of mother-daughter relationships have also created historical and cultural taboos. Mothers are expected to raise good girls. Authority and conservatism become key strategies for mothers to address issues related to their daughters' sexuality (Crawford).

To some extent, the literature suggests these experiences are also connected to social constructions and representations of children and mothers within the Caribbean region. Charmaine Crawford points to the good mother and bad mother archetypes, which have been historically driven by the ideological pervasiveness of this maternal binary, which weighs on the constructions and expectations of mothers. In "Racialized Citizenship, Respectability, and Mothering among Caribbean Mothers in Britain," Elaine Bauer reminds us too of the weight of discussions around the mother's responsibility to ensure her respectability and that of the family within these parental dynamics. However, these expectations for respectability are often framed within Eurocentric notions of social acculturation and achievement orientation, emphasizing educational and occupational mobility but without critical discussion and understanding of how these framings have affected the nature and dynamics of the relationships between mothers and daughters. The expectations for obedience and respectfulness of the child and the mother's protectiveness fall within these oppositional social placements (Best-Cummings). As coauthors, mother and daughter, we are conscious of these narratives and the need to locate the biases within this type of maternal thinking. These narratives have been linked to the tendency for mothers within the region to focus on messages of independence, hard work, and pursuit of education, both as a measure of strength and social mobility (Crawford). We also recognize how these constructions of motherhood and adolescence have been built within key social parameters of race, class, and gender, which make distant the perceptions, interpretations and negotiations of these spaces (see Barrow, *Caribbean Childhoods*; Barrow, *Family in the Caribbean*; Mohammed; Momsen). Though not publicly discussed, these issues are culturally experienced but without a critical and empirical understanding of how mothers and daughters negotiate these changes. Thus, while the literature on adolescent distress is growing (Hickman et al.), there is little research on maternal stress, adaptation, and response during this time (Copeland and Harbaugh).

The evocative and poetic reflections provide snippets of how these relationships can be perceived and negotiated to consciously locate and possibly reframe how adolescence can be located within the framings and experiences of motherhood to make sense of these experiences and dynamics. This work advances in some ways the findings of Orchard et al., who remind us that motherhood remains an extension and consequence of matrescence as a sensitive neurodevelopmental period that continues far beyond this period (313). If not considered, these transitions for the mother also affect how adolescence is experienced, processed, and acted upon. We are also reminded here of the work of Rich, who suggests that "as daughters, we need mothers who want their own freedom and ours" (247) and of O'Reilly, who calls for the empowerment of mothers and young girls. These statements capture the relevance of both actors and their experiences but with a commitment to self-sustaining mindfulness and health. Whether adolescents are striving for more autonomy or for working through the changes in their relationship with their mothers, Cristiano Inguglia et al. calls for a greater understanding of the experiences of emerging adulthood (related to autonomy and relatedness) and the significance of these experiences to relational dynamics and overall wellbeing.

From a Caribbean perspective, examinations of these relational aspects of mothering calls for a broader understanding of the constructions and representations of Black mothers and their mothering practices, which have been historically framed from deficit and functional perspectives. There is little location of the cultural and ideological framings centring the role and significance of the family and, relatedly, the weight of the responsibility for mothers and the wellbeing of the child (Chamberlain). It is against this reality that scholars Claudette Crawford-Brown and J. Melrose Rattray in *Parent-Child Relationships in Caribbean Families* call for deeper examinations of the sociocultural contexts for mother-child relationships that advance the significant ways in which childrearing and upbringing have been grounded within broader communal beliefs and practices, which foster interdependence, perseverance, and fortitude. These values are often reflected in the expectations for the mother, as the one who bears the weight for childrearing and teaches the child survival skills, and the capacity to work in ambiguous spaces and within the broader workings of the community. In such cases, there is a tendency for parents and children to discover their expectations and understandings of their shared spaces do not coincide, a reality that can produce tensions, conflict, and resentment within family relations.

Our evocative and sociopoetic reflections demonstrate this. In this chapter, we call for greater examinations of critical transitionary periods for mothers and daughters that capture some of the cultural and contextual factors and silences that weigh on the relational process for mothers and daughters. However, this type of shift requires more expansive frameworks and open dialogue that locate and deal with the "complex and sometimes contradictory interrelatedness of gender relations and constructions of our gender identities" (Rowley 27–28), which are muddled within ideological, moral, and racialized framings of the family (Esnard, "Towards Matricentric Feminism"). We insist that this type of research remains critical to identifying the thinking and practices emerging through mother-daughter relationships and how mothers and daughters are positioned to improve negotiating the stressful or shifting interactions to ensure the general wellbeing of each other. This type of research remains relatively absent, particularly in the context of the Caribbean and the wider Global South.

Conclusion

Adrienne Rich tells us that "cathexis between mother and daughter, essential, distorted, misused" and "is the great unwritten story" (225). The study advances this conversation. Following Rich's call for mothers to become "outlaws from the institution of motherhood" (195), this chapter has explored the complexities embedded within the relationships that mothers and daughters share and how this affects how mothers and daughters navigate the changes they experience. Through the evocative use of poetry, we point to the many disturbances and strategies of working through adolescence and motherhood.

Our reflection points to the need to locate adolescence within the framework of motherhood to locate mother-daughter relations better and work towards the wellbeing of both. Given these findings, we support the need to dismantle ideological and patriarchal framings of motherhood and for mothers to "act and speak from truth and authentic relationship if they hope to achieve empowerment for themselves and their girl children" (O'Reilly, "Mothering against Motherhood" 170). More contextual location of these truths is needed to situate better the transitions mothers and daughters face and the sociocultural groundings of their experiences.

This requires mothers to process a reflective understanding of themselves from the stance of their daughters. A push is also for greater dialogue between mothers and daughters across generations to unpack some of these tensions and responses (Bernard and Bernard). Doing this also calls for a more feminist type of mothering that is conscious of the cultural ties that bind and that works to allow mothers and daughters to differently and meaningfully construct and experience this relationship.

Endnotes

1. The chapter adopts the World Health Organization's definition of adolescence as constituting persons between the ages of ten and nineteen ("Adolescent Health").
2. Lucy Jones describes matriphagy here as the consumption of a mother by her offspring.
3. The Caroni Swamp is a reserved mangrove area and bird sanctuary in Trinidad and Tobago. It is one of the largest protected wetlands in the country. The poem reflects an actual boat ride through the Caroni Swamp. The poem was written by Faith on July 21, 2023, for the sole purpose of this chapter.
4. Diminuendo in music is a term that refers to a gradual decrease the loudness.

Works Cited

Athan, Aurelia, and Heather Reel. "Maternal psychology: Reflections on the 20th Anniversary of Deconstructing Developmental Psychology." *Feminism & Psychology*, vol. 25, no. 3, 2015, pp. 311–25.

Athan, Aurelia. *Reviving Matrescence: The Developmental Transition to Motherhood*. 2018. Columbia University, dissertation.

Barrow, Christine. *Families in the Caribbean: Themes and Perspectives*. Ian Randle, 1996.

Barrow, Christine. *Caribbean Childhoods "Outside," "Adopted" or "Left Behind": Good Enough Parenting and Moral Families*. Ian Randle, 2010.

Barrow, Christine. "Living in Sin: Church and Common Law Union in Barbados." *The Journal of Caribbean History*, vol. 29, no. 2, 1995, pp. 47–70.

Bauer, Elaine. "Racialized Citizenship, Respectability, and Mothering Among Caribbean Mothers in Britain." *Ethnic and Racial Studies*, vol. 41, no. 1, 2017, pp. 151–69.

Bernard, Wanda T., and Candace Bernard. "Passing the Torch: A Mother and Daughter Reflect on Their Experiences across Generations." *Canadian Women's Studies Journal/Cahier de la femme*, vol. 18, no. 1–3, 1998, pp. 46–50.

Best-Cummings, Christiana. "Transnational Parenting in the African Caribbean Community." *English-Speaking Caribbean Immigrants: Transnational Identities*. Edited by Lear Matthews. University Press of America, 2013, pp. 53–72.

Blakemore, Sarah-Jayne. "The Social Brain in Adolescence." *Nature Reviews Neuroscience*, vol. 9, no. 4, 2008, pp. 267–77.

Blakemore, Sarah-Jayne, and Kathryn Mills. "Is Adolescence a Sensitive Period for Sociocultural Processing?" *Annual Review of Psychology*, vol. 65, no. 1, 2014, pp. 187–207.

Branje, Susan. "Development of Parent-Adolescent Relationships: Conflict Interactions as Mechanisms of Change." *Child Development Perspectives*, vol. 12.3, 2018, pp. 171–176.

Brown, Geraldine. "Let's Talk: African Caribbean Women, Mothering Motherhood, and Well-Being." *Frontiers in Sociology*, vol. 4, no. 88, 2019, pp. 1–8.

Brown, B. Bradford, and Mitchell J. Prinstein, editors. *Encyclopedia of Adolescence*. Academic, 2011.

Bush, Barbara. "African Caribbean Slave Mothers and Children: Traumas of Dislocation and Enslavement Across the Atlantic World." *Caribbean Quarterly*, vol. 56, no. 1–2, 2010, pp. 69–94.

Chamberlain, Mary. "Rethinking Caribbean Families: Extending the Links." *Community, Work & Family*, vol. 6, no. 1, 2003, pp. 63–76.

Coleman, John. *The Nature of Adolescence*. 4th ed. Routledge, 2010.

Collins, W. Andrew, and Brett Laursen. "Changing Relationships, Changing Youth: Interpersonal Contexts of Adolescent Development." *The Journal of Early Adolescence*, vol. 24, issue. 1, 2004, pp. 55–62.

Copeland, Debra B., and Bonnie Lee Harbaugh. "'It's Hard Being a Mama': Validation of the Maternal Distress Concept in Becoming a Mother." *The Journal of Perinatal Education*, vol. 28, no. 1, 2019, pp. 28–42.

Crawford, Charmaine. "Contesting 'Maternal Right': The Impact of Transnational Migration on Caribbean Mother Daughter Relationships." *Feminist and Critical Perspectives on Caribbean Mothering*. Edited by Dorsia Smith Silva and Simone A. James Alexander. Africa World, 2014, pp. 154–79.

Crawford-Brown, Claudette, and J. Melrose Rattray. "Parent-Child Relationships in Caribbean Families". *Culturally Diverse Parent-Child and Family Relationships: A Guide for Social Workers and Other Practitioners*. Edited by Nancy Boyd-Webb. Columbia Press, 2001, pp. 107–30.

Crone, Eveline A., and Andre Fuligni. "Self and Others in Adolescence." *Annual Review of Psychology*, vol. 71, 2020, pp. 447–469.

Goede, Irene de., et al. "Developmental Changes in Adolescents' Perceptions of Relationships with Their Parents." *Journal of Youth and Adolescence*, vol. 38, no. 1, 2009, pp. 75–88.

Esnard, Talia. "(Re)turning to Motherhood and Academe: An Autoethnographic Account. *Journal of the Motherhood Initiative*, vol. 6, no. 2, 2016, pp. 109–24.

Esnard, Talia. "Towards Matricentric Feminism in the Caribbean: Inroads and Opportunities." *Journal of the Motherhood Initiative*, vol. 10, no. 1–2, 2019, pp. 257–72.

Evans, Hyacinth. "Perspectives on the Socialisation of the Working-Class Jamaican Child." *Social and Economic Studies*, vol. 38, no. 3, 1989, pp. 177–203.

Furman, Rich, et al. "Expressive, Research and Reflective Poetry as Qualitative Inquiry: A Study of Adolescent Identity." *Qualitative Research*, vol. 7.3, 2007, pp. 301–15.

Gergen, Mary, and Kenneth Gergen. Performative Social Science and Psychology. *Historical Social Research*, vol. 36, no. 4, 2011, pp. 291–99.

Getfield, Jacqui. "Black Mothering in the Diaspora: Empowerment in the Caribbean Cradle and Resistance in the Canadian Crucible." *Journal of the Motherhood Initiative for Research and Community Involvement*, vol. 13, no. 2, 2022, pp. 139–154.

Giordano, Peggy C. "Relationships in Adolescence." *Annual Review of Sociology*, vol. 29, no. 1, 2003, pp. 257–81.

Hickman, Caroline, et al. "Young People's Voices on Climate Anxiety, Government Betrayal and Moral Injury: A Global Survey." *The Lancet Planetary Health*, vol. 5, issue 12, 2021, e863–e873.

Inguglia, Cristiano, et al. "Autonomy and Relatedness in Adolescence and Emerging Adulthood: Relationships with Parental Support and Psychological Distress." *Journal of Adult Development*, vol. 22, no. 1, 2015, pp. 1–13.

Jones, Lucy. *Matrescence: On Pregnancy, Childbirth, and Motherhood*. Penguin Books, 2023.

Juman, Rahanna A., and Deanesh Ramsewak. "Land Cover Changes in the Caroni Swamp Ramsar Site, Trinidad (1942 And 2007): Implications for Management." *Journal of Coastal Conservation*, vol. 17, no. 1, 2012, pp. 133–141.

Kerr, Madeline. *Personality and Conflict in Jamaica*. Liverpool University Press, 1952.

Landman, Jacqueline, et al. "Child-Rearing Practices in Kingston, Jamaica." *Caribbean Quarterly*, vol. 29, no. 3–4, 1983, pp. 40–52.

Lawson, Erica. "Precautionary Measures: Caribbean-Canadian mothers, Daughters, and Sex Education." *Feminist and Critical Perspectives on Caribbean Mothering*. Edited by Dorsia Smith Silva and Simone A. James Alexander. Africa World, 2013, pp. 111–28.

Laursen, Brett, et al. "Reconsidering Changes in Parent-Child Conflict Across Adolescence: A Meta-Analysis." *Interpersonal Development*. Edited by Rita Zukauskiene. Child Development, 2017, pp. 171–86.

Maxwell, December, et al. "Measuring Becoming a Mother: A Scoping Review of Existing Measures of Matrescence." *Best Practices in Mental Health*, vol. 19, no. 1, 2023, pp. 1–31.

Mohammed, Patricia. "The Caribbean Family Revisited." *Gender in Caribbean Development*. Edited by Patricia Mohammed and Catherine Shepherd. University of the West Indies P, 1988, pp. 170–82.

Momsen, Janet H,. ed. *Women and Change in the Caribbean*. Indiana University Press, 1993.

Mullings, Delores, and Renee Mullings-Lewis. "How Black Mothers 'Successfully' Raise Their Children in the 'Hostile' Canadian Climate."

Journal of the Motherhood Initiative for Research and Community Involvement, vol. 4, no. 2, 2013, pp. 105–19.

Orchard, Edwina R., et al. "Matrescence: Lifetime Impact of Motherhood on Cognition and the Brain." *Trends in Cognitive Sciences*, vol. 27, no. 3, 2023, pp. 302–16.

O'Reilly, Andrea. *Matricentric Feminism: Theory, Activism, and Practice.* Demeter, 2016.

O'Reilly, Andrea. "Mothering Against Motherhood and the Possibility of Empowered Maternity for Mothers and Their Children." *From Motherhood to Mothering: The Legacy of Adrienne Rich's Of Woman Born.* Edited by Andrea O'Reilly. State University of New York Press, 2013, pp. 159–74.

Pillay, Venitha, et al. *Academic Mothers in Developing Countries: Stories from India, Brazil and South Africa.* Africa World, 2017.

Reynolds, Tracey. "Black Mothering, Paid Work, and Identity." *Ethnic and Racial Studies*, vol. 24, no. 6, 2001, pp. 1046–64.

Rich, Adrienne. *Of Woman Born: Motherhood as Experience and Institution.* Norton, 1986.

Richardson, Laurel. "Poetics, Dramatics, and Transgressive Validity: The Case of the Skipped Line." *The Sociological Quarterly*, vol. 34, no. 4, 1993, pp. 695–710.

Rowley, Michelle. "Reconceptualizing Voice: The Role of Matrifocality in Shaping Theories and Caribbean Voices." *Gendered Realities: Essays in Caribbean Feminist Thought.* Edited by Patricia Mohammed. Mona Center for Gender and Development Studies, 2002, pp. 22–43.

Rutter, Virginia B. *Celebrating Girls: Nurturing and Empowering Our Daughters.* Conari Press, 1986.

Serbin Lisa, and Jennifer Karp. "Intergenerational Studies of Parenting and the Transfer of Risk from Parent to Child." *Current Directions in Psychological Science*, vol. 12, no. 4, 2003, pp. 138–42.

Shearer, Cindy L., et al. "Parents' Perceptions of Changes in Mother-Child and Father-Child Relationships During Adolescence." *Journal of Adolescent Research*, vol. 20, no. 6, 2005, pp. 662–84.

Stein, Howard F. "A Window to the Interior of Experience." *Families, Systems, & Health*, vol. 22, no. 2, 2004, pp. 178–79.

Thomas, Truddelle. "Becoming a Mother: Matrescence as Spiritual Formation." *Religious Education*, vol. 96, no. 1, 2001, pp. 88–105.

Whitley, Rob. "Mastery of Mothering Skills and Satisfaction with Associated Health Services: An Ethnocultural Comparison." *Culture, Medicine, and Psychiatry*, vol. 33, no. 3, 2009, pp. 343–65.

World Health Organization. "Adolescent Health." *WHO*, https://www.who.int/health-topics/adolescent-health/#tab=tab_1. Accessed 14 Mar. 2025.

7.

Motherhood Transitions: Menopause, Teenagers, Gender Identity, and Disability

Carmen G. Farrell

October

It's hard to separate what's causing what—I fall into bed as soon as possible after dinner, dishes, driving my eldest to soccer or field hockey practice, a load of laundry, or a slew of emails. Exhausted, I make it through a page and a half of a great book, then lights out. I'm awake ninety minutes later. Like: awake, awake. Turn on the light. Flop around and read for two hours. Try not to wish I was asleep. Turn out the light. Try not to think about fifteen-year-old Jordan failing grade ten math. Turn it on fifteen minutes later. Read 1.5 pages. Try not to think about thirteen-year-old Jess being in a new high school where no one except Jordan knows him. Where he's defined by a diagnosis at the top of his grade eight individual education plan: a syndrome so rare no one comprehends his suite of physical, intellectual, and social disabilities. Turn off the light. If I'm lucky, I'll fall asleep for another hour and a half. This pattern has morphed into months of sleeplessness. Does my head hurt from lack of sleep, or does lack of sleep result from a hurting head?

Most nights, it's three hours of sleep—if the last waking cycle happens at four or anytime after, that's the beginning of my day. My doctor, the one who shepherded me through two pregnancies, prescribed Zopiclone, so I tried various fractions of the little blue sleeping pills to find the sweet spot between effectiveness and addiction. But each time, I woke up drugged and heavy. Gradually, the potency of the sleeping pill crumbs decreased, becoming a quarter of a pill. When that stopped working, half a pill. Then the fractions had morphed towards a whole until the effectiveness of the whole also became less of a sleep-inducing medication and more of a daytime zombie's power source. Getting off them took weeks. Then I tried a natural product called Sleep-Ease until Health Canada pulled it off the market because it contained an undeclared drug, Estazolam. Consultations with a naturopath yielded no help either. No pills or supplements can alleviate my middle-of-the-night sweats, my body's thrumming with a mysterious, hot electric vibration. It seems there's no medical or herbal supplement that works, so I resign myself to a sleep-deprived, jet-lagged state. It's unclear if my brain fog originates from lack of sleep or a hangover from constant, daily head pain. My doctor says the headaches are menopausal and tries to uplift me by saying her sixty-year-old patients feel great. I want to scream: I waited to have children and entered midlife with the solid foundation of an established career, a graduate education, and preschoolers. I didn't realize my choice would mean teenagers plus menopause.

Can I live ten years like this? My children need me, but my intellectual and emotional intelligence is clouded, removed, and unavailable to them and me. I'm physically present, but my judgment and ability to perceive what's happening beneath the surface of my children's behaviours drown and suffocate under the heavy pain in my head. At the end of the workday, I'm no longer a partner to my husband, retreating to the marital bed without him, bowing out of weekend social engagements, so he goes to friends' houses alone. Being horizontal makes my head hurt slightly less, but guilt fires my imagination. Bright, sparkly, unwelcome guilt.

At a time of mothering, when I need all my faculties engaged, they're on the couch with their feet up, watching Netflix. Perimenopause has arrived for these fun years of parenting teens. My eldest, Jordan, at this time, was transitioning from using she/her pronouns but hadn't yet organized her psycho-ed assessment that would eventually pinpoint executive functioning challenges. Yet she's found the courage to have the "how would you feel if I brought home a girlfriend instead of a boyfriend?"

conversation with her—no, their—dad and me. At this point, almost sixteen, it's an academic abstraction—there have been no love interests yet. At least that I've been made aware of.

Which is more than fine. Counselling this child through grade ten academic expectations and friendship realities feels booby-trapped. The wrong word from me, the not-carefully-thought-out slant to an observation or—heaven-forbid—advice, will obliterate our delicate, mutual safe zone. Gifted, this child chose to change high schools for the last three years of secondary school to attend an accelerated academic program. They're a talented writer and thinker but struggle with math. However, with the certainty of adolescence, Jordan is convinced there's no future in the arts and envisions a future STEM career. They insist they love physics. Thanks to their smartphone and its connection to the wide outer world, they are enticed by astronomical breakthroughs like vanishing stars that measure the space-time warp, the discovery of possible habitable planets orbiting the star closest to Earth's own, and the first-ever detection of gravitational waves.

November

"So, Jordan," I begin. It's early Saturday afternoon, post-soccer game, and they've taken me up on a "let's grab a hot chocolate on our way home" invitation. "I know your report card results weren't what you hoped for." All the math and science courses hovered at the barely passing level.

Jordan looks into their cup for what I'm not sure. Something about the hunch of their shoulders and downcast expression makes me momentarily afraid another migraine has descended. "Is your head okay?" I fret. They nod yes, still staring at their drink on the café table. The headache triggers are various and somewhat mysterious: hormone swings, changes in barometric pressure, stress... the neurologist hasn't been specific. I've been called to the school many times over the last two years to collect a beleaguered, wrung-out child. This term, sudden migraines have already sent the number of missed classes into the double digits. The lost instructional time in subjects that aren't a strength is starting to catch up to Jordan.

"You are such a gifted writer. Look at your English and social studies marks," I continue, hoping to focus Jordan on their academic gifts.

"Mom! There's no future in that. I want to be a scientist!" They glare at me defensively—we've been down this road before, and they're protective of their point of view. I miss the days when my advice was gospel to young Jordan. "There's nothing new to learn in the arts—all the exciting inventions are in science!"

"Well, I understand you're interested in scientific subjects, but perhaps careers exist to write about stars, galaxies, and new science for lay people?" I offer, trying to find a middle ground for Jordan to pursue their interests while emphasizing their capabilities.

"I don't want to do that, Mom." Glowers at me. Any postsoccer endorphins have worn off, and the sugar from the hot chocolate hasn't had any positive effect.

"Well, I can't tell you what to do, sweetie; it's your life. But you're not playing to your strengths here, and you're in a tough program. The standards are high. It's November. If this is what you want, you'll have to work that much harder." I can't catch their eye. "Do you really want this? Are you willing to put in the extra time?"

Jordan looks up, eyes hooded with protectiveness. "Yes, Mom. It's what I want."

"Okay then. We're spending a lot of money on a math tutor..."

"I need a physics tutor, too," they interrupt.

"Okay, if you're willing to do the work, all right. But it can't be a crutch to rely on forever. We'll try it through the next term, okay?"

I am not convinced this is a viable plan or that the work required will transpire. But the command-and-control era of mothering is firmly in our rearview mirror. The phase of preschool-aged Jordan wanting to grow up—to be "in charge of me," as they used to say—is over and replaced with teenage determination. I must stand down; I am in charge of nothing and along for the ride, able to make occasional observations about what goes flitting past the window. With school, I'll have to park my doubts, let them try their plan, and not even consider a hint of "I told you so" if marks don't improve.

I am beginning to realize this child—who I used to know so well—will not choose popular, well-trod, and easy paths. This is a painful realization—most of my mothering efforts have been directed at smoothing and easing my children's life paths. I left my paid career to make a profession of mothering them. From toddlerhood, Jess required intensive interventions and a mothering style tailored to his suite of disabilities. First, we had to figure out therapies to help him walk and develop fine and gross motor skills. As he moved past toddlerhood, deciphering his social and speech challenges was added to the mix. By early elementary school, he needed an extensive individual education plan to address his intellectual disabilities. Jordan's needs, to some extent, could be learned from books and adapted to their and our family's circumstances. For Jess, I needed to figure out and participate in every aspect of his conscious life as if I were living his life with him. Interventions for Jordan were also intensive, but once I laid out the scaffolding, they could clamber and navigate the experiences alone, with friends, or in the community. Jess could never do that and will always require his dad or me or a hired replacement for us as his copilot. Another thought bubble for the middle of the night: How will he manage when his parents are gone? In many ways, his high school needs resemble earlier and younger ones he won't grow out of.

Jordan's trajectory—at least through the remainder of this school year—is becoming rocky. All I can do is support where I'm allowed, temper my advice for when it might be tolerated, and travel alongside to the extent I'm permitted. The counsellor I would seek out before Jordan's high school career was complete would say, "You have to come alongside them. Ask yourself how you would want to be treated in this situation." For some time now, permission has been required to enter an occupied bedroom, a blind eye must be turned to the clutter and chaos of teenage belongings, and a tentative détente must be maintained between teenage freedom and motherly supervision. "Pick the hillsides you're prepared to die on," my father used to say, reflecting on his parental experiences of raising my brother and me.

I didn't expect this so soon. And I never imagined it would feel so abrupt. I thought it would be a slow transition—perhaps a gradual and mutual realization that I wouldn't be needed so much. There were times when they were little, hanging off me, mommymommymommy-ing me, that I fantasized about unattainable separateness. I was their runny-nose tissue, their protection from rain, and their source of food and sustenance. I couldn't pee without someone looking at me with big eyes. But the payback was always that I could fix it. Mommy could make a boo-boo feel better, and I was the blue fairy granting fantastical childish wishes who vanquished all their problems with my magic wand. Currently, I'm often cast as the evil witch.

The best I am is neutral. My mothering aims to be inoffensive. I want to influence and guide, but it has to be more from a lived example than from talk. Jordan's hypersensitivity to any actual or perceived hypocrisy means I must always walk the talk. Which is difficult when it's increasingly difficult to imagine the world they will live into. The ways I live and what I prioritize aren't a blueprint for their future. How do I prepare my children for a world with climate change, degradation of late-stage capitalism, and political extremism? The generation I represent is part of their problem. Mine and previous generations are the ones who wrecked the environment, took all the economic stability and good healthcare, and left them with what? Heat domes, atmospheric rivers, a global pandemic, unaffordable housing, postsecondary education systems for the rich, and erosion of the middle class? The systems and infrastructure of my youth and adulthood weren't radically different from my parents', but my children can't see much in my life that might reflect theirs. I'm unprepared for sending Jordan and Jess into a world that increasingly perplexes me. Somehow, when I imagined a future for my babies, it meant a better version of my life. I don't know that anymore.

For now, though, we leave the coffee shop with our tutorial plan and head home, where Jordan disappears into their bedroom with its closed door, per usual, and I find Jess sitting in his customary chair in his father's home office, mesmerized by preschooler-style YouTube videos repeating on his Android phone. With my husband also glued to his computer, working, I hope they haven't spent the last two hours like this, but I decide not to risk marital discord by asking about it.

"Come on Jess, you need to get changed. Coach has a special practice session for the cross-country team this afternoon. We need to get going," "You need to wear running pants, a long-sleeved athletic shirt, and running socks," I say as I follow him up the stairs to help him with parts of dressing that can be problematic: tight socks.

As the day has progressed, my head is increasingly unaligned with my motherly goals. It wants silence, darkness, and quiet. Not noisy cafes, shouts and screams from soccer sidelines, and concentration on traffic logistics. But I want Jess to be a part of this team, so headache notwithstanding, there is no question of my not doing it.

Jordan chose this school for the academic program that's currently adding to my head pain, and their programming for neurodiverse learners with high needs like Jess was well regarded in the community. It seemed a good choice for both kids. But I've logged many sleepless hours over the past several weeks worried for Jess and the quality of his inclusion in grade eight. It's not like elementary school, where we knew many families and kids were used to seeing parents in classrooms and hallways. High school is a dead zone for parent involvement, and I can't hover and engage like I did in Jess's elementary school. With almost no ability to do so, he has to navigate high school himself, with well-intentioned aides who don't know him.

A natural place of inclusion for teenage boys is the sports teams, but Jess's physical disabilities preclude most of that, except cross-country. It's a rare high school sport where all are welcome. And it's unique because kids from several grades train together: boys and girls, grades eight to twelve. In the short weeks of the season so far, Jess has been showing up like a champion, doing all that was asked of him. He's done it without finesse or success, finishing dead last in every training session and every race. But he earns the respect of his teammates with his determination and endurance. With an ungainly and awkward-looking gait, he completes the same workouts they do. He does it with a smile on his face, often laughing as he arrives at the finish line. He loves using his body and being part of the kids' energy. He giggles with pleasure, absorbing the enthusiasm around him. Races offer no incentive to win, just the excitement of the cheering, clapping, and satisfaction of completion.

I am navigating multiple new lines in mothering: negotiations with Jordan, dredging up physical reserves for myself where none exist, and living Jess's teenage life with him but with the added expectation of invisibility. No institutional support exists for students with disabilities to participate in extracurricular activities, so most kids don't because it's up to families. But I want Jess to be seen as a person with dimension, not a resource room kid with an aide in tow. I want him to have a high school life where he's not stuck in a box with a label on it. I sit through every practice, trying to understand what's needed for Jess to be a part of the team. I drive a van full of kids to each after-school race, quietly listen to the conversations of the neurotypical boys in the back and make mental notes about the music they comment on, the movies they watch, the games they play, and what they think of different teachers.

I do this to inform my mothering from the sidelines, to soak in information as I do when I drive for Jordan's volleyball tournaments. These chauffeuring sessions are invaluable portals to the dynamics of high schoolers. Because Jess doesn't notice these things, I observe the kinds of hoodies the kids wear and the brand of sneakers on their feet so he can dress like them. I offer to help time the kids during their practice laps at the after-school practices so I can see them on the forest trails and not worry about Jess tripping over his feet, getting injured, falling behind the group, and getting lost in the unfamiliar neighbourhood. I overfunction so that he can function. Books about adolescent development are of little help. I need immediate context and on-the-ground intel.

In the pouring rain and cold of today's practice, I sit in my puffy long coat, under an umbrella, on the concrete bleachers near the school's athletic fields so I can keep an eye on Jess when their training laps bring them closer. From afar, I glimpse the group dynamics. His teammates notice when he jogs into the group of early finishers and offer Jess their raised palms for the high fives of "yay, we're done." Jess perceives the gesture and responds.

He looks for me at the end of practice, and I wave him over. On the trip home, the heater blasting, my head bellows with pain, expanding and contracting like an accordion. Squeezing and wringing out my brain, leaving it limp and useless. I'm so done with driving: I am ready for teleporting. But it hasn't been invented yet. I glance at the clock: 4:00 p.m. ... how many hours until I can lay down? At the red lights, I bang my forehead on the steering wheel. Probably, I shouldn't be driving—the pain is so distracting—but when I bang my head, at least it's a different pain.

December

Jordan's end-of-term report card is worse than October's, but I have no energy for that fight this month. The low grades on the report card have generated an email from the school's administration. They understand about the headaches and missed classes, but failing is failing. This kind of attention is new. Also new: the flurry of a high school relationship and Jordan's late-night video chats in corners of the house where they think they can't be overheard. More closed doors in my home. I don't know this other girl, Fiona, don't know the family. She seems to be regularly locked out of her house late at night for arbitrariness that is difficult to unravel. Jordan tells me that in addition to school, she's expected to hold a part-time job to pay for groceries. Her half-siblings have different fathers, and the man in the house isn't loving towards her. Jordan, however, is taking Fiona on like a counselling client, and Jordan's romantic feelings mingle with caretaking and a lack of boundaries. Jordan is unequipped to deal with Fiona's drama, which includes threatened suicide. At least Jordan cries to their father and me about this. We're not totally out of the picture.

Jordan's friend circle in this new school, beyond one or two girls from the volleyball team, seems needy and unstable. Relationship boundaries, for Jordan, have always been porous; lost sleep over the elementary school friend playground fights of others was a common occurrence. I feel resentful of the introduction of this unpredictability to our family life. One of Jordan's friends struggles with a brain chemical imbalance—apparently—and threatened Jordan with her knife collection, showing up at our house late at night more than once, necessitating another novel, unwelcome experience: to accompany Jordan to the RCMP detachment to register concern. Words like "restraining order" and "protection services" had never been part of my lexicon.

January

We have a week before Jordan's return to school for our report card conversation. The Christmas tree is down, visiting family has gone home, and guest bed sheets are washed. I know coming down hard on anything—even though my bruised, aching brain shouts profanity, and I want to scream, "Focus on school, not your f-ing girlfriend!"—won't get us closer to understanding or connecting with each other. It will send Jordan further away, perhaps even physically away.

Readying myself for our talk and finding some quiet, I lie on my bed to give my brain a bit of the horizontal rest it craves. But Jess's replaying of his current favourite YouTube tunes wafts up the stairs, and there is no quiet. Instead, for solace, I retreat into some grief to fortify my mental resources. By spending time with my sadness, I can contain it, put it away, to focus on what Jordan needs from me. Being a mom to teenagers isn't what I anticipated. It's so much less: so isolating.

My generation had been raised to believe we could have it all. "We" being cisgender, heterosexual women of the late twentieth century. This meant sex without marriage. Reproductive choice and health. Careers and families. Or not. Opting out of motherhood was equally valid. We could play with Barbies as girls but not be objectified as women, or so Gloria Steinem said. We were second-wave feminists who navigated our versions of Harvey Weinstein but never or rarely said #MeToo to one another. Usually, we dealt with unwanted comments or, worse, unwanted attention from family, friends, classmates, or teachers in isolation. But together, we lauded being women. Firmly entrenched in our genders, we celebrated our differences from men as equals or betters. My generation had it all: no longer barefoot and pregnant in kitchens.

But once pregnant, mothers-to-be like me imagined gendered and equal roles for our baby girls and boys. My boys would play with dolls, and my daughters would play with trucks and blocks! I applaud Jordan's desire for a STEM career, although I struggle to comprehend their understanding of gender. I grieve my assumption that we'd share my gender identity. I'd never thought of gender as fluid, had understood sexual orientation in two terms, maybe three: heterosexual, homosexual with some experimental crossover—but wasn't familiar with the term bisexual or bicurious. In short, it was a pink-and-blue world with she and he pronouns where "they" meant groups of people. Jordan is completely uninterested in understanding my experience and has no patience for my stumbling inaccuracies in navigating pronoun preferences, learning the eleven or more types of sexuality, and accurately affirming Jordan's evolving expressions of gender identity. The reality of mothering teens isn't the "all" my young feminist self had imagined.

I stand at Jordan's bedroom door. "Jordan, can I come in? I need to talk with you," I say to the white composite plywood door. With permission, I enter and sit on the edge of their double bed. I circle my flat palm over the surface of the turquoise paisley-printed duvet we'd picked out together. Not even two years ago. That kind of shopping trip wouldn't happen these days. "The vice principal emailed. You're failing math and physics," I say. "I imagine this isn't news to you," I venture.

Jordan is quiet. "Mom, it's like there's something wrong," they say. "When I'm doing the problems, I know it." They pause. "But then, when I'm in the test, it's like my brain goes somewhere else. I can't remember it," they sigh. This is not completely surprising; we'd dealt with test anxiety for the first time in grade seven. Early high school had seemed to go okay with a modified testing environment. But the missed classes...

"Okay, well, let's get on top of this. Teachers like it when you follow up, stay in communication and are proactive. Can you go see your teachers when school goes back?"

"Okay."

"Let me know when you've set that up. Ms. Sylvester and Mr. Didak want me to participate in it."

"Okay."

This seems to have gone pretty well. Perhaps some comfort will be tolerated. "Jordan, we'll get this sorted out. I know you want to do well."

"I do, Mom." I reach out to give them a hug, and they lean into me, absorbing the comfort. I breathe in their scent to imprint the memory of closeness for later.

February

But then I screw up. My best compromise while I'm learning proper pronoun usage is to use they/them when Jordan is present. But on the telephone with friends of mine, I use she/her to save explaining to these friends—who have known Jordan since preschool—what they/them means to them. I can't. I can't interpret Jordan's experience for them or my friends, and I'm still figuring out my own.

I didn't realize Jordan was home. "Mom," they glare at me. "I heard you on the phone!" Daggers in my direction. They stomp off.

March

Jess's school-based team, which consists of his learning support teacher, speech-language pathologist, aides, and occupational therapist, convenes a meeting to start planning for Jess's posthigh school life. Work experience will become part of his school day next year. With each passing year, they aim that Jess will gradually spend more of his school day in the community, hopefully working and pursuing leisure interests so that by grade twelve, the majority of his day might be in the neighbourhood, with aide support fading to zero. At least this is the optimistic hope we're gathered to discuss.

Unlike his sibling, Jess has no friends or assistance network that his parents or the government don't fund. He cannot generate relationships, maintain friendships, or navigate life choices. Professionals describe him as nonverbal. His speech is completely unintelligible, and he relies on the robotic sound of his voice output software on his Android phone to speak for him. His motor movements are ataxic, and his involuntary limb movement is beyond his control. Therapies have been extensive, expensive, and time-consuming and have filled his schedule and mine and will extend into the rest of his life.

While I might lament the sudden fall from grace in Jordan's life, parenting Jess stretches unchanging and infinite. At a time when my biology is screaming, "Prioritize yourself; it's time to stop this intensity of mothering nonsense," his needs remain almost precisely to when he was six. He requires his nails clipped, his shoelaces tied, his bank accounts managed, and his meals prepared. He always will. Although I've had more than a dozen years to adjust to a high school reality, grieving his dependence never fades. It just changes.

From his babyhood until I die or just can't do it any longer, I spend my time and energy managing his world. I manage the environment around him so that others can see him. So that he can show up as the best version of himself. Without me, cross-country wouldn't exist. But it continues, very successfully, because of him. He shows up with an optimistic attitude, and the good-hearted people around him see his grit and determination and admire and include him. But he needed me to set up the situation. Just like he needs me to find ways for him to spend his days, navigate bureaucracies to try to convince government funders to consider his independent living needs, and help him stay connected with family who don't live nearby. Someday, that may be all he has: extended family younger than me.

Jordan's tutoring sessions have shifted to our kitchen. Driving to tutorials elsewhere didn't provide a window into what was happening, so this term, I paid extra to have tutors come to us. I can see Jordan is struggling with concepts, but also discern their effort. The midterm report is marginally better; they're passing. But these aren't university-level marks. However, they're not giving up, so I need to support them, even if I think they should shift the focus of their studies.

June

Jordan has to have the opportunity to make their own mistakes. Jess just needs any opportunity to try and some support when he does.

With both children, in profound ways, I needed to shift from imposing my expectations and wants on them. For Jordan, I needed to do that so they could evolve into their own identity, separate from mine. So that they could move into the world. With Jess, I needed to let go of expecting that he might do that too, plan for where he's at, and try to advocate for his inclusion in neurotypical circles: to help others see and include him for who he is. I needed to help him be seen in the world. And I needed to see both children differently, separate from me. More equal.

I certainly wouldn't have predicted this when Jess and Jordan were little. I thought mothering Jordan would be easy, and Jess would be the difficult one. Friends said boys were more complex. Jordan was my sparkly little light in the pink or purple skirted dress that "had to twirl" and made the corners of our lives bright and bubbly. Jordan's exuberance pulled us into community relationships.

That brand of motherhood seems simple compared to the daily psychological gymnastics with teenaged Jordan and the physical and mental exhaustion of needing to think about Jess and his life in 360-degree terms. My children are no longer my children. They are becoming my young adults.

But mothering them doesn't go away; it must grow with them.

8.

Outsmarting Giants

Teresa Cavanaugh Donkin

Names have been changed; time has been condensed

There is a moment so indelibly etched in my memory that I both see the image in my mind and feel a flutter in my heart when I think of it. My first child, Ethan, is fourteen months old and has recently learned two new skills: standing alone and stacking wooden blocks. I'm sitting on the floor next to him as he concentrates on bending down to pick up a block and then wobbling back upright to stack it on another. I feel as if I am looking through a long lens, seeing him take his first step towards independence that will eventually take him away from the nest. I know this long journey will seem short when I look back years from now, and I'm filled with a longing to be with him for as many steps as possible.

When he was four, Ethan and I were walking through a wooded park when he asked me, "Mommy, what would you do if we were being chased by giants?" He was sure I had an answer and would know what to do. For this hypothetical question about a fictional problem, I *did* have an answer. I came up with various ways to get away from the giants even as Ethan volleyed one "What if?" after another, probably seeing the mammoth monsters hiding among the trees in his imagination. Eventually, he seemed satisfied that I would indeed know how to outsmart them.

Although I had earned a master's degree and started a career, I stopped working when Ethan was born and stayed home when my daughter, Clara, came along three years later. This decision was made with my husband, Graham, who was willing and able to provide emotional support and to be the primary breadwinner. I was aware of what a privilege it was to have a choice, as many women, including my mother, do not. I loved being there for my children, but it felt like a temporary decision, like someday I would figure out what I would do next, that a path would become clear for me.

Over time, the giants came to represent the challenges I faced as I raised my family. The kids would grow up, the world would change, and I would question my place in all of it. Some giants were gentle, and some were scary, and I didn't always have answers or know how to outsmart them.

Bullies and Super Moms

I knew something wasn't right when Clara started making excuses for staying home during the first few weeks of fifth grade. She pretended to be sick in the morning or went to the nurse's office at lunchtime. She always loved school, but she was caught off guard when the girls who were once her friend group transformed into a clique. Mindy became very popular, and the other girls changed their behaviour to win her approval. Clara didn't follow suit, so Mindy cornered her every day at recess to coerce her into being a loyal member of the posse. The other girls didn't join in the intimidation, but they did not defend Clara either. They stayed silent to remain on Mindy's good side.

"Those girls are not being good friends to you. How about seeking out Beth at recess and lunch?" I suggested. "You used to be so close."

"But, Mom, that's awkward, and those girls are my friends! They invite me to their birthday parties."

My parenting instincts ran short in this situation. I didn't have a good strategy for how Clara should outsmart this colossus disguised as a fifth-grade girl. I went to the bookstore, not knowing what I was looking for. I browsed through a few parenting guides and then wandered into the YA section, where a title caught my eye: *A Smart Girl's Guide to Friendship Troubles* from the American Girl book series. I picked up the slim volume and flipped through its glossy pages filled with colourful illustrations, funny graphics, and quizzes—like the "true friend test." It was an advice book written at the preteen level. I specifically noted the section on how to identify and deal with bullies. Feeling certain Clara would reject it, I bought the book anyway.

The next time Clara told me she didn't want to go to school anymore,

I gently offered it. "I ran across this book and thought you might want to look through it, just to see if there is anything interesting," I said as I held the book out. After pausing to look at the cover illustration—two girls standing back to back and looking angry with each other—Clara silently took it, went straight to her room, closed the door, and emerged an hour later.

"Mom, I read the whole book and figured out that Mindy is a bully and that what bullies want is power. You have to not let them take your power and fight back!"

I was stunned that the book had been so effective. I never found out if Clara said something to Mindy, but within a few days she didn't dread going to school anymore. She simultaneously found the courage to try out for *Fiddler on the Roof* at the local community theatre—something she'd been dreaming of for a couple of years—and got a part. Clara always watched and waited until ready to jump into things. When she was ready, she was really ready and threw herself fully in. The social situation at school was confusing because she still wanted to engage in imaginative play and wasn't interested in the cliques and social games. She found strength in this new-found community of children and adults who, like her, loved expressing their imaginations. Things were still a little lonely at recess, but she had gotten her power back.

I admired Clara's courage and found I needed a little of my own. In social situations, I started to dread the universal first question everyone asks: "What do you do?" If I said, "I'm a mom," it didn't feel adequate because it seemed most mothers were also something else—like doctors or teachers or dental hygienists. I found myself having to qualify that's all I do. I'm a stay-at-home mom. I didn't question their choices, yet I felt they were judging mine.

I began to feel irrelevant because that might be the first and last question someone asked me as if I couldn't possibly have anything interesting to say. Suddenly, they needed to refresh their drink or catch that friend they hadn't yet spoken to. "Excuse me, I have to..." or in other words, "End of discussion!" Or they looked at me quizzically and asked, "How do you spend your days?"

What answer did they expect? "I'm addicted to *General Hospital* and watch soap operas all day?" Or "I sit and eat bon bons while my children happily entertain themselves"? Or, perhaps, "I don't do anything at all; I'm just bored all day"?

From some working parents, I heard about the nanny they employed to help raise their kids or, at least, the mother they dropped their kids off with every morning. I had neither. The way I spent my days was often tedious and I did dream about working outside of the house again. But at that time, I was the full-time caretaker of my kids, house, and yard, the family schedule manager, the head grocery shopper and chef, chauffeur, and chief financial officer of our household, and I was busy!

Still, I had lingering doubts. Was I meeting both my own and society's expectations of me? Although Ethan was already a teenager and Clara would be soon, it still did not seem like a good time to return to work. Graham was putting in long hours, working weekends, and travelling. I did not have family nearby that could help, and my parents and in-laws had all passed away years earlier. Whenever I imagined the scenario of going back to work—juggling after school schedules, scrambling for meals, and hiring help for the house and yard—it didn't seem like a good fit. At the same time, I often felt guilty that I had a master's degree that I wasn't using directly for paid work, although I was doing plenty of volunteering. The super mom messaging was all around me—in the news, magazines, talk shows, television shows, and movies. The mom who works, maybe as an entrepreneur, has fabulous, smart and talented children, volunteers for a good cause, sits on one or more boards, is physically fit, well dressed, and still manages to bake chocolate chip cookies on weekends.

It was not unlike the bullying Clara had experienced in school. I realized I had to take my power back in social conversations and highlight the many things I did without pay, in addition to being a stay-at-home mom. I relied on my education in environmental science to work on climate action initiatives, helped out at my kids' schools, and served as treasurer for a small nonprofit organization. And with Clara's involvement in community theatre, I managed the box office and used my sewing skills to repair costumes. I knew I was a super mom, too.

Social Networks

Because our children were born in the mid-nineties, Graham and I had the challenge of navigating electronic communication in a way that didn't exist when we grew up. Neither of us was eager for our kids to experience the world through screens and push buttons before they experienced it through their senses. We wanted them to look out the window while driving instead of watching a movie screen or playing with a handheld video game, to play outdoors with neighborhood kids instead of watching television, and to learn how to do things like paint a wall or hammer a nail. These and other core instincts for parenting didn't change as Ethan and Clara grew into their teenage years, but we found we had to be more flexible and learn alongside them as changes came about both in their social needs and the world.

The World Wide Web, which barely existed when my children were born, began to infiltrate every aspect of life. By the time Ethan got to middle school, social media had taken off and it seemed all his friends were using *MySpace*. Of course, Ethan wanted to join them. As a person, let alone a parent, this rapid development scared me. I wasn't alone. Flyers were constantly coming home from school, offering parent information meetings, all of which I attended, with themes such as keeping your child safe on the internet. I read terrifying newspaper articles about teenagers making connections with dangerous adults online or through text messaging. Children no longer needed the family home phone to communicate with friends or worse, strangers.

Graham and I didn't want our children to jump right into this unknown and uncontrolled territory. We wanted to take things slowly, armed with as much knowledge as possible. We tried to appease their interest in technology by allowing iPods. They were cool and everyone had them. Most importantly, they seemed safe. We implemented the recommended safeguards on our family computer. I thought this would allow us to control their use of the internet and social media, but I was wrong. By the time we agreed to let Ethan use *MySpace*, he had some news for us.

"I've been using *MySpace* at Mike's house. We created a profile for our band," Ethan admitted.

It was an inflection point. We knew we were at odds with what other parents allowed regarding access to technology. Should we punish Ethan because other kids were allowed to be on social media? I was grateful he had told us—he didn't have to. I knew we would encourage more covert activity if we kept restricting Ethan's use of what was a trend that was here to stay.

Mobile phones were another behemoth. It was 2007, and I still hadn't jumped on that trend myself. I didn't feel the need to make calls while roaming about. If people needed to reach me, email on the computer and voicemail on the home phone seemed sufficient. Here again, Ethan complained that he was missing out on social interactions by not being able to text on a flip phone. We finally allowed him to have one in ninth grade. To moderate his use and reduce the cost, Graham and I insisted on limited text messaging; a few messages a week seemed adequate. That quickly became laughable. He used up the monthly allotment in about three days, and we were faced with either taking the phone away or agreeing to unlimited texting. Once again, we had to choose between sticking to our convictions or risk having our child be a social outcast. We met the giant at its level and chose unlimited texting, with limited contacts.

Bittersweet Sixteen

The front door flew open followed by loud voices and laughter. Ethan had arrived home from school along with several friends. I peeked from the narrow kitchen doorway, through the rounded archway into the living room, and watched as these five tenth-grade boys tried to make themselves comfortable. I shook my head in disbelief as I realized they were too big to fit. They were literally too big for the nest. Although Ethan was now taller than me and was approaching Graham's height of six feet, our whole family of four could still snuggle onto the three-cushion couch. These guys were having trouble arranging their long legs and broad shoulders within the confines of that sofa and two armchairs, none interested in being squeezed in the middle. I made a mental note: We need a bigger couch. I noticed their voices too, taking up more space. Now rich with bass tones, their chatter and laughter seemed to fill the house to capacity.

My perception of those boys outgrowing the house wasn't wrong. Ethan's sixteenth birthday was approaching, and he told me he wanted to have a party. I was all for throwing him a big party—maybe not a blowout, but something memorable to mark this milestone. I happily agreed to plan something special. As time passed, and we got closer to his birthday, Ethan kept shrugging it off when I tried to discuss plans. It seemed he had lost interest. On his birthday, New Year's Eve, I made a chocolate cake for our celebration at home. Late that afternoon, Ethan announced he wanted to go to Patrick's house.

"Patrick's family is flying back from their vacation in Florida this afternoon," Ethan explained. "They're going to pick up supplies for a party on the way home and also pick me up."

I was dumbstruck. After months of trying to plan something, my son's sixteenth birthday party was to be a last-minute affair hosted by someone else's mom with whatever food and supplies they could drum up from whichever stores were open on New Year's Eve. Instead of getting angry, it just made me sad. Fighting back tears, I told him it would be ridiculous for Patrick's family to take this on. Thoughts raced through my mind. *Should I forbid him to go? If I do, will it make everything worse?* Ultimately, I let him go, but I was left with a lump in my throat and a growing feeling of irrelevance.

One day shortly after, I asked him, "Why didn't you want to have the party at home?"

"Because no one wants to come to our house for parties!"

I felt my gut tighten, and I was speechless. I remembered feeling ashamed of my own home growing up because our rugs and furniture were old and worn out. I thought my kids had nothing to be ashamed of in terms of their house. Feeling my throat tighten again, I said, "I don't think that's true. Your friends seem to have fun when they come over."

"But if you and Dad are home, we're all in the same space."

And then I understood. It wasn't about how nice our furniture was. What these teenagers wanted was space remote from adults. Some of Ethan's friends, including Patrick, had much bigger houses and properties. Our smaller house, yard, and open floor plan gave them no privacy.

Even though Ethan was spending less time at home, I was grateful he still talked to me. Family meals helped bring us together. Like my mother, I made sure we all sat down to eat dinner together as often as possible, even when everyone was busy. Having this time to check in with each other helped keep us close. I believe this tradition is one of the reasons why my siblings and I remain a part of each other's lives despite being spread from coast to coast. Although Ethan and Clara often bickered about whose turn it was to set or clear the table, and each accused the other of getting away with less work, when we sat down to eat, they were reasonably successful in keeping the peace and holding a conversation. They often chose to do their homework in the kitchen, so our dinner table brought them together in more ways than one.

In comparing notes with other mothers, I learned that although there was a lot I wasn't privy to, I knew far more about Ethan's day-to-day life and emotions than other parents of boys did. Time after time, mothers pulled me aside to tell me they love my son, how he looks them in the eye and engages in conversation and how he has been a good influence on their sons. I can't take full credit because Ethan has always been drawn to people. Even as a baby, he looked strangers in the eye and melted their hearts with his captivating smile. But I couldn't help but wonder if keeping the lines of communication open through family meals helped to nurture that part of Ethan's personality. I heard from many of these families that they did not prioritize family meals, even if one parent stayed home with the kids, as I did.

First Love

Clara ran through the back door and straight into my arms, sobbing. As I held her tightly, I saw through the window that Andrew's car was pulling out of the driveway. I assumed he said something hurtful to her.

"What happened?" I asked.

"Andrew told me he loves me," she said between sobs.

I was so surprised that I had to restrain myself from laughing. For her, this was a serious matter. She was fifteen, and although she had had other crushes, Andrew was the first boy that came to the house. They had been outside, enjoying the warm weather.

I kissed the top of her head where a blue headband held her wavy brown hair in place. She took a step away from me and wiped her tear-streaked cheeks with her sleeve.

"It scared me, and I didn't know what to say, so I said 'thank you,' and now I feel so stupid!" she said without taking a breath. She ran into the living room, flopped down on the couch, and sobbed some more.

As I pondered what to say, I was amused by the innocent and funny scene that just took place. I imagined Andrew's shock at Clara's reaction. It was as if they backed into each other in the dark and ran scared in opposite directions.

Clara's first love came in the form of a gentle giant, nudging her towards adulthood. I knew it wouldn't always be this easy for her. And it wouldn't be for Ethan either. They had both experienced grief in losing one after another of their beloved grandparents years earlier, but the tectonic challenge of romantic heartbreak is different, an ogre they both would have to face at some point.

Empty Nest

I cried in the shower often those days. It's not that I planned to, but as soon as the water hit my face, I felt sadness wash over me. Ethan was leaving for college soon, and I missed him already. How could his childhood be over? He has a quick wit and makes me laugh almost every day. Maybe I should have laughed at myself, crying there where no one else could see me. At least the water washing over my face made the tears sting less.

When we moved Ethan into his dorm room, I was reluctant to get back in the car and drive the five hours back home. I couldn't stop hugging him. As I watched him walk away from the car and then through his dormitory door, my mind flashed back to that long lens I sensed when he was a baby taking his first step towards independence. It's what I've been expecting him to do—to walk through the door of the university and learn to stand on his own. Still, my eyes welled with tears because I knew he would never fully come back to the nest.

Back home, we had to adjust to being a family of three. It was another busy period at work for Graham. Clara and I found ourselves alone together at mealtimes. It was both a great bonding time for us—we developed some new favourite dishes—but also a phase when we had many disagreements. Clara pushed back on what she felt was too much laser focus on her as I tried to fill the void.

In what seemed like a short time, she too moved into a college dormitory, and I understood why my mother collapsed in the backseat of the car after she dropped her youngest child off at college. A once full house became an empty nest. I noticed how loud silence could be. The door was not slamming shut behind the kids as they ran out. I didn't hear guitar strumming from Ethan's bedroom or Clara's voice singing in the shower. In Clara's room, the fairies Graham painted on her ceiling when she was five were still there. Like portals to childhood, they hovered in the circles Clara brushed around them when she repainted her ceiling in high school.

I had continued volunteering with the community theatre and over the years moved up to serving as producer, a position that came with a modest stipend. It was an immense amount of work; some weeks, I worked more hours than I would have if I had a full-time job. What kept me going was the mothers who confided in me that being involved in that theatre made profound positive changes in their kids' lives, just like it had for Clara. My success with these big musical productions, in addition to my climate action work, caught the attention of the town supervisor, and I was appointed to cochair a volunteer task force considering new environmental regulations. I kept the doors open for what would come next.

Seeds of Change

On a quiet day, I tackled a corner of the basement where junk had accumulated. Among the clutter, I found an old metal box I had once used to store garden seeds. Inside were unopened packets of peas, tomatoes, nasturtiums, and more. I silently admonished myself because that is just so like me—to tuck resources away for the day when I will have time to use them, a day that often never comes. This applies not only to garden seeds but also to fabric and other supplies for unnamed and unimagined projects. *Are these seeds still viable,* I wondered as I turned the packets over, looking for expiry dates. Then I had a startling thought. That question is a perfect metaphor for my current stage of life. After staying home with my children for so long, are other things possible for me?

My thoughts drifted to how I got here. I passionately wanted to be a mother. It was the only path I felt sure about. Perhaps it was because the person I most loved and respected was my mother. She was flawed, as we all are, but I didn't begin to see that until I was almost an adult. To me, she was a beautiful and complex person. She didn't hug and kiss me and my six siblings a lot, but she loved deeply, and I could feel that love emanating from her. She showed it in her devotion to us and in her baking, cooking, sewing, the stories she wrote, and the handmade birthday cards she illustrated. Although stress was always present in my childhood home, so was time to reflect on my day with my mom, her advice and guidance, and help with homework.

By the time I was a teenager, I saw ways in which I wanted to be different from my mother. She struggled all the time with poverty, lack of resources, and lack of support. I knew that to break out of that cycle, I had to get an education and had to leave home. I needed to be self-sufficient and self-supporting. Yet once I had children, I found myself also being the mom who cooked, baked, sewed, and created handmade cards—the one who was there to listen and offer guidance after school. Just like my mother, being a mom became my career and identity.

I looked down at the seed packets and wasn't surprised they were well past their expiration dates, but would they still grow? The only way to find out for the seeds and for myself was to try. It will require conquering a few more giants.

9.

Poems

Victoria Bailey

the other side

i tried
i tried
in oh so very many ways
to be a feminist mother
and when i reached
the other side
when they became
young adults
or thought they were
as i had once
at that same age
they started to
call me out
never in
and all i ever think is
sing all those sweet words
back to me
spit them out
tear me down
i don't care
just make it better

hanging by a thread

there are no such things
as apron strings, when time comes
it's all relative

perfection

i have always tried
to be a feminist mother
but i have never been perfect
thank god
for that

wonder

i still do not know
if you go back
to normal
or you just get used
to it
but i do know
that you just get on
with it
despite
and because
of it all

the eternal maternal

there is a secret
deep in my apron pocket
but let me pull a tissue out first
and wipe your nose
lick-wash your cheek
smooth your hair
tell you to sit up straight
there, there
my cares are endless
but what care i
the cost of having you close
to hear my lifelong lullaby

moving out

are you going
to cry mum
he asked
the day before
moving out
no
i replied because
you're so happy
and excited
and looking forward to it
and it's a good thing
for you
but after he'd gone
i went to make
a cup of tea
just for me
and when i opened
the cupboard door
and saw his mug
i felt hot tears
and these unexpected
moments continued
like the smell
of his left-behind clothes
when i cleaned
his silent room
and the sound
of his voicemail
when i called
and he didn't answer
and the longing
for more than one word
when i texted

to check that he was okay
and the staring
at his kindergarten photo
stuck to the fridge door
when i reached for my milk
and feeling like i had
just gotten off a rollercoaster ride
that had lasted his whole childhood
leaving my legs unsteady
and finally
i realized
the feeling was grief
and it made me cry

glimmers

those wondrous moments
when you see signs of it all
coming together

my eldest coming and going

they arrived
and i bought them a comfy bed
and cozy blankets
and fed them
and hugged them tight
and inhaled their smell
and kissed their cheek
and smiled at them
and wished them well
and a week later i sat
and cried
because it felt like someone had died

they left
and i bought them a comfy bed
and cozy blankets
and fed them
and hugged them tight
and inhaled their smell
and kissed their cheek
and smiled at them
and wished them well
and a week later i sat
and cried
because it felt like someone had died

10.

On Tiger Mothering

Wendy M. Thompson

I grew up with an immigrant mother[1] between two languages.[2] Race/ethnicity, check all that apply:

- Asian or Pacific Islander
  - Asian Indian
  - Chinese
  - Filipino
  - Japanese
  - Korean
  - Vietnamese
  - Native Hawaiian
  - Guamanian or Chamorro
  - Samoan
  - Other Asian—Print race, for example, Hmong, Laotian, Thai, Pakistani, Cambodian, and so on
  - Other Pacific Islander—Print race, for example, Fijian, Tongan, and so on
- Black or African American

Battled her at every turn. In both languages.

I don't want to.   我不想。

I don't know. Figure it out yourself.   我不知道。你自己想办法吧。

I don't care.   我不在乎

I was Black when I wasn't Chinese.
I was Chinese but always seen as Black.
My mother had three Black Chinese daughters. (Emphasis on the Chinese.)

I was the eldest.

As the daughter of a woman whose world stretched over multiple oceanic time zones, whose lifespan was lived on different continents and across multiple fault lines, it was inevitable that there would be tension and mistranslation.

မတူညီသော တိုက်ကြီးများတွင် နေထိုင်ပြီး ပြတ်ရွှေ့ကြောများစွာကိုဖြတ်ကျော်ကာ ကမ္ဘာသည် သမုဒ္ဒရာအချိန်ဇုန်များစွာကို ဖြတ်ကျော်ကာ ကမ္ဘာကို ဆန့်တန်းထားသော အမျိုးသမီးတစ်ဦးအနေဖြင့်၊ တင်းမာမှုနှင့် ဘာသာပြန်ဆိုမှု လွဲမှားခြင်းဖြစ်မည်မှာ မလွဲမသွေပင်ဖြစ်သည်။

This is to say, there was trauma there before she became a mother.
My mother.

People say that Asian immigrant mothers are tough, insisting on extraordinarily high standards for their children, forcing them to always wear a coat when they go out, and forcing them to eat, eat, eat.

"Did you eat yet?"

"Do you want something to eat?"

"Do you want me to cook you some egg, pork, and rice?"

It's more than just the grades, the valedictorian status, the Ivy League schools. Isn't it? It's the fact that when they get old, they'll have someone guaranteed to take care of them. A return on their investment.

They sacrificed so much, came here and worked in restaurants, convenience stores, drive-thru windows, and warehouses, so you had better be their American Dream.

(That college tuition was expensive.　那个大学学费很贵。)

The way an Asian immigrant parent will break you with just words:

(that chicken feather duster strike or slipper thrown across the room provokes laughter once you turn fourteen)

Are you stupid?
Are you deaf?
Are you dumb?
Do you like being a disappointment?
Me and your father are so shame of you.

What did Amy Chua call herself (and her mother before her)?
A tiger mother?

Tiger

A tiger *(Panthera tigris)* is a large cat, one of the largest living cat species on planet Earth, belonging to the genus *Panthera* and native to Asia. Tigers are most commonly identified by their orange fur, long tail, and mostly vertical black stripes. Agile and strong, they can swim across bodies of water up to five miles wide and hunt and kill prey twice their size, wrestling said prey to the ground using their back teeth and canines and holding it close to their body as it dies. In every nature program I've ever seen, the tiger will latch onto the throat of its prey, applying a steady, insatiable bite to the throat, until the animal goes limp and dies of strangulation. The small front incisors are useful in picking through meat, quill, fur, and feathers as they eat clean through the carcass of their kill. Solitary animals, tigers occasionally come together to mate and eat, communicating with other tigers through scent, visual cues signalled through the body, and sound. Producing a range of sounds, a female tiger will roar to call her cubs to her. She will also growl, snarl, and hiss when provoked.

A tiger's moan can be heard up to thirteen hundred feet away.

Male tigers do not raise their young.

In Chinese astrology, the zodiac sign of the tiger is the third animal on a wheel of twelve. It ushers in sudden, monumental, and transformative events and rules the day between 3:00 and 5:00 p.m.

According to the zodiac, tiger people like to be in control of things.

My mother was a controlling presence in the house, always needing to fix, prevent, steer, and direct everything. It was academics. It was food. It was temperament, dress, and appearance. It was other people's opinions and feelings. It always had to be perfect, believable, and on par with the lifestyles and incomes and tastes of other, more affluent Chinese immigrants.

According to the zodiac, tiger people are quick tempered and emotionally intense when upset.

My mother was always angry when things fell outside of her grip of control. A too-short skirt. A hidden boyfriend. A white lie. A dinner rejected by a brutish non-Chinese husband. A lack of application when it came to studiousness and advanced placement achievement at school. A thank you in the form of offering to wash dishes after dinner. An accusation. A smirk. A door slammed shut. "You don't like it, you go live outside!"

According to the zodiac, tiger people never give up when they are frustrated or when there is no hope left.

Did she leave him after he _____? That was over twenty years of closed eyes and a mouth getting fed. Meanwhile, he was all...

According to the zodiac, tiger people tend to be generous, warm hearted, and humorous.

The shirt off her back. Her best cooking pot. The best years of her youth. The only heart she had. She laughed until she cried–at graduations, wedding ceremonies. [Note: There is nothing here that smells like fur and teeth, nothing that sounds like growling or feels like stalking a young village girl in the tall grass, silent, hungry.]

The tiger gave her its last stripes.
The tiger forgave its instinct to kill its prey.
The tiger sat with its hungry children and laughed at its predicament.
(My mother's zodiac sign is the monkey.)

(My) Mother

Having now known in my forties more people who have lost their mothers and who remark feeling anchorless, floating across the surface of a lifespan as vast as the world's oceans, untethered to their primal root, I know I should feel some kind of innate sense of appreciation. I know I should feel some kind of affinity towards a woman who not only birthed me but also washed my hair in a small bucket in a kitchen sink, the water warm and running through the slits between her fingers like a child washing the hair of a doll in practice for the real thing. This, and other loving gestures—pulling my brown arms through the sleeves of a shirt, gently, gently, everything tender, the socks, the soothing voice, the cooing sounds—should be enough to elicit an automatic and wild emotional connection, induce a deeply buried animal sense. My brown face looking into her alabaster face with just a hint of iron patina so it's more golden hued, a young Asian mother, more immigrant than naturalized citizen, and not in a rush to swallow whatever it is that makes America so great.

But, like labour before birth, there were complications.

I now know in my forties that life comes at you like a heavy appliance slipping off a dolly. You've seen the slippage coming in advance so you brace for it and keep it counterweighted. Or it comes like a minor injury that leaves major medical bills in the weight of its correction, what should have been a bruise in your twenties is now a hairline fracture that hurts like a m_____ f_____. I should, I really should forgive my mother for things she did, things she did not do, the way her best was not enough, but it was all that she could give, or whatever it is they say in group therapy about our parents. That, instead, I should, I really should appreciate her for the continental sacrifices she made, projecting her own expected life outcomes—in America, we refer to these as dreams—onto me and my sisters. But what do people tell you about having high expectations (when you're young) or any expectations at all (when you're divorced and middle-aged and shit has literally fallen apart around you)?

The thing that keeps me from being a good, appreciative daughter, from uttering my mother's praises, from giving her flowers on all the days outside of Mother's Day, from paying for all her expenses (despite being a single mother who is daughter of a single mother who is a daughter of a single mother, etc.), is knowing how thoroughly humiliated she felt having to walk through Oakland Chinatown with Black children over the course of our childhoods. "Are they yours?" How thoroughly humiliated I would grow up feeling for being black and having to walk alongside my mother as the source of her shame. 他们是你的吗? How were our blood ties not more powerful than her shamefaced reality of being questioned and stared at by other Chinese people? 他们是你的吗? Of being disowned by her family when they first discovered it?

The discovery: that he was Black, that she was pregnant, that the children were his, and that she would choose ~~him~~ this rather than be a good, dutiful, obedient Chinese daughter.

But, still, she was always a good mother. Always.

A good mother provides for her children: clothes, shoes, notebooks, pencils, three balanced meals a day, birthday gifts, a cake, vacations to the beach, and a pet. She presses them close to her chest, inside that cavity where that beating muscular organ—consistently and with purpose—pumps life and energy across the span of that fragile yet tremendously strong body from which unconditional love and selfless gestures radiate. She will be the last to eat and the last to sleep. She will save her children the last bite. The last morsel. Her survival is unimportant if it means sacrificing herself for her children.

> The airplane manual lies in English when it says mothers should
> fix their masks first before fixing the masks of their children.

(I might be only talking specifically about Asian immigrant mothers here.)

A good mother is nurturing and caring. Cereal poured into a bowl with the exact amount of milk to prevent soggy complaints and teary-eyed stomach pain. Then the bowl and spoon, washed and rinsed, hair braided and unbraided, washed and rinsed, socks and jerseys sweaty from practice, washed and rinsed, and her own bathtime ritual scheduled for after everyone has been put to bed. She provides a safe and supportive environment. A house where electricity may be lacking, food may be lacking, furniture might be lacking, heat might be lacking, toys may be lacking, but in their place, there are stories and laughter and momentous feats like turning bread or cheese or any other one-liner staple in that bare-boned refrigerator into a hundred different meals.

There is no crazy ex-boyfriend trying to break in through the front door, shouting that if she doesn't let him in, he'll shoot up the house.

A good mother creates an environment where her children can thrive and grow. Small scrape-kneed boys shouting across the cul de sac, their leaping bones ricocheting against the face of the wind, their taut limbs bracing onto the back of the metal curve of a bike lifted into the air, handlebars steering them zigzag into traffic. She keeps them safe: pressed against the bread and meat of her body.

One day, they are young and feral. The next, they're grown, having tasted the sobering chapter of heartbreak, a serious, settled grove of boyish men, looming over her like giant redwood trees, still bringing her their empty cereal bowls and sweaty socks and jerseys in adult sizes M-XL.

> She still knows the right amount of milk to pour, the good mother. But she also feels the pull of them away from her body. A magnetic gravitation towards a destiny outside of her expertise, beyond her paygrade.

The way I ran from my mother before I could legally drive.

I would chase after everything that moved just to be out of my father's home.

That is what my teenage years felt like.

Tiger Mother's Stripes

How could a mixed-race Black girl survive school lunches and the ~~delicious~~ horrific surprise of Kam Yen Jan sausages and pork floss over rice packed neatly in a bag with a fork wrapped napkin by her Asian immigrant mother?

All I wanted was ham and cheese on white bread.

All I wanted was for all those kids to stop laughing.

Then at twenty-nine, I became a mother and at forty-two, she turned thirteen. She grew up with a mother who couldn't surprise her with Chinese food tucked lovingly into lunch bags. Instead, I would pack her convenient slices of salami and hot chips until she insisted on me not packing her food to school anymore. Excise any reason for those kids to start laughing.

From my mother, I learned that a balanced meal was important for the body. It kept you healthy and made you mentally ready for rigorous academic study. So, of course, I felt like I was failing. But I also wasn't a Chinese mother.

At least not all the way.

I still expected the grades, A's at best, but I would accept a lonely B. I expected my children to go to college, but I was more lenient about the level of institutional prestige and the medical and engineering degrees. I expected them to be polite and respectful but felt proud chested at their loud, unbridled laughter in public and their bold-faced, singular opinions and desires that they were willing to fight me over. I expected them to not wander curiously into sex until college but also wanted them to feel the first sign that their bodies were theirs and that others could absolutely adore them in the physical form just for existing, especially my daughter.

Then there were no shoes in the house, no outside clothes on the bed, no crumbs on the floor, and no sticky fingers on the couch.

So, in a way, I was also the Black mom I never had.

Scholars have written in depth about the complex relationship between Asian immigrant mothers and their American-born daughters. It's an entire cosmology with its own military, currency, infrastructure, and language where strategic battles and overtures of love are governed by one's own sense of power, identity, wounds, expectations, cultural traditions, and weaponry. In some instances, the mother wins, shooting to kill with deft guilt trips and condescending encouragement. Other times, it is the daughter who goes in like a bomb, razing everything to rubble using a missile in the shape of a refusal to translate into English or a squadron dropping known weaponized chemicals known as "I'm dating interracially to spite you." It is a war fought on all fronts, hot and cold. And despite there being numerous ceasefires, there will be no truce.

But on the outside looking in, these militarized conflicts produce nothing but the best and brightest kids, with the mother—the target aggressor, the colonial empire, the beginning and end of the Cultural Revolution that stole the fat and laughter from the lips of the lost generation so now all they do is nag you about your insufficient salary and insufficient achievements and insufficient parenting—being both heralded and reviled as a tiger. She holds her cubs by their necks, ensuring a lifespan of studiousness, obedience, and respect. Discipline. "Practice it again. From the top." It is not good enough until a first-place award is secured at a national competition. And even then.

The desired outcome is always high-achieving, financially successful adult children. The actualized outcome is always adult people pleasers who never feel good enough and are perpetually entangled in their internal voices that constantly, without fail, ask, no, demand, over and over, *Why am I so stupid? What is wrong with me? Why can't I ever do anything right?* Rhetorical exercises that keep them insecure and bound to their shortcomings and others' stereotypes. But being high-achieving and financially successful and having mastered the art of masking, you would never know those voices provide the cardinal directions of their life choices.

Instead, you focus on those high six figures and the view from the second story redwood deck and the black-haired, early-reading, math-whiz-natural, musical-genius children who—thanks to a strict, regimented family structure, high, unachievable expectations, and a fierce devotion to hard work and collective interdependence—seem so well behaved and smart. Just like their parents.

But my daughter, born from a rebellious half-Black daughter who was lazy in her academics and slacked in music theory application and showed defiance in her displays of filial piety and obedience, could not have been anything like those children.

Black haired, yes. But more wild in spirit and hot at the mouth than obedient and well behaved.

There would be no edge of the American landscape that would not work for overtime pay to kill my daughter.

I had to raise her in preparation for that—for the "You have the right to remain silent" over the "And the highest GPA is awarded to." It was about survival in the midst of her American teenage years, that developmental stage where autonomy, self-discovery, and a recalibration towards peer pressure are all seen as healthy indications of life on the other side of childhood. But in the Asian immigrant parent and American-born child dynamic, this turning towards the self—the choosing one's own path and abandoning one's post at the edge of family expectations to wander into a demilitarized zone full of makeup, boys, baggy pants, and crop tops—made for a personal attack, one that slow burned the fields of millet, rice, and cotton planted and razed between tiger mother and daughter. There were no perfect SAT scores or valedictorian speeches when things were done the American way. Just waves of white freedom that spilled into a river so carefully dammed by the tiger mother, so diligent in her crafting of her children's future, the centre of her future.

A lineage.

Her own personal showcase of black-haired, early-reading, math-whiz-natural, musical genius children.

This wasn't me, though. Nor the territorial boundary I set before my wandering daughter.

Having grown up translating English words to my mother and carrying her across the white divide, I would have to learn to become a Black mother, which meant drawing from what I observed from the women who made my father, the women who were extensions of him. Like a foreigner mimicking the accent of the locals at the coffee shop when they ordered their morning café viennois, I would learn how to hold a pan both as a domestic tool and a murder weapon and how to step in front of the bodies of my children like a US Army M1A2 Abrams when facing enemy combatants, scoffing loudly in the middle of battle when those combatants outranked me and could not be easily put down, making sure my children could hear the crass blackness in my derision. I would learn how to cry in the dark after they had fallen asleep for the things we didn't have and could never have and to twist their rebellion into a submissive compliance with just a click of my tongue and the flash of my eye. For everything else—learning to grease the scalp before turning a headful of hair into knotless braids, the black happy birthday song, and how to make Black-folks approved cookout potato salad—there was the internet.

I would become a version of a mother that was unrecognizable to my own mother while still applying the small touches I learned from her:

"Put on a coat, it's cold outside."

"Make sure you eat something before leaving the house."

"Always come with something in hand when visiting a friend or loved one."

"Make sure you always use your own money—never rely on a man for anything."

Even now, I'm getting it all mixed up.

Tiger Cubs Are Born Blind and Completely Dependent on Their Mother

My daughter would pick and choose from the charcuterie board I presented to her on an artisan acacia serving plank to feed me small ~~lies~~ truths about who she was with and where she was going and what she was doing after I told her good night and turned off the lights. Battling me over the boundary lines, it would feel like I was watching my fifteen-year-old self running circles around my Chinese immigrant mother: the boys, the bruises, the cutting, the weed, the getting into strangers' cars, and the absolute garrish waste of my own preciousness. Yet I would graduate a B-average student and go on to college once I turned eighteen.

I never cared about being a black-haired, early-reading, math-whiz-natural, and musical-genius child. But I wanted both my kids to come close. Especially my daughter: a light-skin girl who wore glasses, had a greedy pleasure for casual reading, was sharply funny to the point of maiming her subjects, and had heart-shaped kissable lips at fourteen.

This was my prize: a chance to live vicariously through my child and curate a better future if only I could steer her to choose the ending on page fourteen of the choose your own adventure book of life. She could devote herself to remaining pretty and Black for men who would initially flood her with flowers and validation and dinner dates and good sex and the eventual "What are we?" and "Where are we going?" conversations before offering a climax of doomed marriageless middle-aged dating cycles at the edge of her early thirties. Or, I issued loudly at every chance I got, she could be what Lorraine Hansberry titled her play about her own layered life: young, gifted, and Black.

Those gifts, I explained, referred to the cerebral, mechanical, and artistic power of the brain. One's raw, limitless intellect and wit. One's serrated sarcasm. One's mastery in survival skills: how to build a shelter in the wilderness, how to exit a brutal man who broke your children when you weren't home. One's tendency to think with common sense and not through a torn, bleeding heart. One's cuss words fitted around her Black woman intuition. One's aptitude for makeshifting.[3] A long tendency to apply enough soft-spoken emotional intelligence to roomful of pale necked skeptics and upper-class nonbelievers while taking in the background noise.

"Sensitivity is a gift," I tell her.
Hardness is a gift.
Drawing one's line in the sand and staying committed is a gift.
Knowing what one should commit to is a gift.

Do you even hear me?

My Chinese mother could never fathom a young me being gifted and Black, as though the two naturally cancelled each other out.

Like married + Black and woman	已婚 + 黑人 and 女性
or successful + Black man	成功 + 黑人

To keep her on the straight and narrow, I would issue a series of decrees, the ones you get to press your shoulders out over as a Black parent but that otherwise come as standard in the operating manual as an Asian one:

1. Get all A's in your classes
2. No phones after 9:00 p.m.
3. Find out what your friends' parents do for a living
4. No dating until eleventh grade (no sex until college)

Each one she would successfully challenge to break, save for the one inside the ().

Each time, I would feel my childhood wounds weeping, with little more than auto-generated daily affirmation and a mantra from my therapist keeping me from becoming the flat-edged shoes of my parents.

No one tells you about the guilt.
No one tells you about the rage.
Or maybe they do, but wǒbù dǒng zhōngwén.
            (I don't understand Chinese.)

As a Black mother, would I tolerate some degree of exploration and independence, some wild streak of rule breaking, some known fabrication of the truth, some expression of sexual pleasure and bodily autonomy outside of being shamed and called "fast"[4] (Ain't I a woman?).[5] Having come from a race of people who held the language of constellations and swamps and daylight and owl calls as integral parts of our collective compass North, it seemed logical to allow the girl to be wild and trust her intuition enough to deliver her safely enough to her purpose in the same way that the many women who came before her, before me, were delivered to conviction, spirit, pleasure, gospel, motive, and everything worth running towards, clean across the clearing. Whereas as an Asian mother, I would celebrate none of this and wonder why she was asking to go outside for nonacademic purposes in the first place.

"Who are these friends?"

"Why are you not working on the things that will get you into college?"

"You still need to study even if there is no upcoming exam!"

There was a degree of competition between value systems in my head but the main parts were consistent: obedience and compliance, intermittent reinforcement, heavy-handed discipline, harsh and indirect gestures of love and affection, deference to elders, almost cultish loyalty to the family, and an undying will to achieve and succeed at the highest level.

My mother could never trust that I was doing it right: being a good enough, hard enough, and selfless enough mother.

"You need to make sure you are checking her homework."

"Did you sign her up for any sport? It helps the brain and will keep her smart"

"You don't want to mess up your kids by bringing the wrong man around"

"Your kids are your priority now. Your life is over. No more fun. Think of the priority."

Even now I can hear my mother talking over me and my good ~~intuition~~ intentions.

In ~~Conclusion~~ Continuity

In the end, I am both a terrible mother and a good mother.
In the end, my own mother was both the same.

Yet despite it all, this girl, born from tigers, keeps on growing.

Endnotes

1. Notice that the author writes "grew up with" rather than "raised by." This is a sentiment often experienced by the children of young immigrant parents who are learning a new country and culture and language and reaching similar developmental milestones as their American-born or 1.5-gen children.
2. She actually spoke three: Burmese, Mandarin, and English.
3. See the context I am referring to in Kimber Thomas's article, "Makeshifting: Black Women and Resilient Creativity in the Rural South."
4. A derogatory label disproportionately applied to Black girls who are considered sexually promiscuous and possessing poor morals and behaviour.
5. This quote was repeated throughout a speech delivered extemporaneously by formerly enslaved abolitionist and orator Sojourner Truth at the Women's Convention in Akron, Ohio, in 1851.

Works Cited

Thomas, Kimber. "Makeshifting: Black Women and Resilient Creativity in the Rural South." *Southern Cultures*, vol. 26, no. 1, 2020, pp. 120–37.

11.

Mothering: The Voices in My Head

Kae Solomon

"What on earth were you thinking?" "Why do I have to keep asking?" When are you going to be more responsible? "How many times have I told you...?" "Why haven't you...?" "Did you hear me?" The loud sighs of disappointment, hissing air of impatience in the back of my throat, my need for her to obey.

One day, I realized I sounded exactly like my mother and cringed. The voice of criticism and judgment, not doing things her way, not measuring up. My daughter stared at me silently, her big brown eyes reflective and wide, taking in my faults without judging, wanting to please because she loves me. What am I teaching her? How have I influenced her sense of self?

From the moment I recognized the voice as my mother's, I vowed never again. But still, at odd inexplicable moments of annoyance and frustration, the voice coming out of my mouth is not mine at all. I feel it before I hear it, grating on my vocal cords, like a cough. No, I will not repeat these mistakes. This precious human being will not be moulded or shaped by my mother's rigid expectations and belief system. I want an entirely different relationship.

My daughter was born in the rec room of our 1970s townhouse in Burnaby, British Columbia. It took nineteen hours, but I was determined. The hottest day of the year at thirty degrees Celsius, and on the advice of the midwives, had the heaters roaring. After hours in the birthing pool, the birthing chair, then crouching, squatting, my body shut down after taking too much Tylenol. One of the downsides of a homebirth, I'd been ten hours in labour before the midwives showed up and couldn't handle the pain on my own.

As soon as all that dark hair emerged, they grabbed her slippery body and placed her on my chest.

"What is it?" I asked.

"A baby," one of the midwives said. I gently moved the little legs apart and saw that it was my dearly longed-for daughter.

I had a world more experience than my young mother, when I gave birth at forty-two, nearly twice her age. When she was forty-two, I had already moved one thousand miles away from home. One thing we did have in common, though, was our inability to have processed our intergenerational traumas before we gave birth.

In my twenties, instead of having my children, which I longed for but was in no way ready for, I worked as a nanny. I looked after infants as young as six weeks old and became an expert at diagnosing cries, soothing, diapering, scheduling, making tasty and nutritious foods, inventing games, intervening between siblings, and helping with homework. I felt assured that, along with studying parenting and child psychology books, I'd be a practised and expert mother.

When my job was over for the day, I went home, played music and wrote songs, read books, went to clubs, hung out with friends, explored the beauty of our coastal city, travelled, and took classes. I expected to still be able to pursue my interests, baby strapped to my back or in a stroller alongside me.

As a newborn, my baby had long naps, rarely cried, and was easily soothed by nursing. My partner worked a lot, so I was alone with her most evenings. I had no idea of the exhaustion that made anything except basic survival seem almost impossible. No idea of the constant demands, details, and the amount of time necessary to be present for a young child's constant needs. On occasion, we got a brief break when my parents visited our city or when we could find a reliable and affordable sitter.

Postpartum depression was my biggest worry. It felled both my mother and grandmother. I nervously awaited the two-month mark. My grandmother had a psychotic break when my mother was that age and was at a mental hospital for seven months.

My mother told me the story when I was young. What she didn't say was how unlikely my grandmother, after receiving months of shock treatments and hydrotherapy, would have been equipped to pick up the pieces of her former life: baby, husband, and a large house.

My mom described her as critical, distant. There was no bond. My grandparents came from "stiff upper lip" families. My mom wanted empathy, compassion, love, and affection. She does not ever remember even a hug or kiss from her parents. Once she got 100 per cent on a test, and her dad, who was a gruff man well into his alcoholism, grumped "Is that all?"

My grandmother related the traumatic events that led to her breakdown when my mother was pregnant with me. I wasn't even born, but absorbed the shock, pain, stress, and worry that my twenty-year-old mother was experiencing. It cast a shadow over her otherwise happy pregnancy, the adored first grandchild in both families.

My mom ended up in the hospital with a nervous breakdown when I was a year old. She had been so afraid she was going to hurt me.

I hung onto the stroller extra tightly when we went downhill. I couldn't look when we went over the little bridge on top of the creek near our home. Only later, a mom friend told me she also could not walk down big hills with her stroller without trepidation. I realized my worries about harming my infant were completely normal.

My daughter took a long time to get into a nap schedule and did not want to sleep at night. I followed advice from parenting books and napped when she napped. The wakings each night got tougher when my year-long maternity leave was over. We tried sleep training, but I couldn't bear hearing her cry when she was so easy to soothe.

She enjoyed stretching out bedtime with many stories and lullabies. I never regretted a moment of those serene cuddles. She nursed until three and a half, much older than I had ever imagined. Her sweet head, silky hair, and eyes bright with love and the future, how could I deny us these moments of closeness, the pure solid weight of her at my side? I grew melty thinking how brief this would be in the timeline of my life and held onto that warm, squishy body until the peace of each night's dreams fluttered behind her eyelids. I buried my nose into her apple cheeks, breathed in the sweet flesh, and squeezed her malleable fingers, which grasped mine in reflex, sighing deeply as she let go. This little creature exhausted me and tested my limits.

I struggled hard to keep myself together with a full-time career as an educator, working busy days with kids, staff, and administering a library.

Some days she stayed in daycare till 5:30 p.m., and then we rushed home to make dinner and then again out the door to activities like gymnastics and ballet. Once home, she was wired and raring to go until after 10:00 p.m. It didn't occur to me that she was hyperactive or ADHD. Her symptoms were nothing like my brother's, who had been diagnosed fifty years ago. I'd worked with lots of ADHD kids. She got glowing reports from all her teachers.

Like many mothers, I regretted how much time I spent away from her. Part-time work would have been ideal, but I started my career late, returning to university in my thirties when my dreams of being a successful musician fell apart. Our lives were more stressful Monday to Friday than they should have been. How could I explain to her why she had to get up so early, rush through the morning routine, and then out the door, always hurry hurry hurry, in opposition to a young child's natural inclination to enjoy the world of her imagination? Her dad was often able to get a weekday off and took her to playgroups and on special adventures. But many mornings, she was thrust into cold reality, with me shoving her little feet into her rainbow-coloured rain boots and then running out into the pouring rain.

What did she think about at daycare when an older girl bullied her? Where were her parents? Why weren't we there to care for her instead of someone else's mommy?

Her dad and I had not yet learned how to turn towards each other to find strength, so in the early years, we turned against each other. We fought and then wouldn't speak to one another for days. We did not know how to resolve our problems and financial difficulties, having just bought a house, which turned into a fixer-upper. In times of stress, the brain reverts to what we learn in our families of origin. Until we become aware of all the patterns ingrained into our DNA, we are doomed to repeat them.

How much was her childhood affected by the discord in our relationship?

My mother sent me to daycare in the afternoons, but she didn't spend the morning doing crafts or pushing me on the swings. She trained me to sleep later, so she didn't have to get up until just before my dad came home at lunch to pick me up. Then I was expected to nap in daycare and lay there, counting shadows on the darkened walls as time seemed interminable.

Could I have done it all differently with my daughter? How can I shape her into the best version of herself?

Or of all of us. She has to overcome the struggles of the women who came before her. This is not the legacy I would like to have passed down. Doesn't she have enough to deal with, the fourth generation of women with mental health problems? Although I was aware of my grandmother and mother's breakdowns, I had not recognized my own, let alone understood that mental illness and trauma are inherited. Mark Woberg's book about epigenetics, *It Didn't Start with You*, says trauma affects three subsequent generations. That means I am the recipient of both my grandmother's and mother's traumas, and I pass along mine and my mother's to my daughter. Does it compound? As my daughter inherits mine, does that mean she takes on my entire burden?

My grandmother's mental illness began long before that seven-month hospital stay. When she was three, the family suffered the accidental death of an older sibling. She had always believed it was her fault. In high school, she was taken out of school because of "problems with her nerves," but she had skipped two grades when younger so still graduated early.

My daughter started her first year of high school during the pandemic. We noticed her moping around, head down, shoulders sloped, and not getting out of bed till 1:00 p.m. or later. Not getting dressed or wearing old, ill-fitting clothing. I told myself, "Oh, teens need more sleep, right? She's staying up late studying; her schedule is turned around. Teens have huge hormonal changes, so aren't mood swings normal?" I didn't want to overreact but also didn't want to miss the signs. But the moping continued. She did not eat much and did not wash her thick shiny mane, usually a source of pride. She finally admitted to a terrible depression she'd been afraid to share.

We promised our full support. She could talk to us. We would get her professional help, and we did. She has an excellent therapist and other mental health support. This is the least we can do, having burdened her with our tainted bloodlines. Her psychologist helps her communicate, identify her feelings and moods, unravel strands of confusion, and unpack the baggage. Unlike our own families of origin, we are constantly evolving. Working through generations of dysfunction takes time and practice.

These are things I cannot protect her from. But there were things I should have protected her from, and that will always hurt me. The helplessness in the face of her dad's and my relationship problems. When I recently expressed my regret she said, "One thing you can be proud of is you broke the cycle." The things she wrote in the handmade Mother's Day card made me cry with relief and gratitude. Then why the hot and cold, like she doesn't even like me sometimes?

The push for independence is protracted. High school was hard. Because of all her physical illnesses and mental struggles, she missed so much. Grades slipped further once her dad's cancer diagnosis compounded her inability to cope. Her friend group made fun of her and then ignored her completely. She struggled through grades eleven and twelve. Finally, a diagnosis of ADHD. The medication has helped her focus, eased her anxiety, and helped a little with insomnia.

How could I teach her about friendships when I put up with being bullied? I wanted to hang out with the popular kids. I was geeky, with acne and braces, until I grew into my looks around fifteen. I felt lucky to be in the orbit of the cool kids and took the bullying as the price paid. It felt wrong but was often passed off as "Can't you take a joke?" or "We didn't mean it." Maybe they didn't, some were nice one-on-one, but to the group, "making fun" of someone was funny. Lots of laughs for them.

Why couldn't I find better friends? Why was I so needy? What was going on in my home life that made me vulnerable? How easily the weak and unprotected can be sniffed out.

I did not want that for my girl. Despite our problems, we were one of the more stable families in her small elementary school where she found herself an unwilling participant in girl drama. After all the talks with other parents, there was no solution, a couple of the girls were from very troubled families. How could I have protected her better?

My parents' mental health problems intensified once my brother was born. My mom's had manifested twice already in their short marriage: just after moving to a tiny town for my dad's first job and then when I was one year old when she couldn't deal with the rage and fear from what her mother had told her just before my birth.

Whatever medication her doctor suggested, Mom agreed. She has never thought to question a doctor, research anything, or seek another opinion or alternative remedies. Decades of antidepressants, calming and addicting sedatives, pills for stomach problems, pills for headaches, the pain in her elbow, her asthma, sore toes.

My brother became extremely ill after my mother stopped breastfeeding at two months and switched to cow's milk. It took the medical system a long time to figure out what was wrong. I remember emergency visits when he was two years old and nearly died. Constant worry, stress, sleep deprivation, trips to hospitals, night vigils. My dad never took a day off work. Would those demons have stayed in the closet if my brother's illnesses had not opened the door? Would another crisis have brought the ghosts into the present?

My teenage rebellion began in grade seven. For some reason, the school thought it was a great idea to separate me from all my friends and put me in a class with three sets of best friends. For an entire year, I was the odd one out, forced to partner with the most unpopular boy in the gym or for projects.

That summer, my young uncle died in an accident. In the days before the funeral, there had been an incident of inappropriate behaviour from my dad. Even before that, there were looks, things said. I told my mom and she confronted him. As she came out of their bathroom where he was shaving, she said, "I asked him if that happened, and he said no."

It had been denied, and then life went on. No discussion, no help. How does this type of trauma change the psyche? You can't tell your friends whom you talk to about everything, except this one thing. You have this horrible secret, and it must stay secret. Somehow despite your best attempt to fit in, you are still marked, something different, not in a good way; something is off.

I always thought I forgave him because he was having a nervous breakdown. A few months later he was hospitalized. Shock treatments, medication.

My parents must have finally noticed something was wrong with me. They sent me to my dad's psychiatrist. He was an old man, portly, with white hair and beard, and a thick Polish accent. My dad went with me to the appointment. The office had the stale smell of mothballs. I don't remember what he and my dad talked about but the only questions he asked me were: "Are you eating? Are you sleeping?" As I answered yes to both questions, he shrugged, and we left the office.

It took decades to process how it impacted me: hundreds of hours of therapy and self-medicating. If it hadn't happened, how different would my world have been? I delved into the dark pit of my psyche to retrieve these displaced memories, pushed into the furthest corner of the closet. Finally able to face, confront, no longer shame, it has fallen like a weight.

At fourteen, my daughter was in quarantine, online schooling in isolation. At her age, I had begun to date, drinking, partying, staying out till the wee hours. At fifteen, I came home drunk, crying, and throwing up. My parents threatened reform school. They were bluffing, but I was terrified they'd follow through. Instead, they grounded me for three months. Somehow, they allowed me out after a miserable month, with strict warnings thwarted by sleepovers when my friend's mom was out of town.

I had more all-night adventures when they vacationed for two weeks, leaving me to care for my eleven-year-old brother. I dropped acid for the first time. The same friend came to check on me. She had just received her driver's license and had the great idea to drive ninety miles to North Battleford to go for coffee. The gas light came on when we were still thirty miles from town, but we made it, laughing and joking about how we'd have to hitchhike, me tripping on acid and her in her fluffy bedroom slippers.

At seventeen, rootless depression swooped in dark and deep. I graduated school a semester early, suddenly adrift. My parents sent me to a different psychiatrist. He asked me to write down my life story. At the next session, I brought out the orange exercise book and read it to him, including the details of what had happened with my dad. He didn't say anything. Riding down in the elevator, I ripped the pages out of the book and tore them all into little pieces. When I got home, I threw all the pieces in the toilet and flushed them down.

My mom wasn't like me as a teen; she was a "goody-two-shoes" as we called girls like that who did not take risks, talk back, or explore outside the norm and expectations parents and teachers set. She continued music lessons after high school. Her parents paid for her to live in a boarding house. Her only rebellion was sneaking my dad in. She was determined to be liberal. By then they were engaged, and at eighteen, my mom was married.

"My mom said she hated sex," she told me once when I was about ten. She showed me her many books and magazines about sex. "I'm not like that, and I don't want you to be either. You can ask me anything you want." She proceeded to go into detail to make sure I knew exactly what went on. We were sitting at the kitchen table when she brought up the Pill.

"It's for when you love someone so much that you just can't wait any longer." She clasped her hands in front of her, sucking in her breath, as she gazed upwards to the ceiling. "You can come and talk to me, and we'll get you a prescription from the doctor." I was only fifteen but had already had much more experience than she knew about.

I kept that in the back of my mind during my sometimes wild but often lonely teenage years. So, at eighteen, I told her I was ready to go on the Pill.

"But you don't even have a boyfriend."

I didn't, I admitted.

"Well of course not then," She acted shocked.

I was hoping that if I went on the Pill, I'd feel more free and relaxed, so maybe sex would just sort of happen. I was desperate for a boyfriend for an emotional connection, but more so for a sexual one. My hormones were going crazy, but I was painfully shy. I took one university literature class, then went home and studied classical music hours each day, taught piano lessons, and babysat, not exactly a way to meet people my age. No wonder I was depressed.

"Why did you get married so young?" I asked her once.

"My dad told me that the first guy that puts a ladder outside my window can have me," she tsked. My dad, with his limited social skills, born on a small farm during the Depression, with a naïve view of the world, would not have had a clue about what he was getting himself into. He put up with her until he couldn't anymore. Divorce was floated a few times, with the end excuse they couldn't afford it. They coped, barely, using their many prescriptions, and for my mom, food. Also lots and lots of sleep. My dad was always napping, and my mom stayed up all night and slept all day.

She slept till noon until I started high school, then later and later until she managed to turn the clock around. My dad came home to make lunch for us. Her depression, but also her narcissism, meant our family's life revolved around her sleep patterns, especially once she began sleeping in the living room, which had to remain dark and quiet all day. Her OCD meant things in the house had to be kept just so. Not neat, often terribly messy, but her piles of junk could not be disrupted

I could not confide in my mother. She betrayed me every time, throwing things back in my face, embarrassing me and making judgements when I had been striving for closeness. I rebelled against her conservative, narrow-minded opinions. Occasionally my dad or brother would side with me for a more reasonable mid-way point. When that happened, she escalated. She threw fits, became hysterical, and cried uncontrollably until it became about calming her down and never about what the problem was in the first place.

We could not protect our daughter from the influences of our families. Big arguments at my in-laws often erupted at the dinner table. No one seemed to understand that screaming and yelling were not good influences for a young child. In my parents' home, there were also arguments. Not as loud, but the digs were deep, just as hurtful, if not more. In the aftermath, we talked it to death, factions breaking off, neutral parties (my dad or brother), then genuine remorse, eventually healing and forgiveness, hugs and expressions of love. Unlike at the in-laws where everyone pretended nothing happened and went on as before.

But inevitably, there would be another clash because my mom has personality disorders; she does not learn from experience. She has no insight into her behaviours and so keeps perpetuating the same unhealthy cycles. Compounded with memory problems and confusion, her anger and sense of victimhood are worse.

On one family visit, several of us were glued to the television, watching an exciting football game. My mother, who needs to be the center of attention, began berating my twelve-year-old because she had not offered to take out the garbage. She then yelled from the kitchen: "Someone left a glass in the sink! More mess for me. I'm never going to get into the bath!" She smashed the glass and threatened to kill herself.

The rest of us stared at each other in shock. My brother turned down the game.

"Okay, Mom. I guess we need to call the police. You are threatening self-harm." I called her bluff. "They will take you to the hospital for a psychiatric evaluation. Is that what you want?"

My mom sounded startled. "No. No, I don't."

My brother called out that we would follow through if we had to and then turned the game back up. My dad went to bed, unable to stomach the drama. My sister-in-law suggested we pack a few things and stay at their house. My mother watched us leave; her glittering eyes radiated dark and hostile. She is at her most vindictive when she feels she is being wronged and keeps a ready list of the many times she has been wronged in her head. This is the version of Mom that I need to avoid.

During my first year in Los Angeles, where I had moved to try to make it in the music scene, I received a letter from my grandmother. My dad's mom had died two years before. I had always regretted not finding out more about her life, so I asked my other grandma to write down her life story. A long brown envelope arrived with "confidential" written across the back.

I sat down to read in the gold velvet wing chair recently purchased from a yard sale. The transparent paper crinkled between my fingers, and I opened it. Her fine spidery penmanship was perfected as a teacher. She wasn't allowed to work after marriage. That would be shameful, as it would appear her husband couldn't support her.

Born outside time and place in her small farming community in rural Saskatchewan in 1918, my grandmother was artistic, creative, extremely pretty, and rebellious. She met and dated my grandpa, but also "so many beaus" she lost track. She eventually became engaged to a man from Scotland. But when she ran into my grandfather again, the affair rekindled. She sent the ring back. She writes, "It took no time at all to fall back into the sex lifestyle." They became engaged.

For how long did she pretend her period was just late? As weeks went by, she would have noticed the bloom in her cheeks, the swelling of her breasts, and the glow in her eyes. Why didn't they marry then? Maybe it would have been the shame of the rushed timing. My grandpa's father was the mayor of their small town. He owned a successful business. There could not be a scandal.

Somehow, they found someone to do the illegal procedure. I don't know how far along she was. How long did she have to wait, wondering if it would even happen? Would she be ostracized from society, with an A on her back?

It went horribly wrong. The bleeding wouldn't stop. She was hospitalized and nearly died. The secret was out. My grandfather's youngest sister's kindness was a lifeline; everyone else was cruel. They accused her of murder, emotionally burned her at the stake. She could not get over the blood, so much blood.

They finally wed. When she became pregnant with my mom, she knew she was mentally ill. She was admitted to the psychiatric ward during the sixth month of pregnancy but released after only a few days. The memories of that traumatic time returned over and over until her mind snapped when my mom was two months old. She saw a baby that should not have been there, must be gotten rid of. In the letter, she says she tried to drown the baby and doesn't remember how she was saved. In my mom's telling, my grandpa had been feeling unwell so came home early from work and stopped her just in time.

Their marriage was not happy. My grandmother had more hospital stays then addiction to medications. My grandfather sought relief through alcohol.

On a recent trip to California, my daughter realized she left her phone in Walmart. We both dashed back. I ran to customer service and then to the checkout stand. No luck. When I got back to the car, she looked at me with annoyance. "Where were you?" Of course, she had found her phone on a shelf right where she left it.

We got back in the car, with my husband remaining strangely calm. It was an expensive phone he had just bought for her eighteenth birthday. Blood rushed through my veins, and a voice shouted in my head: "How could you do that? What were you thinking? You weren't thinking at all, were you?" "When are you going to be more responsible."

I caught myself. I sat and breathed, gazing at the dusty brown hills of the Sierra Nevada Mountains outlined against a hot azure sky. The sun beat down on impossibly green trees. Curious about their water source in this arid landscape, I let go of any other thoughts. The smooth and purring highway calmed my feelings. Deep love and compassion replaced annoyance and anger.

Our fragile girl, delicate flower. She is rare, blooming, and sensitive to conditions around her. We have to give her fresh air, sunshine, and nutrients for the soil so she can eventually push through the doorway into adulthood. For everything she is going through, we also have accelerating climate change and an increasingly dangerous world. How can I continue to protect her?

I left my home in Saskatoon for Vancouver the week after my twenty-first birthday. After I packed the car, I realized my parents had walked down to the driveway to see me off. It was only then I noticed how sad they looked. We would never live together again. I hadn't given a thought to their feelings, only thinking of the adventure before me. If I had taken the time to feel the emotion, the scorching pain wouldn't have let me leave.

In only a few months, my daughter plans to go to university in another city. For now, she remains at home, but this fall, she will have a heavy course load of math and sciences. I'm worried about the strain on her physical and mental health. Why didn't she choose something easier when she has so many talents? I have to trust she knows what she needs. When the going gets tough, I will be there.

I recently returned from a trip to see my mother. With her mental illness, her confusion, memory loss, and mobility problems, it is like caring for a very young and difficult child. My brother and sister-in-law have been saints since Dad died, caring for her needs and neuroses with patience. I feel guilty not doing more, so I try to do as much as possible in the time I'm there. But it's never enough. If I don't meet all her demands, she criticizes me and makes up lies about me to other family members, who roll their eyes and try to change the subject. It is hard to deal with, harder for my daughter who worries about hereditary traits.

I grit my teeth and do breathing techniques my therapist has shown me. I notice certain expressions sound exactly like my mother's despite my best intentions- a laugh or the physical mechanics of my voice like timbre, pitch and resonance.

In these last short weeks of summer, before my job and college begin, my daughter goes to the cabin with her boyfriend's family. The absences are becoming routine as she spends more and more time away.

Last thing at night, before going to bed, I stop in the hallway at her door. My hand rests on the cold knob while I remember the years of tuck-ins, cuddles and books, and the more recent years of moodiness, rebuffing my nightly rituals of affection.

Instead of venturing in to bid goodnight, I open the door to silence but still am surprised by her absence, the empty bed. Could I have kept her here longer? Stopped time? I sniff the air to feel her presence; a sweet astringency smell of nail polish, strawberry body lotion, the heady, feral aroma of hormones. How long will it still smell like this once she has moved out?

Then realize, in many ways, she has already gone.

12.

Spiderlings and Butterfly Wings: A Métis Maternal Response to Teenage Nature Disconnection and Ecoapathy

Josée Bergeron

"I don't want to go," my fourteen-year-old declared. She sat beside me in the passenger's seat of our vehicle, with her arms crossed, shoulders slumped, and icy blue eyes glued to the road ahead. Stunned, I tried to think of the best way to reply.

"Why don't you want to go?" I said, trying to understand her sudden distaste for mountains.

In the past weeks, I had been preparing for a backcountry hike into Mount Robson Provincial Park to scale the tallest peak of the Canadian Rockies. My parents brought my siblings and me camping, hiking and exploring the vast wilderness of Mount Robson, know as Tsyécelcten or "Mountain of the Spiral Road" to the Secwepemc People, almost every summer growing up. Now, more than twenty years later, I wanted to bring my teens to the feet of this magnificent mountain, hoping that they too would be entranced by this mammoth guardian of diverse ecosystems and headwaters of the mighty Fraser River, the biggest river in British Columbia.

"What if something happens? Like, what if someone gets gashed open or something like that?" said Claire.

"Well, both your older brother and I have wilderness first aid. Also, we have a satellite communication device. We'll have the knowledge and resources to deal with it," I replied, trying to assuage her anxious thoughts.

"Really? You don't want to go?" pipped sixteen-year-old Felix from the backseat. "It's going to be fun."

I gave Felix a sidelong look sensing he liked the idea of treating a gnarly gash.

"Can't I stay with auntie?" Claire asked, ignoring our comments and questions. "I just don't want to go."

Over the last year or two, I sensed something pulling my teenagers from "lii lway di la tayr," a Michif term for Land, the animated, spiritual and interconnected being of water, earth, air, and sky that encompasses all plants, animals, insects, fungi, rocks, humans (Schalla; Styres et al.). I clung to this backcountry trek like a sockeye mother battling the currents of the Fraser River determined to bring her offspring to safety.

"You'll have to come with us to Mount Robson. Your aunt won't be home, and your grandparents are out of town, too," I said as gently as I could manage. "You might be surprised by how much you like it there."

"I hope something bad happens, so we don't have to go," she threw into the universe.

A week later, the universe answered.

Two days before our departure from the Okanagan Valley of British Columbia to Mount Robson, an encroaching wildfire forced a full evacuation of Jasper National Park and the town of Jasper. Over ten thousand people were told to leave their homes in the middle of the night, and the road to Mount Robson closed indefinitely. When I broke the news to my teens, Claire smirked, and Felix scowled.

"Your wish came true," said Felix, pointing his thick finger towards Claire.

"I kind of wanted to go," she said, trying to appease her older brother.

"Ya, whatever, I don't believe you," came his reply. I felt the same way. I wanted to believe she had reconsidered, but I sensed more relief than loss.

I spent the day trying to pivot. Between the 435 fires burning across British Columbia that July and reservations made months in advance, there were no easy alternatives. After making a hasty reservation at Manning Provincial Park, only to realize that the Eastgate entrance, which we would have to drive through, was also on evacuation alert, I finally relinquished my efforts and sat glumly on the patio feeling crushed.

"Look what I made," said Claire, thrusting her hand into my gloomy thoughts.

Expertly braided circlets of leafy willow branch graced her finger and wrist.

"I love our willow tree," she said. "Did you see that I hung a hammock in its branches?"

This Claire I knew, the one mesmerized by spiderlings and entranced by the obsidian angular legs of a black-widow spider. The child that only a few years earlier penned a poem about spiders:

Little Spider
by Claire Bergeron (age eleven)

We coward over little spider,
not knowing how he cowards over us.
While he hides all day,
creeping away,
looking for things to do.
We play all day keeping away,
from little spider and his web of glue,
How ironic what we do.

I wanted this version of Claire to stay forever, but I knew a contradiction stood in front of me. No longer a friend of spiderlings, fourteen-year-old Claire declared she hated spiders a year ago. A teenager wreathed in willow yet disgusted by most creepy-crawlies. The chrysalis of her nature-connected childhood had split open—a fissure.

In early spring, I had spoken to Sean Blenkinsop, professor in the Faculty of Education and Codirector of Imaginative Education Research Group at Simon Fraser University, about how his philosophical approach to education could help families coparent with nature for a parenting book I'm writing. Near the end of our chat, I offhandedly asked him about teenagers and nature, and his answer surprised me: "There's a pre-adolescent psychological split that occurs, when youth realize that a relational way of being with nature is weird according to our culture. They must choose a belonging. Belong with the natural world or belong with a group of human beings (peers)."

Rationally, my brain understood this information. This reorientation made sense from an evolutionary perspective. Our ancestors depended on each other for survival, being rejected from the tribe meant not only ostracization but death. Teenagers become increasingly aware of being part of *the tribe*, or not. If today's adolescents find spiders "scary" and backcountry adventures "boring," no matter how much nature they were steeped in during childhood, a disconnection from nature will occur. In fact, Miles Richardson, professor of human factors and nature connectedness at the University of Derby, discovered that a decrease in connection with nature starts around the age of seven and hits a low point in mid-adolescence, earning the name the "teenage dip" in nature connectedness, or nature relationship (Price). To protect themselves, teenagers knot the umbilical cord between Land and themselves, choking a reciprocal flow of health and wellbeing.

Logically, I want to accept, but my hands pick at the knot trying to restore flow. My maternal heart won't let go. Like watching a toddler fall onto the hard ground, out of arm's reach, time slows, but I can't stop the hurt from happening. My hands don't move quickly enough and instead strangle myself in self-accusations: I should have known better. What could I have done differently? Could I have stopped this from happening? Can it be undone?

Later that day, I spotted Claire's small frame cocooned in blue nylon fabric high up the tree. She swayed back and forth, floating among wispy willow branches caught up in gusting westerlies—a protective chrysalis against the world's anxieties. Eventually, like a newly born butterfly, she will have to crawl out of the cracked chrysalis and hang her wings to extend and dry. Her childhood identity will merge with new possible identities, new narratives. This process takes time. Two hours for butterflies. How long for teenagers? I can already see it taking place with Felix at sixteen.

Looking up at Claire swinging in the tree made me want to wrap my arms around her delicate frame, tuck flowers into that honey brown hair, and carry her to safety, but new wings are delicate. Rough handling, even with good intent, could cause a crinkle which could be catastrophic. I have seen it happen before.

In 2021, when Felix and Claire were thirteen and eleven, I purchased a painted lady butterfly larvae kit. I wanted them to experience the bewitching magic of metamorphosis up close. The rearing kit came with eight little caterpillars and all the food they would need to enter the pupal stage. We set up these little caterpillars in our living room, protected by a soft mesh flight cage, which the caterpillars clung to in their chrysalis form. After a week, the chrysalis turned transparent, wiggled around, and birthed orange and brown butterflies with dots of white on their wing tips. My children marvelled at these winged insects, until they spotted something amiss. Not all the butterflies' wings extended.

A newly born butterfly must climb up and allow its wings to hang and fill with blood. If something stops this process from happening, the wing will harden into a crumpled mess.

"What happened to those wings?" Claire pointed to the struggling painted lady.

"I don't know," I said honestly. "Sometimes a butterfly can't straighten its wings properly. Maybe this butterfly couldn't climb up to straighten its wings or the wings got damaged somehow."

Claire bit her lip. I wondered if perhaps she had tried to help the butterfly emerge, but an accusation at this point wouldn't help.

"Can it be fixed?" asked Felix. He has always been my hands-on, figure-out-how-it-works, and fix-it child.

"Unfortunately, it can't," I said sadly. "The wings are stuck that way."

"What will happen to the butterfly?" said Claire, a watery film glazing her eyes.

I suspected she already knew the answer, but I said it anyway. "It will be released outside with the other butterflies. Maybe we can place it on special flowers in our garden. It won't live long."

This scene played through my memory as I watched Claire cocoon in the willow tree, perfectly perched, fully trusting the willow to support her. The tree held her without judgment, leaves flickering in the wind, soothing. The willow reached out to me, showing me how to hold space for my teenager so that when she emerges from the chrysalis, her wings can extend unrestricted.

The fires continued to rage in Jasper National Park, destroying 358 structures in the historic town of Jasper. Information about the devastation rolled endlessly on the news while accusations filled the air like thick wildfire smoke. Did the federal government, which oversees the park, do enough forest management and fire mitigation to prevent this catastrophe? Was this devastation a symptom of climate change? Droughts, pine beetles, winds, storms, lightning... fire. I worried this extreme fire would push my teens further from the mountains, filling their hearts with anxiety about our planet, ecoanxiety, but instead of anxiety something even more concerning came forth: apathy. Both Felix and Claire seemed unphased by the explosive Jasper wildfire complex.

"Forests need to burn. It's natural. It's sad that the city burned though," said Felix, one afternoon when the topic came up. "Is it because of climate change?" he rattled on. "Ya, maybe. I don't know, but I'm not that worried. I think we should be aware of climate change, and do stuff, but panicking isn't going to help."

Claire echoed Felix, "Forests burn, it's normal. Why is everyone freaking out? I don't get it. They blame climate change for everything, but they don't really care about nature. Is climate change real? Does it matter? People don't do anything about it anyways."

Huh. Where did that come from?

I wondered if living in the Okanagan Valley, often labelled Smokanagan, because of the wildfires that burn our forests regularly, resulted in my teenagers' wildfire apathy, but it went deeper than that. When I pressed my teens for more of their thoughts, to find out how they felt about climate change in general, they shrugged at the conversation. They did not care. I almost wondered if they believed climate change existed.

The perception that teenagers are enthusiastic environmental activists, the likes of Greta Thunburg who made headlines for school strikes for climate in 2019, doesn't always hold true. While teens seem to be more aware of environmental issues compared to past generations (my teens know more about climate change than I did at their age), they tend to be less concerned and motivated to take personal proenvironmental actions (Wray-Lake et al.; Lehnert et al.). My teens included. When I prompted them to consider actions they could take, they gave me blank stares and walked away. It's as if they emerged from the protected chrysalis of their nature-connected childhood with wet and crumpled wings, and I worried that they would dry that way. After all, those leading the kaleidoscope are also maimed. Most adults today believe that climate change is real but feel powerless to make change (Eise; Tyson).

In late August, one month after wildfires sabotaged our backcountry plans at Mount Robson, I drove my children north to my hometown of Prince George, British Columbia. From there, we prepared for a three-day backpacking hike into Sugarbowl-Grizzly Den Provincial Park, an area covered in thick old growth cedar, hemlock, and spruce forests that capitulate to sweeping alpine meadows and rocky ridges.

In the week leading up to our hike, I braced myself for teenage resistance, extreme weather, and wildfire events. I watched Felix and Claire from a distance, noting their body language when the topic of our adventure came up. Strangely, no complaints came forth. I kept an eye on the weather and on wildfire reports, but no extreme events popped up. The night before our adventure, I held my breath waiting, watching, and expecting something to happen, but nothing occurred. As my brother-in-law, who would be joining us along with my sister, their toddler, and his father, laid out strict weight restrictions on the snacks my teenagers could bring, Felix and Claire didn't complain. They weighed their allotted three hundred grams of trail mix, one hundred grams of dried fruit, and six granola bars each, laughing and joking throughout.

What's going on here? Why are my teens so jovial about this upcoming trek, especially knowing they had a limited number of snacks (a teen's worst nightmare!).

A mixture of suspicion, hope, and anticipation swirled in my belly making it difficult to sleep that night.

At the trailhead, an hour-and-a-half east of Prince George, my teenagers heaved heavy packs onto their backs. Claire raked her neon pink fingernails through her hair, trying to fix the part while giving me a metallic grin. Hair in place, she joined stride with Felix and entered the thick verdant forest, moving deftly along the overgrown trail.

Despite the expected rain, and the weight they carried, my teenagers walked along the trail with an energetic anticipation I could only describe as joy. I could hear the swish of ostrich ferns, thimbleberry, and blueberry bushes against their coats as they scaled the increasingly steep and rocky path through towering spruce trees. With each step, space increased between us. At first, I could hear snippets of shared stories siphon through the branches, but soon these were swallowed by the forest. Another soundscape emerged. One filled with raindrops bouncing off the devil's club and the trickle of streamlets connecting our footsteps through the mud. Theirs, then mine. My mother's heart wanted to run ahead and to hold them close. Instead, I allowed space to emerge between us, remembering my father's lessons.

My father, a Red River Métis, showed me how to love Land, not in words but in actions. As a child, we walked through forests without maps, followed creeks down ravines, and stomped through snow covered trails.

He showed me how to skin a road-killed fox in our backyard shed, find wild blueberries along trails, and suck nectar from Indian paintbrush flowers. Most importantly, he encouraged me to go outside in all seasons, giving me space to connect with nature on my own. I needed to do the same with my teenagers and trust in *lii lway di la tayr* to show them the way.

The steep trek up to Raven Lake took longer than planned. The constant rain turned the root-bound rocky path into a slippery maze for our feet, forcing us to move slowly. What should have taken us two-and-a-half hours turned into four. Those four hours of difficult hiking offered plenty to complain about, but my teenagers remained stoic and engaged.

Over the next three days in the backcountry, I witnessed a reorientation. My teenagers settled into Land, remembering their unique ways of relating. At the top of the mountain, Claire stooped over. Initially thinking she had stopped to tie her boot; I noticed white rocks cradled in her hands.

"Look at this quartz," she said, awe in her voice.

She had come across a vein of exposed white quartz on the ridge of Raven Peak. A kilometer past she discovered bumblebees napping in wildflowers. Later that day, my teens dove into the icy waters of Raven Lake, played with abandon in a trickling creek surrounded by purple wild monkshood, and watched the sun set over alpine peaks. Rocks found their way into pockets where smartphones usually sit, and my smartphone, which I carried for taking photos only, filled with hundreds of pictures of flowers, insects, and sunsets taken by Claire.

Three days in the mountains, I wanted to stay longer but the end of August meant back to school and back to overfilled schedules. On our descent from Raven Lake on the third day, I asked my teens, "What was your favourite part of our time in the mountains?"

"The sunsets," said Claire.

"The rocks," said Felix. "You know," he went on, "We should do this again next month and bring friends next time. It would be good for them."

Felix's reflection hinted at a truth recently recognized by researchers. Contact and connection with nature has a positive impact on adolescents' health and wellbeing (Arola et al.). I saw this reality unfold firsthand watching my teens touch, breath, taste, and know the mountains they traversed. They seemed happier and more grounded, for the moment.

Would this experience draw them closer to *lii lway di la tayr*? Will it strengthen their wings for flight? Would it propel them into a renewed connection with nature? Will it make them care more about Land?

I knew a single tryst into the forest wouldn't immediately heal their growing disconnection from nature, yet I hoped it would spur a remembering in their hearts. A longing, a desire, to swap out screens for spruce trees. To seek out songbirds and sunsets. To climb above the din of social media doom scrolling into the sun and let wings unfurl and strengthen for flight. When we returned home, my teens fell into familiar patterns bereft of nature. Curious to see if anything had changed, I asked Felix about his closeness to Land: "Uh, well, I guess I feel weird just being outside with nothing to do, like there has to be a purpose to going out. I have to be doing something. When I was younger, I would just play outside or sit in a tree. I don't really do that anymore. It feels weird. I guess I don't have time. Nature isn't easy to get to... you know."

I didn't know. From my perspective, Felix had time and access to nature. I asked Claire the same question: "I don't know. I feel like my relationship with nature is kind of similar. I'm still curious. I still like looking at all the little things. I guess I'm not in nature as much. I'm not touching it and playing with it much anymore. I mean I want to, but I guess most of my friends don't just go out and play with mud like little kids anymore." She chuckled.

On the Sunday before the start of the school year, I brought my teens to a small stream just south of Peachland, British Columbia. It's a well-known spawning area, and the first salmon were making their way upstream. We watched the salmon swimming, scales faded to reveal bright red.

"Maman, we do this every year," Felix complained as he peeked over the bridge and watched the salmon with fascination.

I saw myself in those sockeye mothers, in the struggle of the stream, in the mother's sacrifice to bring her offspring home and then letting go.

"Let's do this again," Felix's words sit on my heart. When I return home, I open my computer and type the words "Spectrum Lake Backcountry Hike" into the search bar.

Works Cited

Arola, T., et al. "The Impacts of Nature Connectedness on Children's Well-Being: Systematic Literature Review." *Journal of Environmental Psychology*, vol. 85, 2023, https://doi.org/10.1016/j.jenvp.2022.101913.

Blinkensop, Sean. Personal interview. 23 Mar. 2024.

Eise, Jessica. "Americans Love Nature but Don't Feel Empowered to Protect It, New Research Shows." *The Conversation*, 28 Aug. 2024, theconversation.com/americans-love-nature-but-dont-feel-empowered-to-protect-it-new-research-shows-231256. Accessed 15 Mar. 2025.

Lehnert, M., et al. "Czech Students and Mitigation of Global Warming: Beliefs and Willingness to Take Action." *Environmental Education Research*, vol. 26, no, 6, 2019, pp. 864–89.

Price, E., et al. Factors Associated with Nature Connectedness in School-Aged Children." *Current Research in Ecological and Social Psychology*, vol. 3, 2022, https://doi.org/10.1016/j.cresp.2022.100037.

Schalla, M. "Metis Relationality of lii lway di la tayr through the Teachings of Interconnectedness and Balance." *Pawaatamihk: Journal of Métis Thinkers*, vol. 1, no. 2, 2024, pp. 171–74.

Styres, S., et al. "Towards a Pedagogy of Land: The Urban Context." *Canadian Journal of Education*, vol. 36, no. 2, 2013, pp. 34–67.

Tyson, Alec. "What the Data Says about Americans' Views of Climate Change." *Pew Research Center*, Pew Research Center, 9 Aug. 2023, www.pewresearch.org/short-reads/2023/08/09/what-the-data-says-about-americans-views-of-climate-change/. Accessed 15 Mar. 2025.

Wray-Lake, L., et al. "Examining Trends in Adolescent Environmental Attitudes, Beliefs, and Behaviors Aaross Three Decades. Environment and Behavior." *Environment and Behavior*, vol. 42, no. 1, 2010, pp. 61–85.

13.

Healing the Blame and Shame in Motherhood: Tokens of Resistance

Vanessa Marr

Tokens of Resistance

We live in a world where society's expectations of mothers have never been so extreme; perfectionism trends mask patriarchal and misogynistic constructs that hold mothers answerable for every element of their children's wellbeing, often well into adulthood. This pressure to be perfect hurts new mothers who struggle under the weight of unachievable goals while mothers of older children are often weighed down with regret. As a mother of four daughters aged from their teens to thirties, I've experienced these pressures keenly. They have come not just through media and society but also from my children themselves as they've transitioned from viewing me as the all-powerful centre of their world towards (I hope) accepting me as a mere mortal who has messed up sometimes.

Knowing Motherhood through Creative Research Practice

As a practice-based scholar and autoethnographer, I have created artwork to know these experiences inwardly (Marr) while enticing change-making conversations outwardly (Ellis). I've engaged in this methodology practically (Gray and Mallins), reflexively, vulnerably (Bochner and Ellis), imaginatively (Metta), creatively, and with feminist intent (Acker et al.) to challenge the construct of my society that sets mothers up for perceived failure through unachievable expectations. Autoethnography provides a means of 'manoeuvring through [the] pain, confusion, anger and uncertainty' (Holman Jones et al. 34) of mothering and in breaking the silence surrounding the invisible pressures myself and others experience.

I use craft, stories, and socially motivated research to make sense of the world around me and critically engage with carefully chosen cloth objects that reflect the historical or cultural context pertinent to the theme. Other research I've completed through this method includes a collaborative community project embroidering yellow dusting cloths (Marr) to challenge gendered domestic inequalities because as culturally gendered objects (Kirkham), these cloths share the invisibility of housework and care. I've also used embroidery to tell personal stories, for example, a stitched illustration of my womb documenting my first period, births, traumas, and various medical procedures on a vintage dressing tablecloth to make sense of a surgical menopause and full hysterotomy (Fig. 1); and a series of work on vintage tray cloths exploring the conflicting expectations that society imposes upon mothers for Andrea O'Reilly's 2023 book *Normative Motherhood* by Demeter Press.

Figure 1. Womb diary. Vintage textile, embroidered by the author, 2020.

The work discussed here was inspired by the tokens left by mothers at the Foundling Hospital in London from 1739 to 1955, an experience I relate to because I was a young mother whose fate could so easily have been the same had I been born a generation or so earlier. Creating each piece has been an act of embodied healing and resistance against the blame and shame that have been constant shadows in my mothering experience. They embody the story of how I became a mother, how I was mothered myself, and have been a means of navigating this new phase of motherhood I now find myself in. They are a tangible reminder of my children's love for me, an affirmation of mine for them, an apology to my mother, and an act of resistance against dominant patriarchal narratives that can lead us to forget that a mother's love is always there, even when blame and shame get in the way.

Treasures

I visited the London Foundling Museum, formerly the Foundling Hospital, in 2023; it made me cry. They have boxes and boxes of tokens given by mothers as a means of identifying the babies they were forced to give up so that one day they could come back and claim them. They rarely did. The tokens are scraps of cloth, buttons, beads, a conker, and a coin. They are worthless but also beyond worth, embodied as they are with the meanings they hold. Reflecting on that visit, I was drawn to the things I've held onto, a reverse token of sorts. These are the treasured gifts from when I was my children's everything and the unconditional focus of their affection. My treasures include homemade bracelets made from plastic, coloured children's beads, a teddy bear pin gifted to me one Mother's Day (Figure 2), a drawing traced from a pile of pictures I've saved for over twenty years (Figure 3), and a remembered necklace made from pasta tubes (Figure 4).

Figure 2. Tokens of resistance: a homemade bracelet made from children's beads and a teddy bear pin. The bracelets remind me of their small hands slowly threading bead after bead onto a gift that I treasure more than any gold.

Figure 3. A drawing from my daughter from when she was six. She is now thirty-two. I discovered this phrase repeated over and over again in the pile of cards and pictures that I'd saved. It embodies the reassurance I wanted her to carry into adulthood: the knowledge my love is there, no matter what.

HEALING THE BLAME AND SHAME IN MOTHERHOOD

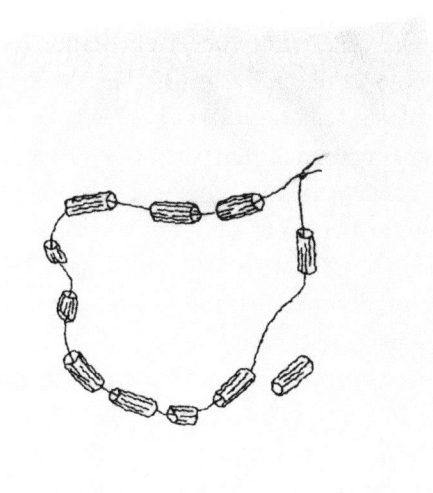

Figure 4. A remembered pasta necklace. All my daughters made these at preschool playgroup; they are coloured pasta tubes held on a string that flaked paint and glitter everywhere from the moment they were thrust around my neck. Sadly, they all have since disintegrated, so this is a memory, a moment recreated, now held in time.

As my children have grown into adulthood and forged their paths in the world, I have clung to these tokens of the love that I've saved. I have done so not to hold my daughters back, for I want them to be the strong independent women I've raised them to be, but because through the process of their detachment, I've experienced what some psychoanalysts call "matricide" (Stone), the murder of the mother, a notion also rooted in Greek mythology. This is not a murder in a physical sense but a breaking away. It is forced estrangement by the grown-up child towards the mother, which has been my experience more than once. I say this with great shame and difficulty, deleting and retyping the words several times. I blame myself, of course I do. This is not an experience of motherhood that I was prepared for. It is shameful to admit.

In 2023, I met other mothers who had or did still experience the same rejection at the annual Museum of Motherhood (MOM) conference, held in Florida, US, which was themed around healing the blame and shame sometimes associated with motherhood. They, like me, are good mothers.

We care deeply about our children. We kept them warm and nourished and as safe as we could while they grew despite hardships. These teens and young people were, and are still cherished, so why, we all asked, have they pushed us so firmly away? Why have they chosen to give us up? One mother recounted how she no longer recognized her twenty-year-old daughter because her behaviour towards her was so far from the way she'd brought her up to be; I felt the same. Another shared how they'd now come out the other side, but she still couldn't explain it. We were all hurt and confused. Where had it all gone so wrong? It was a relief to be in a space where the shame and blame we carried everywhere, a burden that weighed us down and interrupted our every thought, could be safely shared for a few days without judgment. Where we could find solace and hope in each other.

Donald Winnicott writes of the good enough mother, suggesting that tolerable failure by one's mother helps one to function in an imperfect society. Maybe we were trying too hard? Perhaps the messages sold to the generation of girls I belonged to had become confused with our mothering. We were told that we were the first women who could do and become anything we liked, but there was a silent catch. We had to do it perfectly, exceptionally, and relentlessly. The women at the conference and I were all high (perhaps over) achievers. Success for us looks like the outcomes of our labour being exceptional and praiseworthy, so when those outcomes are our children who then say we have done everything wrong, the roots go deep and beyond our mothering. They reach the value we place on our very own selves. Perhaps we need to give ourselves a break and care for ourselves just as much as for our children—to allow ourselves to be good enough.

Embroidering Resistance and Resilience

I've titled this work *Tokens of Resistance*, capturing the spirit of craftivism (Greer) and embroidery as an act of feminist emancipation (Parker) because making each one has been an act of love, memory, and personal activism that helps me move beyond the blame. As Roszita Parker writes in her seminal book *The Subversive Stitch*, "Feminists in their embroidery showed that the personal was the political—that personal and domestic life is as much the product of the institutions and ideologies of our society as is public life" (205). Embroidery is my primary methodology; it is my means of thinking and coming to know and understand the challenges I face as a woman, mother, and academic. Through this process of quiet contemplation, observation, and reflection, I embody experiences and memories with stitches that tell stories and entice conversations with other women, building a solidarity of experience uniting us.

I often refer to my embroidery as drawing with thread or stitch because it is more than the skill of embellishment (Goggin and Tobin), more than mark-making with my needle for representation; it is a means of capturing the experience of all and everything that it means to be me. As David Rosand writes on the phenomenology of drawing, "The drawing asserts itself as the main object of concern, the primary other in the subject-object relation" (13). In my case, stitch as a mode of drawing asserts itself and the meaning of the object and the subject of the experience I attach to it take over as the main object of concern.

It takes hours to complete every line with my needle and thread, and as I do so, the words or images forming on the cloth repeat in my head. It is a mediative and healing experience. It is an embodiment of conscious and unconscious knowledge held in each thread, covered in the DNA that I share with my daughters. Creating this work has made a space, literally and figuratively, to hold the complex combination of love, hope, and pain that this phase of motherhood brings. Letting go, whilst still being there to soothe, support, encourage and pick up the pieces is a challenging conundrum. It's a reality that hits you in the face as you struggle to find a new way of keeping them safe, a monster that creeps into your dreams as you wait for the click of the door when they return late from a party, an absence in a bedroom now deserted, and a hole in your heart when they push you away. It is also joy when they flourish, a comfort when they return (albeit often briefly), and moments of pride fit to burst as the wonderful human that grew in your body steps bright and brilliant into the unknown. My stitches hold all of this. Each piercing of cloth is a hole my heart, each tug of thread a hope, each line of thread a memory; each reproduction a connection to mothers the world over who have and do and will experience the same.

Blame and Shame

Becoming a mother when I was very young was (apparently) shameful, being a mother in an abusive marriage was difficult, being a single mother was hard, building a stepfamily and having another child with my new husband was challenging, but nothing prepared me for rejection by my grown-up child. Give me sleepless nights, no time for myself, and the endless pressure of being all and everything to my children. Anything other than this.

There is much talk of and advice for new mothers, and rightly so, and some about mothering teenagers, but little for those of us whose children are in their twenties. It's not empty nest syndrome. I have plenty to fill my time, and my youngest daughter from my second marriage is still in her teens; it is the utter black desolation when I have been cut out and blamed for things beyond my control. I need to learn to bear this, to build myself back up so that when she returns, I am ready for her. The only way I know how is to stitch myself some hope.

Reflecting on this blame and shame, I've also stitched fragments of text onto pieces of handkerchief that embody the internal monologue of my mothering experience. These words have come from notes I've typed into my phone, as is my habit when my mind wanders while I'm stitching. Warnings, pleas, reflections, and memories—the things I cannot say out loud:

Figure 5. "Bite my tongue." A note to self: Do not react if she says something hurtful.

Figure 6. "Your silence is deafening." The thing I dare not say in case I make it worse.

Figure 7. "Tell me where it hurts." I long to make it better, to hold you.

Figure 8. "I hold you as a lump in my throat." You are always here. I am close to tears. I still hold you.

Healing Objects

Sherry Turkle's book *Evocative Objects* explores our human relationships with objects as a positive force in our lives because they connect us through memory to experiences and people that have been significant to us. Turkle's analysis of the object-self relationships explores how the defamiliarization of an object through theory helps us to "extend the reach of our inner sympathies" (307) towards it. In other words, our relationship with an object evolves to become something more than it first appeared to be because we bring theoretical knowledge to how we think about and engage with it. Her theory that objects are things we think with provides the basis for a framework informing how I engage in my research method because she connects our human need for meaning and story to these inanimate things we share our lives with.

I chose lace handkerchiefs to hold this work about the complex history of handkerchiefs as a token of memory and endearment (Mirabella) and because many of the tokens left at the Foundling Hospital were cloth, too. As a simple cotton square, edged with lace but intended for the dirty task of blowing one's nose, a handkerchief embodies the messy labour and beautiful joy of motherhood. It is feminine, historically precious, and nostalgic. I am old enough to have been gifted them by my Granny as something special but young enough to use tissues myself instead. They hark back to a previous time and, in doing so, hold memories of times gone by that were precious to me, too.

Breaking the Cycle

I also asked my mother for a token. She sent me a photo of my baby dress she'd saved for over fifty years. We've had our challenges, too, but stitching the outline of that dress (Figure 9) and the hours it took helped remind me of her love for me, as imperfect as it may be, as is my own. Blame and shame have travelled down family lines from my grandmother to her mother, too.

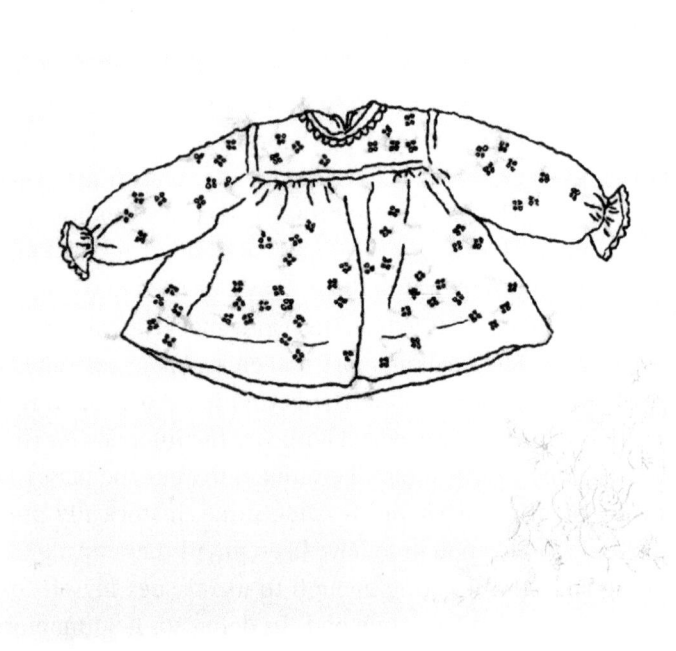

Figure 9. My baby dress, saved by my mother.

I am determined to break this cycle, and so in hope for the future, and having discovered that granny-knitting was a force of nature when my eldest gave birth a couple of years ago, I've traced the crocheted square I made for my granddaughter's blanket in chain stitch (Figure 10), mirroring the legacy of all the other grandmothers who have done the same, binding my love into every stitch.

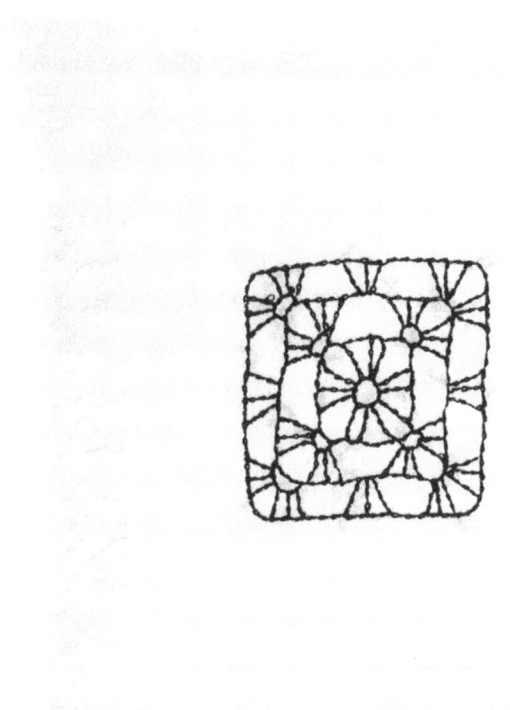

Figure. 10. A crochet square. Remembering the blanket knitted for my granddaughter.

Stitching my mothering autoethnographically has provided an intellectual, rigorous, emotional, and creative framework where I can "name and interrogate" these "intersections between [my] self and society, the particular and the general, the personal and the political" (Adams et al. 2). My story is my own, but in this context it bears witness to the lives of others too, creating change both for myself and for other women, and acknowledging our need to be visible and valued as our children grow into adulthood. This is my motivation and my everyday reality; I hope this will be enough to grow some new threads of connection.

Works Cited

Acker, Joan., et al. "Objectivity and Truth: Problems in Doing Feminist Research." *Women's Studies International Forum,* vol. 6, no. 4, 1983, pp. 423–35.

Adams, Tony, et al. *Autoethnography: Understanding Qualitative Research.* Oxford, 2015.

Bochner, Arthur, and Carolyn Ellis. "An Introduction to the Arts and Narrative Research: Art as Inquiry." *Qualitative Inquiry,* vol. 9, no. 4, 506–14. https://doi.org/10.1177/1077800403254394. Accessed 23 Mar. 2025.

Ellis, Carolyn. *The Ethnographic I.* Altamira Press, 2004.

Gray, Carole, and Julian Mallins. *Visualising Research: A Guide to the Research Process in Art & Design.* Routledge, 2004.

Greer, Betsy. *Craftivism.* Arsenal Pulp Press, 2014.

Goggin, Maureen Daly, Beth Fowkes Tobin, editors. *Women and the Material Culture of Needlework and Textiles, 1750–1950.* Ashgate Publishing, 2009.

Holman Jones, Stacy, et al. *Handbook of Autoethnography.* Routledge, 2013.

Kirkham, Pat, ed. *The Gendered Object.* Manchester University Press, 1996.

Marr, Vanessa. "Drawing with Thread Upon a Duster: A Phenomenological Investigation of Female Domestic Experience." *Tracey,* vol. 14, no. 1, 2019, https://ojs.lboro.ac.uk/TRACEY/issue/view/208. Accessed 23 Mar. 2025.

Marr, Vanessa. "Stitch-Drawing (a Duster) as Autoethnographic Practice for Health and Wellbeing: A Personal Case." *Manual Drawing in Health and Wellbeing: Marks, Signs, and Traces.* Edited by Philippa Lyon and Curie Scott. Bloomsbury, 2025, pp. 179–98.

Marr, Vanessa. "The Domestic Academic." *Storying the Self.* Edited by Ross Adamson and Jess Moriarty. Intellect Books, 2023, pp. 89–105.

Metta, Marilyn. *Writing Against, Alongside and Beyond Memory.* Peter Lang. 2010.

Mirabella, Bella. "Embellishing Herself with a Cloth: The Contradictory

Life of The Handkerchief." Ornamentalism: The Art of Renaissance Accessories. Edited by Bella Mirabella, University of Michigan Press, 2011, pp. 59–82.

Parker, Roszita. *The Subversive Stitch*. Tauris & Co. Ltd, 1984.

Rosand, D. *Drawing Acts: Studies in Graphic Expression and Representation*. Cambridge University Press, 2002.

Stone, Alison. "Against Matricide: Rethinking Subjectivity and the Maternal Body." *Hypatia*, vol. 27, no. 1, 2012, pp. 118–38.

Turkle, Sherry. *Evocative Objects: The Things We Think With*. MIT Press, 2007.

Winnicott, Donald. "Transitional Objects and Transitional Phenomena." *The International Journal of Psychoanalysis*, no. 34, 1953, pp. 89–97.

Epilogue

Maya E. Bhave, Talia Esnard, and Kae Solomon

As we reflect on this completed volume, we are thankful, first and foremost, to Andrea O'Reilly for spearheading the call regarding work on mothers and emerging adults and for bringing us as editors together. We enjoyed the chance to read, evaluate, and analyze the work of women and mothers from around the globe. Our Zoom meetings would often start slowly, and then one of us would jump upon a comment made by a contributing author. We would all start talking—from different social, racial, and professional locations—about the value of the idea and how it related to us as mothers. These episodic moments were invigorating and stimulating for us as co-editors and authors. Thus, creating this volume was an exciting and collaborative process. We feel honoured to have these contributions in this co-edited volume. In every way, the submissions deepened and extended the conversations on maternal thinking, action, and scholarship.

Matricentric feminist research has come a long way since Adrienne Rich's pivotal work *Of Woman Born: Motherhood as Experience and Institution* (1986). Thankfully, O'Reilly's scholarly leadership within the matricentric community has brought the field to new heights. Yet, as mothers, writers, and readers, we know there is always more to be done—gaps to be filled and more problems to be solved. The contributors here significantly add to the complexity, breadth, and width of the ever-growing matricentric literature. Through their contributions, they address some of those gaps, including eco disconnect, non-proximate, e-mothering, tiger mothering, mothering and neurodiversity, as well as racialized understandings of teenagers' lives, and abuse by teens.

What is most significant, however, is this volume's contextual discussion, which remains paramount as to how we advance maternal scholarship. The multilayered relationship between human thought, social context, and the effects of such knowledge on society affects the lives of mothers, as well as the social location of that knowledge and the behaviour that follows from it. The contributors show that regardless of whether we are examining emotional and social narcissism of mothering, non-proximate mothering, cross-cultural analyses, or maternal expectations vis-a-vis their reality, mothers deeply analyze and think about the fluidity and complexity of their mothering roles.

We see the microlevel issues and analyses, which remain central to this volume, as a critical aspect of advancing these conversations and representations of motherhood. This is particularly so given that mothering literature has often been dominated and bounded by broad and overarching academic theories, frameworks, and analyses. While this type of work is necessary to advance the frameworks being developed and applied to shape this burgeoning field, we also see the need for diverse levels of analyses with attention to spatial and temporal complexities. This volume advances these maternal perspectives and their contextualization. The volume makes visible some of the taken-for-granted, uncomfortable, and disruptive experiences that mothers encounter in their daily lives and how they shape what emerges as an intimate and deeply contextual type of maternal thinking. We show through the volume not just the reality around how they think about their mothering experiences, which are often captured in hidden, emotional, intimate, and meaningful ways, but also the contexts wherein and through which these experiences unfold.

To some extent, this type of analysis is reflected within the current mothering literature. O'Reilly has recently argued that mommy lit has grown over the last few years yet notes that too often this discourse "ultimately reinscribes, or more accurately naturalizes and normalizes, the very patriarchal conditions of motherhood that feminists, including the motherhood memoir writers themselves, seek to dismantle" ("Motherhood Memoir" 481). This statement certainly alludes to the social and cultural relevance of maternal experience. O'Reilly also argues that we must push beyond such frameworks to see structural and familial inequities within mothering and offer more critiques of new momism. Examples of this kind of research can be found in O'Reilly's edited volume entitled *Maternal Regret: Resistances, Renunciations and Reflections*. Here we find deeply revealing, open, creative essays by Kanchan Tripathi in which the author writes about her mother who regretted having the author as a child, and Jessica Jennrich's piece, in which she ponders what she would have told her twenty-year-old self, who grew up as a daughter with a violent mother.

Additionally, we find an intimate analysis of mothering in Andrea O'Reilly and Fiona Green's edited volume on mothering during COVID-19. Here, we see Haile Eshe Cole's diary and memoir essay on the stress of caregiving as a mother during the pandemic. Cole writes vividly and explicitly about the stressors of illness, worry, and exhaustion for her and her children. Similarly, we see the complexity of how mothering affects women's personal lives in the 2018 poem by Adrianne Kalfopoulou. In this powerful, short poem, the author struggles to make sense of raising an eight-year-old daughter while navigating her failing intimate relationship with an unnamed male companion. Such pieces point to similar themes shown in this edited current volume, such as emotional and social narcissism of mothering, non-proximate mothering, cross-cultural analyses, and maternal expectations vis-a-vis their reality. Yet, there is still a need for more of these creative and intimate pieces. O'Reilly calls writers to be more critical, daring, and innovative. She pleads that memoir authors must "bite the hand that feeds them" ("Motherhood Memoir" 488). Mothers must address issues that are often unspoken, difficult, and messy. This current edited volume does just that. It centers these intimate stories and thus is a fresh, innovative step toward what O'Reilly is asking motherhood studies to do.

As such, this volume on mothering emerging adults brings intimate voices to subjects—such as neurodiversity, various levels of maternal loss, and abuse—into the motherhood canon in ways never seen before. We see this in the empirical pieces but even more clearly in the creative ones. Seemingly, the opportunity for mothers to reveal through creative essays, memoirs, poetry and hybrid pieces the depth of their joy, coupled with deep pain, is what we believe to be the beauty and uniqueness of this volume. These experiences capture the ways in which these emotional and perceptual responses are rooted in the relational dynamics between mothers and daughters and, by extension, how that are connected to broader constructions of social relations and connections. It is these relational, micro level aspects, and processes that collectively demonstrate that we are not alone as mothers, and that in fact, that sharing these deep thoughts and emotions help not only to understand and locate ourselves as individuals, but as social beings within the structural and relational spaces that we occupy. Thus, while we recognize that it is the power of our feelings and thoughts about "how" and "why" we mother that matter, we also advance the need for more scholarship that contextualizes the structures and relational conditions through which these perceptive and constructive framings of mothers and emerging adults develop. These relational and structural dynamics are critical to the advancement of maternal theorizations.

Overall, we advance a volume revealing unspoken and unpacked ways of thinking, feeling, and responding to mothering thinking and expectations. We see these complexities as significant within the advancement of motherhood studies. In this case, the volume also breaks the usual tide of academic expression by including creative pieces about maternal thinking, expression, and questioning. These elements of academic expression and resistance have allowed mothers and writers to communicate authentically to their own experiences, relevant to their cultural and relational expressions, and beyond the confines of accepted communication or written form. It has also assisted mothers in their search for ways of being, seeing, experiencing, and responding outside the confines of social isomorphic parameters. By so doing, the volume situates and celebrates the value of creative expression as meaningful and provocative ways of communicating and adding to not just the scholarship on maternal thought and practice but also the practice of resisting and advocating for change around these. These represent powerful messages and expressions of emotions and actions tied to oppressive lived realities that need greater exploration, visibility, deconstruction, and resistance. These are also important to highlight the significance of language, culture, and expression and the connection of all of these to politicized contexts. These contributions are also necessary to elucidate the social construction of maternal knowledge through expression, meaning, practice, and experience.

Although the volume has merit and value, we believe that there are still several areas that need to be investigated further:

1. Contextual or situated mothering. While the contributions in this volume show some common ways of thinking and working through maternal experience, they also suggest that some cultural

and social nuances need further exploration. More is needed within maternal theorizations to uncover and unpack some of the social structural foundations of maternal thought and practice and to situate the relevance of place and space, where the social and racial contexts and the meanings of practices are located to make sense of the experiences.

2. Emotive or affective aspects of mothering. Maternal literature has extensively discussed the relevance of maternal thought and praxis. Our contributors have also signalled the need for more research about the emotional and affective aspects of maternal experience, especially how mothers are impacted by motherhood.

3. Shame and grief as silenced. This emerged as one of the aspects of maternal experience centred within the stories and contributions within this volume. In some cases, shame has been storied as an internalized aspect of what it means to experience and maintain the often privatized aspects of mothering, which, unfortunately, has been normalized to create certain degrees of silence. The conversations also touch on varied understandings of what constitutes grief and how these unfold for mothers, whether based on emotional outbursts, lack of control, or silence. To some extent, these conversations have been captured in the literature on unmet expectations, voices, and representations for mothers. Although the literature has extensively addressed the normalized aspects of maternal thinking and practice, more is needed to tease through and problematize the expectations around how mothers respond to these stories, expectations, and experiences. More work is also needed to theorize how the expectations affect maternal responses, whether as a reproduction or embodiment of the thinking or as a form of resistance. More is also needed to empower more mothers and writers to boldly speak out against some of the epistemic forms of violence that follow these subtle and not-so-subtle silencers that obtain around material experience.

4. Decolonialized Representations of Mothering: The literature on maternal thinking and practice is deeply seated within Eurocentric framing and advancement. Such theorizations, however, silence the many experiences and practices existing outside of these frames of reference that affect the realities for mothers beyond

the Global North. The contributions from the Caribbean speak to the importance of the historical and colonized experiences for how mothers have been situated. The chapter on maternal scholarship in Brazil also speaks to the specificities of contexts that offer diverse insights into the field. More is needed to situate the relevance of these historical experiences across contexts and to make sense of maternal realities that are both culturally relevant and situated.

Our epilogue is not meant to be prescriptive but to discursively tease through problematic aspects of maternal thinking and experience and build on their existing theorization, contextualization, and reconstruction. Our calls for further exploration around the representation, expression, and protection of mothers unfold within a broader commitment to maternal freedoms. While we remain open to new explorations around these, we stand committed to this work and look forward to the solidarity within this intellectual and radical process.

Works Cited

Cole, Haile Eshe. "Breathe. Exhale. Repeat: A Reflection on Love, Caretaking, and COVID- 19." *Mothers, Mothering, and COVID-19: Dispatches from a Pandemic*. Edited by Andrea O'Reilly and Fiona Joy Green. Demeter Press, 2021, pp. 187–94.

Jennrich, Jessica. "Time Machine." *Maternal Regret: Resistances, Renunciations, and Reflections*. Edited by Andrea O'Reilly. Demeter Press, 2022, pp. 193–200.

Kalfopoulou, Adrianne. "Growing." *Journal of the Motherhood Initiative*, vol. 9, no. 2, 2018, p. 187.

O'Reilly, Andrea. "The Motherhood Memoir and the "New Momism": Biting the Hand That Feeds You." *In (M)other Words: Writings on Mothering and Motherhood 2009–2024*. Edited by Andrea O'Reilly. Demeter Press, 2024, pp. 479–89.

O'Reilly, Andrea. *Maternal Regret: Resistances, Renunciations, and Reflections*. Demeter Press, 2022.

O'Reilly, Andrea, and Fiona Joy Green. *Mothers, Mothering, and COVID-19: Dispatches from a Pandemic*. Demeter Press, 2021.

Rich, Adrienne. *Of Woman Born: Motherhood as Experience and Institution.* W. W. Norton and Company, 1976.

Tripathi, Kanchan. "My Mother's Story." *Maternal Regret: Resistances, Renunciations, and Reflections.* Edited by Andrea O'Reilly. Demeter Press, 2022, pp. 161-74.

Notes on Contributors

Editors

Maya E. Bhave's PhD in sociology (Loyola University, Chicago) focussed on Ethiopian immigrant women. After teaching sociology at North Park University for ten years, she moved to Vermont, where she has explored gender identity among female players in soccer; motherhood and child loss; and mothers' struggle for work-life-family balance. Her most recent book is titled *War and Cleats: Women in Soccer in the United States*. She is currently working on a book manuscript titled *Mothering College-Aged Children: Strategies and Patterns of Maternal Influence, Investment and Sustained Social Bonds*. She has taught for many years as an adjunct professor at Saint Michael's College and, most recently was a visiting assistant professor of sociology at Middlebury College.

Talia Esnard (PhD sociology) is a senior lecturer and sociologist working within the Department of Behavioural Sciences at the University of the West Indies, St. Augustine Campus, Trinidad and Tobago. As a researcher, she focusses on issues of women, work, and organizations, particularly within entrepreneurial and educational spheres. She has also published sole, co-authored, multiple-authored, and edited books on entrepreneurship, motherhood, social justice and higher education, and equity, diversity, and inclusion. She is the coeditor of the *Caribbean Educational Research Journal* (CERJ) and associate editor for the *Journal of Organizational Sociology, Gender, Work and Organization,* and the *Caribbean Journal of Multicultural Studies*. She is a past recipient of the Taiwan

Research Fellowship (2012) and the Canada-CARICOM Faculty Leadership Program (Brock University [2015] and Ryerson University [2018]).

Kae Solomon holds a master's of education from the University of British Columbia and has completed graduate studies in Creative Nonfiction at Simon Fraser University's The Writer's Studio (TWS) Program. After graduating, she worked as a teacher's assistant in this program. She has published with *Barren Magazine*, *Little Fish Magazine*, TWS's *emerge 21*, and is featured in the anthology *Don't Tell: Family Secrets*. She has completed her first memoir and is working on a second memoir and novel. Kae is also a musician and is in the process of recording an album of original songs. Kae works as an elementary teacher librarian on the unceded territory of the Musqueam, Tseil-waututh and Squamish. She lives in the Lower Mainland, British Columbia with her family.

Contributors

Victoria Bailey has a PhD in creative writing and an MA in women's studies. Her poetry has been included in a wide variety of feminist publications, including other Demeter Press anthologies. She is also a feminist mother of three.

Josée Bergeron, a Métis from British Columbia, helps parents connect with nature. Living in the Okanagan Valley with her husband and five children, she is currently writing her first parenting book, *Beyond the Front Door*. Learn more at backwoodsmama.com.

Savannah Dali is a graduate student at Texas Woman's University currently pursuing her master's in psychological science. She primarily studies the cross-disciplinary development of adolescent mental health disorders with a specific focus on the influence of mother-daughter relationships on the prognosis of disordered eating.

Teresa Cavanaugh Donkin is a recent graduate of The Writer's Studio (TWS) at Simon Fraser University. An excerpt of her creative nonfiction work appears in *emerge 24*, the annual anthology published by TWS. Teresa previously worked in New York state as a freelance journalist focussed on climate action.

Carmen G. Farrell (she/her), https://carmengfarrell.com, is a force behind community initiatives for neurodiverse youth, from elementary school through college. Her other published creative nonfiction (*Grain, filling Station,* and *The Globe & Mail*) focusses on disability and inclusion, questioning assumptions that a normal way to be with each other exists. North Vancouver is home.

Faith Flavius is a final-year undergraduate student at the University of the West Indies, double majoring in history and sociology. Studying these disciplines has enabled her to assess phenomena and situate them within their nexus of socio-historical contexts. Moreover, her lens of perception expands to a third dimension with her poetic abilities. Writing poetry for twelve years, Faith attempts to capture the raw emotions of her life and those around her. Together, she crafts the complex contextual realities of Caribbean life with a quill pen.

Isabella Iven is a specialist-level graduate student in school psychology at Texas Woman's University. She engages in research related to bilingualism in children, family-school relationships, and parent-child interactions.

Dante Jackson is a graduate counselling psychology student at Texas Woman's University. He engages in research related to the experiences of Black students majoring in STEM disciplines at HBCUs and understanding protective factors Black people use when seeking mental health services.

Irene Rocha Kalil has PhD in Health Information and Communication. She is a researcher and professor of the graduate program in Health Information and Communication at the Oswaldo Cruz Foundation, Brazil. She conducts research at the interface of gender, communication and health, and her academic research currently focuses on women's health, especially maternal mental health.

Catherine Ma (she/her/hers), MA, MPhil, PhD, is a dedicated scholar, the first Chinese full professor of psychology at Kingsborough Community College, City University of New York, a board member of the Asian American/Asian Research Institute, and cofounder of AAMPOWER (Asian American Mentorship Providing Opportunities to Women for Empowerment and Resilience).

Vanessa Marr is a principal lecturer at the University of Brighton, a senior fellow of Advanced HE, and a fellow of the Royal Society of Arts, UK. Her practice-based research uses embroidery to weave together practices of autoethnography, drawing, creative writing, and craftivism as collaborative art projects, personal artwork, and academic publications.

Maritza Marquez is a graduate counselling psychology student at Texas Woman's University. She engages in research related to transnational mothers and coping strategies, Latino/x/e youth, and feminist border theory.

Laura Rite is a final year PhD candidate at the University of Warwick, where she is researching the lived experiences of mothers who have been abused by their children. Her research focusses on social constructions, such as mother blaming and shaming, and how professional responses shape victim-survivors' help-seeking behaviours.

Lisa H. Rosen is a professor and director of the undergraduate psychology program at Texas Woman's University. Her research focusses on parent-child communication, exploring ways parents can best support victimized youth, and promoting resilience in mothers.

Linda J. Rubin is a professor of psychology and licensed psychologist at Texas Woman's University. Her research, clinical, and teaching interests target traumatic stress and violence against women. She has offered empirically-based intervention to college students who experience domestic and dating violence, sexual assault, and stalking.

Martha Silvia Martinez-Silveira has a PhD in Health Information and Communication. She is a researcher and professor of the graduate program in Clinical and Translational Research at the Oswaldo Cruz Foundation, Brazil. She has expertise in systematic reviews and evidence synthesis for Public Health Policies. She has published several articles in various areas of medicine, public health and social sciences. Her research area is on scientific evidence in health decisions and policies.

Wendy M. Thompson is an associate professor of African American Studies at San José State University. Her creative work has most recently appeared in *Juked, Hayden's Ferry Review,* and *Obsidian: Literature & Arts in the African Diaspora*. Her first poetry book, *Black California Gold,* is forthcoming from Bucknell University Press.